Wall Street
in the American Novel

THE GOTHAM LIBRARY
OF THE NEW YORK UNIVERSITY PRESS

The Gotham Library is a series of original works and critical studies, published in paperback primarily for student use. The Gotham hardcover edition is primarily for use by libraries and the general reader. Devoted to significant works and major authors and to literary topics of enduring importance, Gotham Library texts offer the best in literature and criticism.

Comparative and Foreign Language Literature:
  Robert J. Clements, Editor

Comparative and English Language Literature:
  James W. Tuttleton, Editor

Wall Street
in the American Novel

Wayne W. Westbrook

New York University Press · New York *and* London

Oh! the might of money and the entanglement of art with it—the dollar as the soul's husband: a marriage nobody has had the curiosity to study.

—Von Humboldt Fleisher's
prefatory letter to Humboldt's gift

Humboldt's Gift, Saul Bellow

Copyright © 1980 by New York University

Library of Congress Cataloging in Publication Data

Westbrook, Wayne W   1939-
    Wall Street in the American Novel.

    (The Gotham library of the New York University Press)
    Includes bibliographical references and index.
    1. American fiction—History and criticism.
2. Wall Street in literature.   3. Finance in literature.   I. Title.
PS374.W34W4   813'.009'355   79-47997
ISBN 0-8147-9194-8
ISBN 0-8147-9195-6 (pbk.)

Manufactured in the United States of America

ACKNOWLEDGMENTS

Parts of this book appeared, in different form, in *Critique: Studies in Modern Fiction, Ball State University Forum, Jack London Newsletter,* and *The Mississippi Quarterly.* I wish to thank the editors of these journals for permission to use the material here.

Contents

1.

Introduction

"The business of America is business," said Calvin Coolidge. "Not art!" he might have added. Business and Art. Two different worlds. Seemingly by nature opposed, as Van Wyck Brooks believed in *America's Coming of Age,* when he discovered the perennial war between man's acquisitive and creative impulses. The pragmatic and poetic mind are separated by a divide. Businessmen prefer practical matters and daily greetings in the marketplace. Writers eschew the eight-to-five life-style, happiest seeking creative solitude. While businessmen skeptically regard writers as eccentric and of too odd a character, writers generally look upon businessmen as concentric, with too little character. One sees the other as a little off, a little funny—sometimes a kook. The other views the first as a little devious, a little selfish—sometimes a crook.

Yet business and art have walked common ground, if not shared a common purpose in American history. Anyone who regards them as totally estranged fails to see, really, that the fundamental economic structure of society extends its influence over more than just the annual figures of the Gross National Product or daily fluctuations in the Dow Jones industrial average. William Dean Howells,

1

who wrote novels at a time when robber barons were making millions, in an essay entitled "The Man of Letters as a Man of Business," felt that "at present business is the only human solidarity; we are all bound together with that chain, whatever interests, tastes and principles separate us." Business is that common ground and purpose, as Howells suggests. Business and art are bound together with that chain.

As he gazed upon Wall Street during a revisit to America, novelist Henry James was struck by the bustle, the singleness of purpose of multitudes as they hurried along the streets, the heroic mood that seemed to enliven the whole financial district. He sensed at once an "epic order suspended in the New York atmosphere." But that epic order, as well as Wall Street and the businessmen who figured there, remained quite beyond James. It was as if his own artistic interests, tastes, and principles separated, even alienated him from business and commerce. James yearned for but always felt shut out of the busy world "downtown." Also, he admittedly quailed before the businessman. Finding no avenue of approach that would open him up to understanding, he called instead for a rare "Zola of manners" to capture the vast and complex world of practical affairs.

New York and Wall Street were inspiring. That James knew. He would have wanted their inspiration for Emile Zola's *Money,* he says in *The American Scene,* rather than the Bourse in Paris, where Zola's novel does take place. The Bourse as well as the Royal Stock Exchange in London, James also knew, simply failed to stir novelists' imaginations, perhaps because paltry dealings in small lots and fortnightly settlements were not on a scale with the vast sales made in a breath on the New York Stock Exchange. Wall Street fired the mind and passions! It had helped turn America into an industrial and manufacturing beehive! It had spawned millionaires! It had shaped an aristocracy out of the plutocracy!

Wall Street traces a volatile path through American history, a repetitive cycle of ups and downs of business activity. The fact that the stock market had gone through such boom and bust periods fired many minds and passions into believing a good story is there. Henry James called for an epic novelist to write such a story. Another American writer, Lafcadio Hearn, pleaded for a romanticist.

In an 1894 letter, Hearn wrote, "There is, of course, a tremendous romance there; but only a financier can really know the machinery, and his knowledge is technical. But what can the mere *littérateur* do, walled up to heaven in a world of mathematical mystery and machinery?"

Although James and Hearn lamented their own failures to see "downtown" beyond a "plate-glass window," fortunately a few writers penetrated the mystery. Frank Norris and Theodore Dreiser, for instance, rolled up their sleeves and got to know the businessman in his Wall Street habitat, as well as the complex machinery of high finance. Norris painstakingly delved into the career of twenty-nine-year-old Joseph Leiter (the "boy plunger"), gathering material primarily about his spectacular 1897 corner on wheat. He based the financial feats of Curtis Jadwin in *The Pit* on Leiter's dramatic history. A *littérateur* who never had a mathematical mind and ardently disliked numbers, Norris also consulted a commodity broker in Chicago and a financial reporter in New York to comprehend "short selling," a trading technique vital to many of his plots. Seven years after *The Financier* was published, first novel in the Cowperwood trilogy, Dreiser was still bemoaning his ignorance about finance. In *Hey Rub-A-Dub-Dub*, he admitted he hadn't the least faculty for making money, not the least. "No, I am not brilliant financially," the novelist owned. Yet so accurately does he master the details of high finance in *The Financier*—from hypothecation of securities and pyramiding of loans down to the smallest technicality of floating a bond issue—it requires a reader with his own experience in investing to fully recognize and appreciate the hero's financial resourcefulness. For his titanic character of Frank Algernon Cowperwood, Dreiser looked into the careers of twenty American capitalists, including Morgan, Carnegie, Gould, Sage, Stanford, and Frick, before choosing Philadelphia traction tycoon Charles Tyson Yerkes, because he was the "most interesting." The novelist subsequently fell into so deep a fascination with, even envy of Yerkes, he made a clumsy attempt to imitate the financier's libertine life-style.

Other writers, luckier perhaps than James or Hearn, or Norris and Dreiser for that matter, incorporated firsthand knowledge of Wall Street and the stock exchange into their literature. These men are unique because they represent a sort of literary and financial half-breed. Edmund Clarence Stedman virtually linked the two worlds of business and art for almost three decades late in the nineteenth century ("Don't call me 'broker and poet,' " he warned. "Let me gamble as much as I choose, so long as I don't mix stock quotations with my verse"). Stedman ran his own brokerage firm in Wall Street with a seat on the exchange, while also a critic and member of the Century Association, a fashionable literary group that included Richard Henry Stoddard, Bayard Taylor, and Thomas Bailey Aldrich. Novelist David Graham Phillips, reporter for several New York newspapers and frequenter of Delmonico's restaurant, came to know financial and business types from years of studying and rubbing elbows with them. Matthew Josephson, historian of American financiers and robber barons (a term he recoined after it was used by Kansas farmers in an antirailroad monopoly pamphlet of 1880), started out as a statistician, broker, and writer of weekly stock market letters on Wall Street in the 1920s. Finally, Louis Auchincloss—maybe not the Zola of manners Henry James prescribed, though he felt himself stamped again and again with that determinist tag, but a novelist of manners nevertheless—sustained a Wall Street law career much like the lawyer-narrator of Herman Melville's *Bartleby the Scrivener: A Story of Wall Street*, in the cool tranquillity of a snug retreat doing a snug business among rich men's bonds, mortgages, and title deeds.

Willa Cather may have been right when she contended that art and economics are strangers, for strangers they truly seem. Yet her novelistic sense fails her when she argues in an essay, "The Novel Démeublé"—"But are the banking system and the Stock Exchange worth being written about at all? Have such things any proper place in imaginative art?" The reader must answer these questions for himself as he comes to know what Wall Street in the American novel is all about.

2.

The Wall Street Novel

National Woolens 33¼—up 1½; Apex Consolidated 18—down ⅜; Ward Valley Copper 34⅞—down 2¾; Transcontinental Common 63¼—up 6. Closing prices of stocks on the Big Board? In a way, they are. But you can't buy or sell them. Although listed on the New York Stock Exchange, they're not companies whose symbols you will find moving across the ticker tape in tomorrow's market, or about which you might pick up a research report. They are stocks traded only in the pages of American fiction, whose prices have been reported on imaginary ticker tapes and whose news items have been carried in the financial sections of fictitious dailies. Shares in these companies have been cornered by bull syndicates, sold short by bear consortiums, watered and manipulated by ruthless, money-mad gamblers. Financiers in American fiction have gotten rich on these stocks, fallen into bankruptcy, and turned to corruption, evil, revenge, and suicide. The game is called speculation, or the devil's game, and it is played for high stakes on Wall Street.

Wall Street. A narrow thoroughfare slicing the toe of Manhattan between Trinity Church and the East River. Destined for more

5

fame than its busy neighbors Broad, Pine, or Nassau Streets, it is the symbol of the stock market, investments, and American free enterprise. It is boom and bust, bull and bear, prosperity and panic. Since the first exchange agreement between brokers under the Buttonwood Tree in 1792, which replaced the old free-for-all Tontine Coffee House market, Wall Street has mushroomed into a huge financial center where millions of stock and bond shares are traded daily. In the history of American fiction, it has grown as well into a rich literary arena, peopled with a multitude of fictive financiers, wild-eyed speculators, and crass stock-market players. Muckrakers, populists, progressivists, and utopian reformists, romanticists, naturalists, and novelists of manners have variously portrayed Wall Street. Standing astride the corners of Broad and Wall, like Colossi of Lower Manhattan, American writers have not always been able to perceive it steadily or whole. Purblindness, a want of sympathy, lack of a mathematical mind—such things as these too often obscured their vision. Nonetheless, novelists have repeatedly drawn from Wall Street, not always to communicate matters as shallow as mere stock trading or money making, but often to portray deeper attitudes about American culture as well as insights into man's heart.

The Wall Street novel, or novel of high finance, is an anomalous literary creature, a species difficult to label or type. It is as diverse and varied as the nation's money centers themselves, an archipelago stretching from Wall Street at the edge of Manhattan to Pine Street in San Francisco. First, there is the Wall Street novel as myth, in which the businessman-hero ascends like Prometheus to the heavens, steals fire from the gods, and returns to establish a kingdom on earth. With the stock exchange as the ethereal field of battle, the Titan scatters opposing forces into disarray on the strength of a bull campaign, or outwits his enemies by laying a treacherous bear trap. Then there is the Wall Street novel as "dime" Western or Wild West tale. The rogue-financier in this picaresque story rises from a lowly and unillustrious birth to the highest levels of wealth and society. A roughshod and reckless fellow, he finds that only amorality and dishonesty beget riches on the open frontier of Wall Street. The Wall Street novel is also the novel of local color and lore, the novel of social protest, and the genteel novel of manners. In fact, the Wall Street novel is just about everything except the modern psychological novel. At least one critic of American fiction has found fault with the novel of high finance for exactly this reason. Looking for a psychological study of the businessman in Frank Norris's *The Pit* (1902), Granville Hicks writes:

> But for the reader who wants to understand the mind of the businessman, and wants to see how speculative operations actually affect human lives, for the reader who asks that this novel should help him to understand the forces it deals with and to realize their expression in credible characters and events, for such a reader there is little but disappointment—some stirring descriptions of the Pit, some insight into the lust of the gambler, a few pictures of Chicago society, and not much more.[1]

The Wall Street novel is never a casebook or psychological study, just as it isn't a guide or handbook on how to be a millionaire. The novelist studies speculation and moneymaking not so much as they affect the psyche as by the way they darken the heart and soul. The mind of the fictional financier, whether he is god or demigod, clod or well-bred man of culture, suffers only insofar as the conscience is pained or distressed. And rarely does the conscience of the financier in American fiction become uneasy or prove to be more than a blind and indifferent witness to evil. Rather, the severe and transforming effects of Wall Street and high finance are more vividly seen on the heart. In fiction, when moneymaking is guilt-producing, the heart pays the dearest penalty.

A more serious view of money and success is portrayed in the American novel of high finance than the Cinderella story with the fairy tale ending recast into the popular Horatio Alger formula. Few figures in fiction emerge from the dark and foreboding canyons of Wall Street to build majestic castles upon airy mountaintops. For instance, Silas Lapham is not a Ragged Dick (or even an anti-Ragged Dick, such as one scholar presumes W. D. Howells deliberately created in *The Rise of Silas Lapham*).[2] Nor is Frank Algernon Cowperwood, Theodore Dreiser's titanic financier, an eternal dweller upon some financial Olympus, consorting with other gods of immortal riches. The Wall Street novel rarely draws from popular culture or myth. Rather, it taps a deep cultural root trailing back through history to Puritan times. The vicarious sense of guilt that prompted economist Jesse Sprague to penitently remark about the bull market of the 1920s, "We are all miserable sinners," or urged Alfred E. Smith to credit the causes of the subsequent 1929 Crash to be "as old as original sin," is the same spirit seen in the writings of the seventeenth-century Puritan divines. Like the biblical prophet Ezekiel, the Puritans warned about the preeminence of commerce and evil. When the "sinners" were cast out of the financial marketplace in the Great Crash, Cotton Mather and Jonathan Edwards would have agreed that biblical Tyre had risen and fallen again. Puritan notions have determined in large part the attitudes of American novelists toward money. Cotton Mather, for example, was emphatic in declaring that "gains of money or estate by games, be the games what they will, are a sinful violation of the laws of honesty and industry which God has given us."[3] Playing or gaming for money was strictly forbidden in the Puritan colonies, and their censure and penalty were written into the *General Laws of the Massachusetts Colony, 1658*. The Puritan prejudice against gambling and speculation as a way to wealth, and as a form of corruption and debauchery, has been an innate and lasting prejudice of the American novelist against high finance as well as success on Wall Street.

After the Civil War, the nation swiftly developed into a mercantile and competitive society. During this period of historic economic growth, the Puritan ethic was forced to undergo a steady secularization. Change occurred so rapidly that not only were Puritan values and ideals made obsolete, but even the native tradition of the Protestant work ethic lost its sacred character. Hard work and individual initiative were supposed to have been the means to material prosperity. The system of monopolistic enterprise, however, spawned and nurtured on Wall Street in the late nineteenth century, violated traditional Puritan-Protestant beliefs. Wealth and power became concentrated in the hands of a small minority, while the vast numbers of the public spent their lives in serfdom, subjected to the money lords and barons. The evil inherently associated with excessive money and commerce in the seventeenth-century Puritan mind revived and became symbolized by the modern financial marketplace. Sexual fertility and fecundity, fearfully repressed by the Puritans as symbolic of profligacy and degeneration, were transmuted into the sin of financial fertility, while the traditional Christian argument against usury and increase, that they represented an unnatural sex act because they forced inert coinage to breed and multiply, was renewed. Financial gain and its attendant lusts for power and domination were regarded once again as demonic forces within man himself, of which money was the cause and catalyst.

Wall Street bore the blame for economic injustices and inequities. It became "that devil's chasm" (H. L. Mencken), a murky realm haunted by demons and witches. Financiers and stockbrokers were emissaries of the devil, fiends of finance who issued and dealt in beguiling paper certificates. Why else, for instance, was Hetty Green, the country's wealthiest woman and most stubborn bear, called the "Witch of Wall Street" in the late nineteenth century? Or, how does it happen that each new epoch of prosperity or every new bull market brings a more dazzling and fabulous "wizard" to Wall Street? Instead of the straight and narrow way to wealth, riches, and the American Dream, Wall Street, in the popular mind as well as in literature, is a broad road that leads to destruction and ends in nightmare.

Ralph Waldo Emerson never got too excited about Wall Street. He philosophically disregarded the financial marketplace, finding it added no new insights into the nature of man. Emerson felt that the merchant who figured there "so much to his own satisfaction & to the admiration or fear or hatred of younger or weaker competitors, is a very old business. You shall find him, his way that is of thinking concerning the world & men & property . . . the whole concatenation of his opinions, the[ir] very shade of their colour, the same laughter, the same knowingness, the same unbelief, & the same ability & taste, in Rabelais and Aristophanes. Panurge was good Wall Street." [4] Even though the nature of society slowly changed, Emerson concluded that man's worldly nature remained the same down through the ages.

The works of Nathaniel Hawthorne and Herman Melville bear the first major witness to the association of evil with money and condemnation of the financial marketplace in American literature. Emerson celebrated man's mind and the light of reason, but Hawthorne and Melville looked into man's heart and studied the darkness lurking there. Each knew the writings of Increase Mather and other Puritan divines, and had immersed themselves in the dark Puritan history of demonology and supernatural folklore. The devil or his demonic lieutenants haunt the pages of Hawthorne's fiction, appearing in various shapes as the horseman ("a fiend of fire and a fiend of darkness," who is in charge of the procession of Major Molineux), the devil-father who lures Young Goodman Brown away from Faith into the forest one night, or the dusky shade of old Roger Chillingworth in *The Scarlet Letter*. Evil and money, however, seem to coalesce in Judge Jaffrey Pyncheon, Hawthorne's accursed capitalist in *The House of the Seven Gables* (1851). Innately evil, Judge Pyncheon inherits the curse of his great-great grandfather, Colonel Pyncheon, Governor of Massachusetts, who sold his soul to the devil when he urged the persecution and hanging of Matthew Maule in order to obtain his property. The devil collected his due from the Colonel, but Pyncheon's descendants also came under Maule's curse. One, Judge Pyncheon, is motivated by overweening ambition and possessed by a Faustian desire for wealth and power. Yet, closely as he is associated with evil, Judge Pyncheon is also linked with the financial marketplace. His gifts are emphatically those of a man of finance, prompt, acute, clear-minded. A prosperous man, on the very morning of his death he lies in bed still cherishing his schemes, "planning the business of the day, and speculating on the probabilities of the next fifteen years." [5] He confidently thinks of the enjoyment that "his real estate in town and country, his railroad, bank, and insurance shares, his United States stock,—his wealth, in short, however invested, now in possession, or soon to be acquired" [6] would bring in the years ahead. But, later that day, motionless in his chair, dead, he leaves his business affairs waiting—a bank directors' meeting, an appointment with a State Street broker in Boston, and an auction for a piece of real estate. "Let him go thither, and loll at ease upon his moneybags! He has lounged long enough in the old chair!" [7] Hawthorne sardonically mocks him. Money and finance, symbolized by Judge Pyncheon, are made as evil and ugly as the organ grinder's monkey that performs under the arched window of the house on Pyncheon Street. A product of the deviltry of nature, that wrinkled and abominable creature supplicates each passerby, "holding out his small black palm, and otherwise plainly signifying his excessive desire for whatever filthy lucre might happen to be in anybody's pocket." [8] "Take this monkey just as he was, in short," writes Hawthorne, "and you could desire no better image of the Mammon of copper coins, symbolizing the grossest form of the love of money." [9]

Deviltry and money are parallel themes throughout Melville's *Moby-Dick* (1851). Ahab, the captain of a profit-making commercial enterprise, is really a Yankee Faust who has struck a bargain with the diabolic fireworshiper, Fedallah. Closely involved with the devil, Ahab baptizes his newly forged harpoon in the blood of the three pagans, Queequeg, Tashtego, and Dagoo, as he pronounces the witches' heretical renunciation of God and Christianity: "Ego non baptizo te in nomine patris, sed in nomine diaboli!" His namesake, the wicked king of the northern dominion of Israel in the days of the prophet Elijah, was also associated with evil and money. The biblical Ahab sold himself to work villainy in the sight of the Lord (1 Kings 21:25). Failing to purchase Naboth's vineyard for money, Ahab finally obtained his desire through Jezebel's wiles, which included murder of the vineyard owner. Melville's Ahab, who just as wickedly drives his economic enterprise in search of gain, represents a prevision of the late nineteenth-century robber baron or captain of industry. The whaling ship *Pequod* is the "joint-stock company of humanity," or the stockholder-owned ship of American investment. It epitomizes a capitalistic venture in which the two major shareowners, rather than the rank-and-file employees, unjustly receive the lion's share of the profits. Peleg and Bildad, the ship's owners, horde the largest number of shares in the vessel, leaving only a paltry few in the hands of "a crowd of old annuitants; widows, fatherless children, and chancery wards; each owning about the value of timber head, or a foot of plank, or a nail or two in the ship." It is young Ishmael who considers that "people in Nantucket invest their money in whaling vessels, the same way that you do yours in approved state stocks bringing in good interest." [10] The *Pequod* is an American corporation, stock-owned, ill-managed, and fated for bankruptcy.

Another Melvillian vessel about whose decks stalks a money-devil figure is the passenger steamboat *Fidèle,* which quietly plies the Mississippi River between St. Louis and New Orleans in *The Confidence Man: His Masquerade* (1857). The time is the age of "joint-stock companies and free-and-easies"; the day April 1, the Feast of All Fools. The *Fidèle* represents the world. The confidence man is Satan, who wanders about like a subtle serpent, seeking whomever he may devour. Disguised in various shapes and weeds, the confidence man diddles, gulls, tricks, and cons suspicious but foolish humanity aboard the boat. Posing as Messrs. Ringman, Goodman, and Truman (Ring Good and True?), among other false identities, he duns one moral-minded gentleman for alms on behalf of Seminole widows and orphans. He then bilks by turns a college sophomore (a wise fool), and a country merchant, selling them shares of bogus stock. In the guise of the president and transfer agent of the supposedly well-known Black Rapids Coal Company, he carries about a black transfer book, register of the devil or ledger of the damned, upon whose pages he records his victims' names. When asked about the low price of Black Rapids stock—if there hadn't been a recent sell-off—the confidence man admits there was a depression but blames the bears in a glowing paraphrase of Satan's first speech in hell in *Paradise Lost.* He heatedly calls them

> hypocrites by inversion; hypocrites in the simulation of things dark instead of bright; souls that thrive, less upon depression, than the fiction of depression; professors of the wicked art of manufacturing depressions; spurious Jeremiahs; sham Heraclituses, who, the lugubrious day done, return, like sham Lazaruses among the beggars, to make merry over the gains got by their pretended sore heads—scoundrelly bears! [11]

—describing none other than himself!

The confidence man, rather than invoke Ahab's renunciation of God, calls upon the spirit of Wall Street to redeem the world on strict Wall Street principles. His philanthropic scheme is to merge all the world's charities into one huge organization, a monopoly or trust called "The World's Charity." Benevolence would thereby be methodized and one grand benevolence tax levied upon all mankind. Ultimately, the bewildering sum raised would be "eleven thousand two hundred millions," enough to eliminate every pauper and heathen "the round world over." The charlatan philanthropist goes even further, proposing to quicken all the world's missions with the "Wall Street spirit." Once quickened, charity could be "let out on contract" or auctioned off to the highest bidder, as if it were to take place on the New York Stock Exchange:

> So much by bid for converting India, so much for Borneo, so much for Africa. Competition allowed, stimulus would be given. There would be no lethargy of monopoly. We should have no mission-house or tract-house of which slanderers could, with any plausibility, say that it had degenerated in its clerkships into a sort of custom-house. But the main point is the Archimedean money-power that would be brought to bear.[12]

The confidence man, who is from the East, is a satirical version of a well-established American stereotype, the native Yankee peddler or Yankee trickster. With his multifarious financial schemes for duping his fellow man, he is extremely shrewd, commercial, and self-seeking. Stubb, the second mate aboard the *Pequod* in *Moby-Dick*, is a somewhat earlier example of the ingenious Yankee trader. Although free of the evil connotations of the confidence man, Stubb nevertheless doesn't exactly lack native guile. It is he, remember, who talks the captain of the French whaler, *Rose-Bud*, out of the foul-smelling whale they have fastened alongside. When the *Rose-Bud* cuts the whale away and sails off, the *Pequod* moves in, picks it up, and the crafty second mate rifles the fish for its precious ambergris. Another exponent of the devil-as-Yankee trickster is Melville's lightning rod salesman in "The Lightning-Rod Man" (1856). Along with Stubb, and also Dr. Long Ghost in *Omoo* (1847), he is the forerunner of the confidence man. A clever stranger, the lightning rod peddler turns Ben Franklin's honest invention into a diabolical tool, dealing in rods at a dollar per foot and driving "a brave trade with the fears of man."

In primitive mythologies, the devil is the lineal descendant of the trickster. However, the mysterious salesmen in "The Lightning-Rod Man" and *The Confidence Man*—fiendish masters of deception and duplicity—are the devil and Yankee trickster in one. They demonstrate how a native American mythology combines with innate Puritan suspicions and prejudices to produce a view of money and commerce as forms of evil. These suspicions and prejudices are carried on in American fiction, although they are transferred later from the individual in commerce to the individual in high finance and the financial marketplace in general. Instead of the peddler or trader, the stockbroker or financier on Wall Street is the villain, the trickster, the devil in disguise. In fact, the confidence man masquerading as a businessman and broker is the prototype in the American novel of the stockbroker as devil or tempter. Melville is the first novelist to employ this type, which recurs with striking consistency throughout American financial fiction. His bogus broker with a bag full of tricks evolves into a long line of stockbroker-as-devil figures, which includes Darius Dorman in John De Forest's *Honest John Vane*, Sam Gretry in Frank Norris's *The Pit*, or Gus Trenor in Edith Wharton's *The House of Mirth*, and stockbroker surrogates such as Milton K. Rogers in W. D. Howells's *The Rise of Silas Lapham*, or the quack Dr. Tamkin in Saul Bellow's *Seize the Day*. Melville's conception of the demonic confidence man selling phony stock in the pre-Civil War period of America's commercial history reflects even then the suspicion with which stock financing and speculation, as well as the broker or financier, were held by the literary artist.

Melville's tale of Bartleby the scrivener, despite its subtitle *A Story of Wall Street*, is not precisely about money, commerce, or the financial marketplace. Setting the story in the financial district at the lower end of Manhattan, the author seems more interested in the pun than in economics. The financial setting, however, does provide a perfect atmosphere for Melville's metaphysical inquiry into the meaning of life and death in *Bartleby the Scrivener* (1856). A maze of walls within walls envelops and imprisons Bartleby. Wall Street is a street of alienation, isolation, and emptiness. The walls

of Wall Street also bear a resemblance to "the dead, blind wall" in
Moby-Dick, which "butts all inquiring heads at last." In a sterile
and void world of bonds, mortgages, and title deeds, the individual, like Bartleby, is reduced to the pathetic insignificance of a
human copying machine, creating nothing, contributing nothing,
thinking nothing. A key figure in the story is the lawyer-narrator,
who employs Bartleby. He is part of the dead, blind wall and
exemplifies a money-conscious society. "I am a man who, from his
youth upward, has been filled with a profound conviction that the
easiest way of life is the best," the lawyer unashamedly admits.
One of his patrons and saints was the late John Jacob Astor, infamous for debauching and swindling American Indians, defraud-
ing the city of New York out of land and taxes, and becoming a
major property owner in the city by swiftly foreclosing mortgages
if interest was not paid exactly on time. Astor, who inflated his
enormous fortune with securities purchased in the panic of 1837
and was the richest man in America a decade later, is a name the
lawyer boasts, "I love to repeat; for it hath a rounded and orbicu-
lar sound to it, and rings like unto bullion." Bartleby's plight is to
be trapped in the financial and commercial milieu of Wall Street.
Like the minstrel Pan in Edmund Clarence Stedman's poem, "Pan
in Wall Street" (1866)—the heart and symbol of nature in the
financial district who pipes his pastoral lays before a gathering
crowd until a policeman pushes him away—Bartleby is out of place
in this moribund world.

3.

Apple Eating, Demon Hunting, and Other Themes

I

Money and religion have had a curious relationship throughout the history of civilization. The original coinage in Lydia in the seventh century B.C., officially stamped by the state as legal tender, were metal pieces that may have been used as religious tokens. The first money markets were sacred markets. Banks and mints were temples. The first to issue money were priests or priest-kings. Through history, just as money markets never lost their ancient sanctity, neither has money relinquished its sacrosanct role. Gold has always vied with God as man's hope. Wealth is man's confidence, uncertain riches his trust. Great gain itself is supposed godliness. Satirist Juvenal hailed the *sanctissima divitiarum maiestas,* or "the holy majesty of wealth." Seventeenth-century poet George Herbert in his Poem "Avarice" scolded base money for exalting itself above man—"Nay, thou hast got the face of man; for we / Have with our stamp and seal transferr'd our right: / Thou art the man, and man but drosse to thee."

Since the mid-1800s, when capitalism transformed America

from its ecclesiastical and mercantile beginnings into a thriving industrial nation, money and profit have become twin gods. Washington Irving, who in the pre-machine age saw the growing glory and omnipotence of money, prophetically coined the phrase "the almighty Dollar." Ben Franklin tied not only time to money but money to God, calling economy "holy." Mark Twain summed up the credo of the Gilded Age, "Money is God. Gold and Greenbacks and Stock—father, son and the ghost of same—three persons in one; these are the true and only God." The motto "In God We Trust," stamped on all U.S. currency, seems to bring full circle man's original impulse to mark religious tokens with the state seal. So inborn is the American people's instinct to confuse money and religion that this association has managed to creep even into everyday matters of business and finance. When the Swedish Immanuel Congregational Church in New York City launched a fund-raising drive in the 1920s, church elders promised each contributor that God would certainly not forget him, that He would lay aside in His kingdom an engraved certificate of investment in preferred capital stock. Years earlier, Philip Armour, the Chicago meatpacking magnate, when secretly "bulling" the stock of the St. Paul Railway, openly encouraged a journalist during an interview to report that "every man who holds 100 shares of St. Paul has a joint account with God Almighty." John D. Rockfeller, Sr., oil baron and ardent Baptist who not only had a joint account but seemed God's anointed broker, steadfastly believed "God gave me my money." God's gold, in fact, was carried by Rockefeller and others from the marketplace and laid at church altars in magnificent sacrifices, for many American money lords, apparently mindful of the camel and needle's eye, were curiously religious. Bible-reading Daniel Drew, Jay Cooke, the Astors, the William Vanderbilts, the Morgans, the Wanamakers (wealthy department store owners who first sponsored the Young Men's Christian Association), the Armours, and the Pullmans were all seemingly true believers who feared God's disfavor, particularly if their native parsimony excluded Him.

Money and religion are themes closely linked in the Wall Street novel. But Mammon, alas, whose chief temple is the holy city of New York, is the only god worshiped by businessmen and financiers in fiction. Earthly goods in such transitory forms as bank accounts, stock portfolios, mortgage holdings, and real estate investments are the only treasures stored up. Scripture is the daily financial page, where the principles of stern expedience and urgent necessity, whimsical fortune and sudden chance, merciless revenge and deadly annihilation are sanctified. Businessmen or financiers in the Wall Street novel, who make pilgrimage to the marketplace in search of the fatted calf, are often types of Adam, prelapsarian men whose innocence leaves them unprepared for the American commercial and financial world. Boys from the boondocks or outlands, like Ishmael, Huck Finn, and Henry Fleming, these fictional money men seek adventure as well as fortune. They set out at first as a sort of country bumpkin, uncut, unkempt and uncultured, lacking in worldliness and social grace, yet full of backwoods savvy. Instead of the call of the sea, river, or battle, however, they are led by impulse into the great city—that bewildering Big Town which haunts the American literary mind—to find their niches in commerce. There, alluringly arrayed in the pale green garments of wealth and success, High Finance coyly beckons. Out of the folds of her sumptuous robes steals the deadly serpent, bearing the promise, "Ye shall be as gods." A struggle rages within the innocent's breast. Yet the dark fascination of the stock market proves too enchanting. They who had set out to serve both God and Mammon soon discover there is no God.

Give the American writer a story about the stock market or high finance, and he turns it into an allegory. Wall Street is a type of paradise, the Garden planted eastward in Eden, filled with enough fruits of the tree of life to satisfy all man's needs. Yet there is knowledge forbidden to man in this world, knowledge not of good and evil but of speculation and high finance. Against a Puritan background long suspicious of money and commerce, which viewed speculation and gambling as taboo, Wall Street becomes the battlefield on which man's soul is lost. The stock market, not woman, is the agent of his Fall. Stockbrokers, bill changers, and money men, those demons who inhabit and haunt Wall Street, are the devil's minions, tools for conveying sin and death into the business world.

The association of money with the devil is strong in the Wall

Street novel. Its origin, though, is found in biblical typology. Wherever merchandising and commerce flourish in scripture, it seems Satan flourishes. The wealthy prince of Tyre in Ezekiel is a shadow of Satan. He reigns over his coastal city, a region blessed and enriched by traffic in merchandise. Wallowing in prosperity, however, he lifts his heart up in pride and boasts, "I am a God, I sit in the seat of God" (Ezekiel 28:2). The prince of Tyre, like Satan, had been the "anointed cherub" in Eden and was "perfect in his ways" until a multitude of commerce filled him with violence and sin. He is cast to the ground by God. Similarly, the king of Babylon in Isaiah, wealthy beyond measure, is punished for his pride and iniquity. Again, like Satan, he is shaken from heaven down to the ground. Babylon, the golden city that was the glory of kingdoms and beauty of the Chaldees, ceases evermore to exist (Isaiah 13, 14). Also, in its abundance and wealth, Babylon in Revelation is utterly destroyed and cast into the sea. A habitation of devils and hold of every foul spirit, Babylon is so corrupted by fornication and violence that the merchants of the earth weep, "for in one hour so great riches is come to nought" (Revelation 18:17). Although we cannot be sure how much the devil made for beguiling Eve, we do know what Judas Iscariot earned. Of the twelve original apostles, Judas was the group's bagman or treasurer, the money man who always looked at things from a financial angle. Those thirty pieces of silver that were dangled before him as blood money appeared far more attractive at the time than Christ's life. Even before the betrayal, he objected that the spikenard Mary used to anoint Jesus' feet was too costly and wanted to sell it for 300 pence.

Brokers, bill changers, note takers, paper merchants, and money men, Judas figures all, personify evil in the Wall Street novel. In fact, evil in its own shape is less hideous than when it rages in the breast of the money man or broker. His origin and identity are peculiarly linked to and derived from Wall Street, which is a natural habitat. Because he haunts the financial marketplace and persists in selling fruits of the stock market, he becomes the devil or Tempter. But, unlike the Old Testament prince of Tyre or king of Babylon, brilliant Luciferian types who fall in a blaze of light, the broker as devil is modified into a lesser fallen angel. Rather than a roaring lion seeking whom he may devour, he is cast in the subordinate role of a lowly seducing spirit, an enticing serpent. His assignment is to wait upon the Adamic financier, trap him into an involvement with high finance, and encourage a sinful commitment to speculate in the stock market.

Belief that the United States had been an economic Eden in the period before the Civil War, the age of the Golden Day, lies behind the novelist's vision of a nation also fallen from innocence and violated by high finance. When robber barons and industrialists operating out of Wall Street manipulated, plundered, and bled young industry in its formative stage, a new age of competitive capitalism was ushered in. Rather than good, these men dedicated themselves to profit, and used Wall Street and stock exchange as diabolical tools. The figure of Adam that reappears throughout financial fiction, therefore, is a reaction against whatever unsettled economic conditions happened to have been current. The portrait of the bumpkin as a money hero, uncomfortably stuffed into a business suit with starched shirt, high collar, and cravat, is really a vision of America coming of age into financial and economic manhood, yet resisting this growing up because it transgresses a whole religious and cultural tradition.

Death and rebirth are also predominant themes in the Wall Street novel. Money exerts a tremendous disintegrative influence upon the financier in fiction. Curtis Jadwin makes his way from the provinces to the city in Frank Norris's *The Pit,* for example, but is snatched up by the Giant Despair and cast into the Valley of the Shadow of Death. His journey turns into a nightmarish fall from innocence and a frightening descent into the pit. The Pit or trading room of the Chicago Board of Trade itself represents a place of death. Before the fall of Tyre, Ezekiel prophesies that strange nations will "bring thee down to the pit, and thou shalt die the deaths of them that are slain in the midst of the seas" (Ezekiel 28:8). The king of Babylon, who exalts his throne above the stars like Lucifer, is similarly "brought down to hell, to the sides of the pit" (Isaiah 14:15). In Norris's novel of high finance, commitment to speculation and a prideful attempt to corner the world's wheat supply and be like a god bring about a fall for Jadwin. Significantly, he is cast into the Pit of the Wheat Exchange, where mad-

ness, sickness, and rapid aging, all outward signs of death, overtake
the financier.

The process of rebirth, on the other hand, is the countertheme to
death in the financial novel. Not unlike the New Testament pre-
scription for salvation of turning away from the world, the flesh,
and the devil, rebirth for a Wall Street sinner consists of a conscious and specific rejection of the financial marketplace. The sinner is brought up out of the horrible pit of the stock exchange, out
of the miry clay, and his feet are set upon firm ground. But first,
the old financier must die and the new man must emerge. Contri-
tion and a broken spirit, necessary conditions for salvation, usually
occur after the financier has been punished for his iniquities with
bankruptcy and failure. To salvage his life amidst the ruins, he
must acknowledge his sin of speculation on the exchange, then
turn away from the evil marketplace. Curtis Jadwin or Silas
Lapham in W. D. Howells's *The Rise of Silas Lapham,* financiers cast
into ruin and facing certain death, penitently leave La Salle and
State Streets and humbly return to the country. Able to flee Satan
and the City of Destruction, they are new men, free to shape new
beginnings.

The themes of money and death are closely related in the Wall
Street novel. *Moby-Dick,* story of an ill-fated Yankee commercial
venture, is in many ways an early version of the economic novel.
Melville constantly reminds the reader that whaling is big business
in preindustrial America, that money and profit are the twin motives behind the voyage of the *Pequod.* Ishmael translates the business of whaling into sheer numbers and dollars:

> And lastly, how comes it that we whalemen of America
> now outnumber all the rest of the banded whalemen in
> the world; sail a navy upwards of seven hundred vessels;
> manned by eighteen thousand men; yearly consuming
> 4,000,000 of dollars; the ships worth, at the time of sail-
> ing, $20,000,000; and every year importing into our har-
> bors a well reaped harvest of $7,000,000. How comes all
> this, if there be not something puissant in whaling? [1]

If the *Pequod* is a commercial enterprise, then Starbuck, the calm
and pragmatic first mate, is the foreman of the factory who keeps a

close eye on the business at hand. He is forced to admonish even Ahab, who is preoccupied with Moby-Dick, that "I came here to hunt whales, not my commander's vengeance. How many barrels will thy vengeance yield thee even if thou gettest it, Captain Ahab? it will not fetch thee much in our Nantucket market." [2] The boss's responsibility, in Starbuck's mind, is to make profits for the stockholders and employees, not to satisfy his own selfish interests. Ahab reluctantly accedes to the primary goal of the voyage, which is to make money—"I will not strip these men . . . of all hopes of cash— aye, cash. They may scorn cash now; but let some months go by, and no perspective (sic) promise of it to them, and then this same quiescent cash all at once mutinying in them, this same cash would soon cashier Ahab." [3] Ahab, however, never forgets his private motive. What is the gold piece nailed to the masthead but a signification of incentive pay for overtime, the Yankee idea of a bonus to the first crewman who sights the white whale? Nor does the crew ever forget its purpose in originally signing on board the *Pequod.* What is Flask's shout, "There goes three thousand dollars, men!—a bank!—a whole bank! The bank of England!" but a delirious cry for profit as he urges his oarsmen to outrace the boats of the *Jungfrau* in pursuit of a crippled sperm whale.

Yet, just as Melville reminds the reader of the money in whaling, he also keeps us aware of the death. "Yes, there is death in this business of whaling—a speechlessly quick chaotic bundling of man into Eternity," Ishmael philosophically acknowledges. Money and death, two basic postulates, are linked inseparably by American novelists as they explore the search for the dollar and see the effects of this search upon man's soul and spirit. The quest for the white whale in *Moby-Dick* is replaced in the Wall Street novel by the obsessive pursuit of wealth and power, which are just further dead, blind walls. Ahab, prophetic of the industrial titans who rose so mightily in late nineteenth-century America, also foreshadows the financial monomaniacs in fiction. Characters like Norris's Curtis Jadwin, Jack Dumont in David Graham Phillips's *The Cost,* or Frank A. Cowperwood in Dreiser's trilogy *The Financier, The Titan,* and *The Stoic* spring out of the American imagination to chase illusive riches across uncharted financial seas. Death, destruction, and ruin are the rewards for these heroes of the stock exchange, no less certainly than they were for Captain Ahab.

II

Mammon, the false god, awakens a powerful money lust in the Wall Street novel. Once conceived, that lust brings forth speculation or financial sin. When financial sin is completed, death and its companion forms, decay, sickness, even madness, are the issue. The fictional financier who quests solely after riches is unfailingly subjected to these forms of death. Meanwhile, as the individual suffers from the effects of financial sin, society as a whole suffers. Speculation is not limited among financiers and businessmen to the game of fleecing one another or getting rich, but is bound to touch the general public as well. The theme, in this event, is the Fall of society—or the "corruption of Hadleyburg." The moral character of town, city, or society in general is weakened when infected with the Wall Street malaise of speculation. Mark Twain's peaceful village, Hadleyburg, is a microcosm of American society. Before the arrival of the passing stranger, it is the most honest and upright town in all the region. Yet, Eden though it is, the money lust befouls it. The village's principles of honest dealing succumb to open greed and vulgar deceit when the sack of gold ("gambler's money" or "wages of sin," as it is called) is dangled within the townspeople's grasp. The "Nineteen" in Hadleyburg, the very best of society, is corrupted by this gold, for each family believes the specific right to it is theirs. This debasement of the Nineteen resembles the dissolution of New York's Four Hundred, which is tainted with the commercial and financial instinct later in Edith Wharton's fiction. Novelists such as William Dean Howells, Robert Herrick, David Graham Phillips, Upton Sinclair, and William Faulkner, as well as Wharton, portray the theme of the obliquitous influence of money and finance as a cause of society's moral decay.

Closely related to the theme of the corruption of Hadleyburg in the Wall Street novel is the pessimistic view that society overall is decadent and declining. German philosopher Oswald Spengler, in *The Decline of the West* (1918), theorizes that the "expression forms" of world history—historical eras, epochs, or situations—constantly reappear and repeat themselves true to type. One such historical expression form that Spengler sees repeated is the era of commercial Rome in the second and third centuries A.D. Its shadow is the late nineteenth-century era of American capitalism. The type of the Roman financial magnate is repeated in the Yankee business-man. Spengler believes that the decline of modern Western civilization is inevitable, because its fall has already been seen in history in the dissolution of commercial Rome. From the first century B.C. to the first century A.D., Rome was the financial center of the world. Accumulated capital and surplus monies did not lie idle but were put to work by industrious financiers and businessmen. Banking and lending practices grew to chief importance in the economic system, and sophisticated credit operations and sensitive interest rates were fully utilized. The main sources of prosperity were a thriving domestic commerce and an international sea trade. Investments in land and industry were common. A bourgeoisie society came into existence, therefore, as the wealth and ownership were distributed more widely among its citizens. The economic strength of the system became its eventual weakness, however. Gradual decline and breakdown, when the provinces lost faith in Rome, marked the end of a great commercial era. If the satire in Petronius's novel *The Satyricon,* written in the first century A.D., is based on truth, then the city of Rome, like the biblical city of Tyre, had already at the height of its splendor begun to fall into profligacy and corruption.

Spenglerian ideas about the decline of modern civilization, as well as the epoch of American capitalism, being a historical reproduction of Roman commercialism, are at least implicit in the Wall Street novelist's picture of the deterioration of society. America's opulent Gilded Age had already been compared with commercial Rome by Mark Twain. In a journal entry dated in the early 1900s, Twain cited Roman conditions then, particularly the stupendous wealth that brought corruption and moral blight, and the power of money that bribed and influenced thousands of men, turning them into alms receivers. Charles Dudley Warner, in the turn-of-the-century novel *That Fortune,* looked at the rich foreign parvenu Murad Ault living in a palace and thought of the barbarians occupying Rome, as well as of the emperor Caligula. Upton Sinclair, Theodore Dreiser, and Louis Auchincloss also have mentioned and specifically made the parallel between Rome in its heyday and capitalist twentieth-century America, emphasizing the moral weaknesses of our modern Romanesque commercial society.

Dreiser, for one, pondered America's future by looking back at ancient Rome. America in its own good time may come to a great end—and again it may not—he mused. "It may be—who knows?—a mere money machine, a honey gatherer like the bee, a material welter like Rome, without the slightest vision as to what to do or how to act once it has its great store." He goes on, "Rome has gone; Greece has gone; and many, many another. . . . And may not America perchance be one such? One hopes not. But—" [4]

The Freudian view of money and its power to emasculate is another theme in the Wall Street novel. American novelists of high finance usually see the money lust in a moral sense as a destructive work of the flesh. But often, money is portrayed as gaining so complete a sway over the financier that all human feeling and emotion is deadened. Nullified are not only the hero's affinities for brotherly love, but worse, even love for wife and children. The passion for money controverts the passion for love. Agape is subverted by Eros, Eros is frozen by greed. Wasn't it a character in Edith Wharton's *The Custom of the Country* who argued that the real *crime passionel* in money-minded America is a "big steal," that businessmen get more kicks out of wrecking railways than homes? Yet the money lust can also arouse sexual lust and awaken aggression. The Wall Street novel is strewn with figures who carry the heartless methods of moneymaking into the drawing room. It is there they pursue a woman as they would chase after a large block of stock on the exchange, for the thrill of victory, the pleasure of possession, even the delight of inflicting defeat and loss. The generous instincts are wholly replaced by the will to power and control.

Father-son rivalry is another theme that recurs in the Wall Street novel. The Oedipal pattern in a way is incorporated into the modern financial drama. The myth of Oedipus, earliest of all human dramas, is the revolt of the son against his father and consummation of love for his mother. In the novel of high finance, a struggle often takes place between the two male generations of a family for dominance and authority. When the financier father is a despotic and tyrannical figure who rules the household with as iron a hand as that with which he presides over his fortune, the son looks up to him not as the exemplar of success and achievement, but as an immediate enemy and rival. The son first notices that his father stands in the way, not between him and his mother—which would be the mythical pattern—but between him and moneymaking or the stock market. The stock market, successfully courted and manipulated by the father for so long, has been the source of the family's well-being and prosperity. Jealous of his father's successes in the market as well as his dominant role in the family, the son effectively sets out to remove him from the ruling position. He turns, himself, to the stock market to prove his worth in these important matters of speculation, manipulation, and moneymaking. A "killing" in the market with either bull or bear maneuver represents a victory over the father, in a sense supplanting him as the financial authority figure. The son wants the stock market—source of the family's strength—all to himself. More particularly, he needs control of the family fortune with which to woo and play the market, and the formidable presence of the financier father is an obstruction.

There are variations on the father-son rivalry theme. The Horatio Alger tales, for example, stories about the American myth or dream of rags to riches, are also melodramas illustrating this rivalry. The young hero of these tales is a poor, fatherless country boy who comes to the city and finds fortune suddenly thrust upon him. At the moment the boy meets his riches, he also usually discovers his adoptive father or uncle. Yet the first thing he does is rush home to provide for and protect his mother. As a result of his unexpected wealth, the boy thinks only of his place of authority in the family, which he can now assume and defend. Ultimately, the truth behind the father-son rivalry theme is that money, an important factor in the American family structure, is vital even in the maturation of the young American man.

George Bernard Shaw's *Major Barbara* offers a dialogue between Andrew Undershaft, wealthy munitions maker, and Adolphus Cusins, professor of Greek, about the advantages of having a Jewish business partner. Undershaft asserts that a Jew is suggestive of financial stability and also can receive the blame when profits are considered too exorbitant. Cusins pipes up, "A scapegoat, then?" "Exactly: a scapegoat," Undershaft concurs. Cusins replies, "That

is the role of the Jew in modern capitalism." The role of the Jew on
Wall Street, if not in modern capitalism, is scapegoat—another
theme in the American novel of high finance. The figure of Jewish
capitalist or money man is treated rather harshly, in fact. Worse
than scapegoat, he is cast in the dubious role of outsider, antagonist, pariah, or villain. These roles, however (not precisely in-
ventions of either Undershaft or the American novelist), date back
into Renaissance, even Medieval literature. Anti-Zionist sentiment
crept into the image of the economic Jew in the Middle Ages as
peddler, note changer, poisoner of the wells, and then bloomed
into such Renaissance portraits as Christopher Marlowe's Jew of
Malta or Shakespeare's Venetian moneylender. Wealthy Machia-
vels, with bags and coffers crammed full, Barabbas and Shylock
are pictured as greedy, miserly, and vindictive. They take their
authority from Deuteronomic principles to justify mean and
vengeful practices in lending to stranger or Gentile. The Jew as a
relentless usurer, a cheat or thief who would spite his own pride
and name to save a ducat, therefore became a commonplace figure
in literature. When he invades Wall Street—already fixed in the
novelist's mind as a symbolic haunt of demons and evil spirits—the
Jew conforms to the stereotype of devilish merchant of credit and
paper certificates. Like Marlowe and Shakespeare's usurers, the
Jewish money merchant in the financial novel contributes to or
causes the downfall of the innocent Christian hero.

Beyond the symbolic associations of the Jew as devil on Wall
Street, a historical anti-Semitic bias also persuaded the novelist.
German Jews had come to America in the 1840s and 1850s, form-
ing a class of traders as aggressive and unerring in money instincts
as the Yankee businessman. After the Civil War, rich Jews operating from the money center of Frankfurt invested in and controlled
a large portion of United States bonds, including the gold six-
percenters, floated by Jay Cooke in 1869. The Yankee-Jew cleav-
age that has often characterized American commerce and finance
dates from these early years. Since then, the Jew in matters of
money and finance has frequently been looked upon as a dangerous denizen of the back streets, a treacherous Fagin on Wall
Street. Those epic turn-of-the-century skirmishes for control over

the Northern Pacific Railroad (eventually culminating in the Northern Pacific corner and panic of 1901), for example, were fought out between the Gentile House of Morgan in one camp and the Jewish investment banking firm of Kuhn, Loeb & Company in another. Although WASP Morgan's complicity in the corner was never publicly decried, hostility toward Jewish financiers intensified. Steel king Andrew Carnegie, elated about victory over J. Pierpont Morgan, Sr., in the deal that led to formation of the United States Steel Corporation in 1901, gloated "It takes a Yankee to beat a Jew, and it takes a Scot to beat a Yankee." Even Henry Adams, member of Boston's staid Brahmin class, openly displayed bias in his autobiography when he contemptuously referred to the infamous Wall Street financier Jay Gould as "the complex Jew." Actually Gould, born in Roxbury, New York, was from Yankee stock that for the most part was a poor farming class. Adams was misled no doubt by Gould's original family name, which was Gold, changed many years after emigration from England in the seventeenth century, or by the popular stereotype of the dissimulating Jew that fit Gould perfectly, with his subtle machinations and subterfuges on Wall Street and an ominous and furtive look suggested by his bushy black beard, short stooped posture, piercing dark eyes, and hooked nose. Edmund Clarence Stedman, the Wall Street "broker-poet," in his popular poem "Israel Freyer's Bid for Gold," which is about the smash of the great gold corner on Black Friday (September 24, 1869), deliberately altered the name of the broker who was actually involved, Albert Speyer, to Israel Freyer. Stedman's theme in the poem is the lunacy and absurdity of this wild plan by a small group of speculators led by Gould to buy up the available float of gold, forcing higher prices. He hoped, perhaps, that using a more Semitic-sounding name would call attention to the underlying greed and evil that prompted such a scheme. Stedman described in one scene the hell-like setting of the exchange and the devilish broker, Israel Freyer, who was urging the price of the metal upward:

> Up from the gold Pit's nether hell,
> While the innocent fountain rose and fell,
> Loud and higher the biddings rose,

> And the bulls, triumphant, faced their foes.
> It seemed as if Satan himself were in it:
> Lifting it—one percent a minute—.

Not only is the Jew disdained as an individual financier or money man in the Wall Street novel, but he is also distrusted as a tight and unified group of international bankers who rule Wall Street, Lombard Street, and the world. The Rothschild banking dynasty in England did virtually control the monetary systems of the West during most of the nineteenth century. The founder of the empire, Meyer Amschel Rothschild, boldly stated: "Permit me to issue and control the money of a nation, and I care not who makes its laws." The Rothschilds, no doubt, learned their banking lessons well from the historical feats of the Medici family who, in the fourteenth, fifteenth, and sixteenth centuries, controlled Europe. A habit of the Medicis was to establish a powerful bank in each European country, as well as one family member in the ruling class. The House of Rothschild, like the Medicis, exerted tremendous influence on the course of the world's economic and political development. So powerful were they that by exercising control over European central banks they were able to contract or expand credit, contriving alternate periods of inflation and deflation. The Rothschilds also were able to create widespread financial panic whenever they saw the opportunity for vast profits. In the United States, the panic of 1893 may have been engineered not by the Rothschilds directly, but by one of their top agents and apostles, J. Pierpont Morgan, Sr. Morgan commanded the major New York banks to retire a third of their money in circulation and call half of their outstanding loans, a carefully calculated move that wreaked economic havoc, collapsed the stock market, and produced more than six hundred bank failures across the country. The Great Panic of 1907 was also ascribed to Morgan, not by the public but by knowledgeable Wall Street insiders, even though Morgan partner Thomas W. Lamont later dismissed that notion as pure demagoguery. At any rate, Paul M. Warburg, employed by Kuhn, Loeb & Company and also considered a Morgan accomplice, was a cousin of the English Rothschilds. When Warburg, a brilliant student of European banking, was named vice-governor of the Fed-eral Reserve Board in Washington after that banking system came into operation in 1914 (seven years after the Panic and under stress of the Great War), skeptics feared this appointment would enormously extend the influence of the House of Rothschild over American finance. The idea in the Wall Street novel, therefore, of the existence of a clique of international Jewish bankers—unpublicized and unseen but omnipotent—although exaggerated, has some basis in historical fact. The Jew in modern capitalism, with coals of fire heaped on his head during boom or bust times, does seem, as Cusins summed it up, to play the role of scapegoat.

4.

Road to Destruction

I

After the Civil War, the United States embarked upon an epoch of economic expansion unparalleled in modern history. The "Era of Triumphant Business Enterprise" changed the country from an agrarian into urban society. Americans fled the farms to the factories. Industry superseded agriculture as the economic base. Also, stimulated by the war, with enormous issues of depreciating currency by Congress and reckless waste of money and credit, speculation grew to stages of mania America had never before known. Not only on Wall Street, center of speculation, but throughout the Northern states, nearly everyone who had money at all began buying stocks on margin in gold, copper, petroleum, and railroad companies. Only a scattered handful of novels reflected this burgeoning economic growth and burning stock market fever. Not until the late 1880s and 1890s did a real flux of fiction about business and finance appear, portraying the vast changes that were reshaping the country. In 1875, however, while economic change was taking root, two novels were published that still stand as landmarks of the Wall Street novel—*Honest John Vane* by John W. De Forest, and Josiah G. Holland's *Sevenoaks: A Story of To-Day*.

Honest John Vane breaks ground for the modern financial novel. The hero, John Vane, after a successful career as a small-town businessman, comes to the city with his innocence and principles intact. There he falls into the temptation of easy riches promised by stocks and bonds, only to plunge into financial sin. If De Forest is the first American novelist to see tragedy on Wall Street as the Fall of Man, William Dean Howells brings this vision to fruition and maturity only ten years later in *The Rise of Silas Lapham* (1885). *Silas Lapham* is, in fact, the *locus classicus* novel of American finance.

Sevenoaks, on the other hand, diverges from the story of Adam as well as from the Christian allegorical pattern established by De Forest's novel. A second or alternate version of the Wall Street novel is presented. Published in twelve issues of *Scribner's Monthly* during 1875, *Sevenoaks* is the prototype for Wall Street fiction in which the central character, rather than the good or innocent businessman, personifies evil. Instead of Adam, the financier is a type of Satan. J. G. Holland's villainous financier, Mr. Robert Belcher, is the devil incarnate. He is a direct literary descendant of Jaffrey Pyncheon, the evil capitalist in *The House of the Seven Gables,* as well as the forerunner of such fallen financial titans as John Dumont in David Graham Phillips's *The Cost* (1904), Dan Waterman in Upton Sinclair's *The Moneychangers* (1908), and Frank A. Cowperwood in Dreiser's trilogy *The Financier* (1912), *The Titan* (1914), and *The Stoic* (1947). A more commonplace but no less evil money figure is Jason Compson in William Faulkner's *The Sound and the Fury* (1929). Sons of Belial, these unregenerate money men are warped and demonic. Wealth and power are their idols. Grabbing and getting are the cornerstones of their ethical systems. They refute the romantic idea implicit in the Adamic version of the Wall Street novel that man is naturally good and made bad only by institutions. Satanic capitalists, they are corrupt long before they consort with the stock exchange, and remain damned with not a shred of hope of finding peace or salvation. Wall Street, a nether world of shades and darkness, is the sphere in which these evil financiers most naturally adapt.

Honest John Vane is Adam, the natural man originating in a prefallen world. He is good, innocent, uncorrupted. Yet, in his goodness and innocence lie weakness and susceptibility. Like Melville's Good-Enough-Morgan in *The Confidence Man*, who represents any "corpse of calamity" victimized by the "gloomy philosopher" or "destroyer of confidence," Vane is singled out as an easy prey and relentlessly stalked by the devil. At first, corruption creeps up quietly and unnoticed as he is lured away from his small prosperous business into politics. Then, when Honest John is elected congressman and comes to Washington, worldly lusts and appetites, once unknown to him, are awakened. Riches dazzle him as well. Vane's subsequent complicity in a massive financial scheme in the nation's capital that pivots around stocks and bonds completes his fall into evil. Back-corridor politics, high finance, and easy money, tendered in the proper dosages, readily corrupt him.

The Gilded Age was a prolific time for scandal. The attempted gold corner by Jay Gould and Jim Fisk that culminated in the panic of "Black Friday" in 1869, the watering of the Erie Railroad, the Whiskey Ring, the Crédit Mobilier, these and a thousand other business piracies clouded the dawn of the age of Big Business. The plot of many an economic novel in the 1880s and 1890s turns on the illegitimate efforts of financiers and businessmen to compile fortunes. *Honest John Vane* accordingly was inspired not by the wave of speculation that flung the whole nation into the stock exchange in the 1870s, but by one of these scandals—the infamous Union Pacific-Crédit Mobilier—uncovered a few years earlier.

The Crédit Mobilier was a joint-stock company organized in 1863 (reorganized in 1867) to build the Union Pacific Railroad. Scandal broke out openly in 1872, when high government officials were found to have been accepting bribes from the company. Novelist De Forest subsequently saw in the Crédit Mobilier the chance to write an overt political satire, a scathing allegory in which Washington lawmakers as well as lobbyists are represented as opportunists and public malefactors. Assigning them names such as Christian, Faithful, Hopeful, and Greatheart, De Forest classified the principals in the scheme according to their tastes and fondness for corruption. He pointed out that his novel was "a new and perversely reversed and altogether bedeviled rendering of the *Pilgrim's Progress* into American politics." [1]

Honest John Vane is not only one of the first bedeviled renderings of Bunyan's *Pilgrim's Progress* into politics, but also, quite by chance, into American financial fiction. The counter or reverse path that the hero travels toward the city of Destruction, *not* the Heavenly City, and toward evil, *not* good, is the course followed by many financial innocents. Honest John's is the story of the businessman or financier in American fiction who, like moth to candle, strays too close to the glowing fires of the stock exchange. Whenever moral resistance to sin and evil is broken down, particularly by greed, the devil's victory is sure. Vane is the literary forebear of a long list of Good-Enough-Morgans, from Howells's Colonel Lapham to Louis Auchincloss's Guy Prime, victims of the devil who fall into the money bondage and try speculating their way out of financial crises. The American novel of high finance, therefore, set forth and established by John De Forest, transmutes the figurative and symbolic action of the Bunyanesque journey into a Christian allegorical version of the Fall.

John De Forest modeled his disgraced hero, John Vane, after Oakes Ames, a wealthy manufacturer from Easton, Massachusetts who inherited a shovel and tool factory from his father. Ames, whose brother Oliver Ames was president of the Union Pacific Railroad, won election to the U.S. Congress in 1863. Subsequently he became a kingpin in the Crédit Mobilier when an insider and front man was needed in Washington by the scheme's organizers to ensure success of the fraud. Congressman Ames doled out free shares of stock in the company to important House colleagues in an effort to thwart any adverse legislation against the Crédit Mobilier. The scheme was, as he indiscreetly boasted, "a diamond mine." That "diamond mine" in essence was an independent construction company formed to build roadbed and lay track west from Omaha for the Union Pacific Railroad. It was a company within the original company, contrived to siphon off millions. The construction scheme relied on two main sources for revenue. One was rigging estimates 'way above actual costs and thus overcharging the Union Pacific for track. A second was an ingenious system of double payments, in which long stretches of line already built by the Union Pacific with stock and bondholders' money were paid for again by the U.S. government. When the first dividends were declared and paid out from the company's exploding profits,

Crédit Mobilier stock soared to $260, making many insiders in the company—businessmen, financiers, senators, congressmen and, alas, the Speaker of the House (James G. Blaine), the vice president (Schuyler Colfax) and a future president (James A. Garfield)—instantly wealthy. Overall, Union Pacific paid the Crédit Mobilier $93 million to build road worth only $50 million, a "take" of $43 million. Small wonder New York speculator and plunger Jim Fisk had gone to court in the early years of the scheme to declare Union Pacific's contract with Crédit Mobilier fraudulent and to seek a restraint on the railroad from paying for construction. No white knight himself, Fisk had a knack for chicanery that enabled him to spot a spade when he saw one—and he also had enough cash tied up in Union Pacific securities to give him the courage to call it as such. A congressional investigation of this silk-hat and kid-glove operation eventually took place in 1873, eight years after the swindle had been in full swing. When this investigation ended, however, it produced nothing more than an official whitewash. Ringleader Oakes Ames, proclaiming his honesty to the end while protecting the real masterminds behind the scenes, merely received a reprimand from the committee. He died three months later. De Forest was not the only novelist who thereafter vilified Ames. Mark Twain took a swipe at him in *The Gilded Age,* published several months before *Honest John Vane.* In that novel, New York dandy Harry Brierly (a caricature of Jim Fisk) spies lobbyist Laura Hawkins at a political reception in Washington hobnobbing with "that stuffy Congressman from Massachusetts—vulgar, ungrammatical shovel-maker—greasy knave of spades."

Like Oakes Ames, John Vane is ungrammatical, though a maker of refrigerators, not shovels. A businessman in a small New England town, Vane is honest, upright, and seemingly incorruptible. So naive is Honest John about the world and so devoid of guile that De Forest is compelled to qualify his image of spotlessness: "I am exaggerating Mr. Vane's Eden-like nakedness and innocence; but I do solemnly and sadly assure the reader that I have not robbed him of a single fig-leaf of knowledge which belonged to him." [2] Honest John's fortunes dramatically change when he is approached by a mysterious stockbroker and financier named Darius Dorman. Dorman, whose origin is undetermined, coaxes

Vane to attend a Republican caucus in his district. An unassailable reputation for honesty and integrity makes "awnest Jawn" an ideal candidate for Congress, and a perfect tool for the devil. This Adamic businessman is marked by Dorman for a future role in a much grander scheme of evil than the petty day-to-day affairs of Washington. Meanwhile, Honest John wins the election and subsequently marries the coquettish Miss Olympia Smiles. Like Dorman, Olympia finds Vane an easy mark, particularly after she knows he'll be going to Congress. Miss Smiles is all part of the devil's plan, apparently, for it is her fascination with the big city social swirl and her prodigal spending that soon after creates a drain on her congressman-husband's meager bank account, weakening also his dedication to probity and honor.

Love-bewitched by Olympia, Honest John Vane becomes money-bewitched and captivated by the devil. Darius Dorman reappears on the scene in Washington and wastes little time counseling Vane to "Go into finance," rather than bother with less important committees in Congress. The newly elected congressman's reply—"I've thought of that already. . . . It's my line, you know,—business, money-matters, practical finance" [3]—is characteristically vain, yet comically unsuspecting. "Practical finance" he may be familiar with, but high finance, Dorman's realm and the exclusive province of the devil in American financial fiction, Honest John knows little or nothing about. A demon-stockbroker, Dorman is prototypical of the tempter or devil in the Wall Street novel. A tint of ashes and dust discolors his smirched appearance to the extent that "a vivid fancy might easily impute to him a subterranean origin and a highly heated history." [4] Openly fiendish and satanic, Dorman "had absorbed all the evil that he could find in business, politics, and lobbying." [5] Like Milton K. Rogers, who entices Silas Lapham into accepting cheap stocks, the devil in *Honest John Vane* helps establish the innocent hero, then sets about undermining his moral resistance. Dorman offers stock in the proposed project of the Subfluvial Tunnel Road—a cabal that promises huge returns if Vane would see it generously funded by Congress. Sensing that the Subfluvial is a plot to defraud, Congressman Vane, however, balks at the stock offer. The initial interview between Adam and Satan, financial innocent and evil money man, thus ends "with virtue still unshaken, but vice undiscouraged." [6]

The Subfluvial conceals a smaller corporation within it, whose ostensible object is to unite Lake Superior with the Gulf of Mexico by means of an inland waterway, but whose real object is to make money and divide the profits for insiders. In the dusky shadows is the scheme's real brain, Simon Sharp, a financier and practical statesman. The Honorable Mr. Sharp, "one of the oldest sailors in this ship of state" who "knows all the ropes," vaguely suggests financier Russell Sage, known as the Money King of Wall Street during the last half of the nineteenth century. Sage had served in the Thirty-Third Congress and knew the ropes so well that, while in office, he enriched himself and fellow politicians with consolidation of the New York railroads into the "Central," a deal that also quickly cost him his political career. Nevertheless, twenty years later, after the Crédit Mobilier had been exposed and investigated, and Congressman Ames had died with the secret of who the real leaders were forever sealed on his lips, who wound up with control of the Union Pacific Railroad? Money King Russell Sage!

A figure of Adam who is weakened by an indulgent and ambitious Eve, then corrupted by the devil, Honest John Vane also suggests Faust. In the traditional legend, Faust was a denier of God, preferring worldly knowledge and power. The American financial novel, however, employs only the popular mechanics of the Faust legend, emphasizing the devil's pact and subsequent damnation of the soul. Vane, as well as Silas Lapham, are financial Fausts in the sense that they have already tasted moderate riches and success but wish to acquire more. Through an agreement with Mephistopheles, they become rich in worldly assets for a time, as Faust became rich in worldly experience. Honest John at length makes a deal with Dorman, but not without further resistance. His resolve, though, like his money, is soon spent, a fact not unnoticed or left untried by the stockbroker.

> The eyes of the Mephistopheles of the lobby glowed with
> a lurid excitement which bore an infernal resemblance to
> joy. He had a detestable hope that at last he was about to
> strike a bargain with his simple Faust. There was more

than the greed of lucre in his murky countenance; there was seemingly a longing to buy up honesty, character, and self-respect; there was eagerness to purchase a soul.[7]

The stockbroker-lobbyist-demon, who has peered into the "very bottom of John Vane's thimbleful of soul," again offers his victim shares of stock. Vane reluctantly confesses he is "awfully hard up," as if to apologize for even considering the offer. Soon after he accepts the gift and seals his fate.

Scandal eventually breaks out in the nation's capital, and foul winds around the Subfluvial scheme shift Vane's way. But the fictional congressman, like his real-life model, ducks behind a façade of honesty to escape public exposure and remain above condemnation.

II

Sevenoaks: A Story of To-Day, published in 1875, is one of the cornerstones of Wall Street fiction. Its author, Josiah Gilbert Holland (1819-1881), was a physician until twenty-nine years old, then turned poet, lecturer, editor of the *Springfield Republican,* and later editor of *Scribner's Monthly* as well as novelist. Dr. Holland was more widely known by his nom de plume, "Timothy Titcomb," which he used for a popular series of letters offering middling moral advice in the Richardsonian manner to young bachelors, maidens, and married folks. But he was known more particularly by Emily Dickinson as a reigning authority on literary matters, and by William Dean Howells as a rival editor who tried to lure such contributors as Henry James away from the *Atlantic Monthly.*

Sevenoaks presents a Calvinistic view of high finance, saturated with a banal and pervasive moralism. Holland rebukes the growing vice of business in the Gilded Age, an issue he had previously raised in an article for *Scribner's.* Robert Belcher, the capitalist in *Sevenoaks* who is congenitally wicked and inherently malign, represents the dark side of the financier in American fiction. He foreshadows those capitalists and financiers who enter the world in a fallen condition, already corrupt. Past redemption, the dollar is their only Word, the wrath of it their only fear. Holland concludes about this type of businessman that "when known evil seems absolutely good to a man, and conscious falsehood takes on the semblance and authority of truth, the Devil has him fast." [8] During Holland's day the devil had many businessmen fast, and new recruits were springing up everywhere. One acolyte was James Fisk, Jr., the same who blew the whistle on the Crédit Mobilier crowd. Vermont-born Fisk started out as a traveling country peddler, then moved on to Boston, and eventually New York. He fell in with that shady Zacchaeus of the stock exchange, Jay Gould. Fisk's reputation as a financier and also a "high liver" grew to gaudy proportions, until he was murdered in 1872 by a former associate over a love affair. Holland was quick to moralize in an editorial in *Scribner's Monthly* entitled "Easy Lessons from Hard Lives." "No man ever died a more natural death than James Fisk, Jr.," he wrote, "excepting, perhaps, Judas Iscariot." Even Henry Ward Beecher, minister of Plymouth Church, Brooklyn, whose own reputation was under a cloud, had a few thoughts about Fisk's death, denouncing him as "that supreme mountebank of fortune . . . absolutely devoid of moral sense as the desert of Sahara is of grass. . . . God's providence struck him to the ground." Jim Fisk reaped what he had sown, and Holland and Beecher no doubt along with a good many others were content God's word was justified. The memory of Fisk was still fresh in the public's mind, making him a "hot topic" when the novelist wrote *Sevenoaks* three years later. J. G. Holland exploited the lingering charisma and legend, modeling his evil capitalist, Colonel Robert Belcher, after Jubilee Jim. *Sevenoaks* rapidly became a bestseller as well as a fixture on every middle-class reading table, holding place with *Pilgrim's Progress* and the Bible. Scribner's, in fact, kept the novel in print as late as 1922.

High finance, the province of the devil-stockbroker Darius Dorman in *Honest John Vane,* is also the murky realm of evil in *Sevenoaks.* The satanic Robert Belcher sucks and feeds on the dank corruption that breeds in the darkness of Wall Street. A greedy and malcontent manufacturer in a small mill town in New England, Belcher is impatient with the slow day-to-day pace of making a fortune. He'd rather compile riches in a hurry, so he resorts to wildcat stock scheming. The evildoer promotes absolutely worthless shares in the

Continental Petroleum Company to widows, orphans, clergymen, small tradesmen, and farmers. Inflating a mammoth bubble in the price of Continental stock, Belcher skips town before it bursts, and, with enough money from the scheme to purchase a mansion on Fifth Avenue, he gravitates to New York and the more lucrative climes of Wall Street. The stock exchange demoniacally attracts Belcher (as it did Jim Fisk), who darkly vows, "I'm going to be in the middle of this thing, one of these days. . . . If anybody supposes that I've come here to lie still, they don't know me. They'll wake up some fine morning and find a new hand at the bellows." [9] Determined to reign over this hell-like region, the financier furiously dives into the inferno. Not long after, he is fearfully spoken of in the highest banking and brokerage circles as "the General" (Fisk was nicknamed "Commodore" after he purchased his own steamboat line), while he boldly buys stocks in a rising market and then unloads them, "sweeping into his capacious coffers his crops of profit." But, secretly, Belcher really lusts for a railroad, ownership or control of which is visible proof of financial authority and a ticket for membership in the elite robber baron class. He does manage to grab controlling interest in the Crooked Valley Railroad (a portrait of the crooked Erie Railroad, known as the "Scarlet Woman of Wall Street"). Then, gorging his appetite on the public's gullibility, he pulls the same stock swindle in Crooked Valley shares with which he launched his nefarious financial career years earlier in Sevenoaks. Belcher's fame as a manipulator and plunger on Wall Street spreads far and wide. He is lionized, fawned upon, flattered, and worshiped by his retinue of toadies, all devil followers, as "a kind of god, to whom they all bowed down."

The highest seat in Wall Street, however, fails to protect Belcher from financial sins sown back in Sevenoaks. He had stolen patent rights and a share of the profits from his former business partner, Paul Benedict, who had invented the "Belcher" rifle (Holland's own father had been cheated out of profits from a textile invention for which he never secured a patent). Benedict's lawyer eventually brings the Wall Street luminary to public trial, in a scandal as bothersome yet ridiculous as if Satan himself were being tried and sentenced for a minor breach of Hadean law. Nevertheless, either his financial acumen is paralyzed by moral depravity or the market itself finally disgorges and exorcises its own evil demon, because Belcher suffers dramatic reverses on Wall Street. Unregenerate, the financier tries to restore and redeem himself, not by atoning for his sins and abandoning the marketplace as Silas Lapham and Curtis Jadwin choose to do later, but by attempting one more financial coup, a corner in Muscogee Air Line. When this last-ditch plot fails, he is cast out of Wall Street. Real-life financier Jim Fisk died from a jealous rival's bullet. Holland, however, refuses to risk any such martyrdom or fanfare for his villain. Instead of a sensational end, Robert Belcher is reduced to bankruptcy and exile in Canada, where he is heard of no more.

III

"Hadleyburg," or society, is corrupted by the pernicious influence of Wall Street. Financial fever spreads infectiously outward in both *Honest John Vane* and *Sevenoaks,* threatening whole communities. Washington, center of the nation's government and showplace of the nation's character, is pictured by John W. De Forest as a malignant and cankerous nest of venality, where each political fowl sits incubating his own financial egg. An elaborate structure of graft, bribery, payoff, and kickbacks fosters greed, allowing lobbyists to hold the key to every legislator and encourage them to dip into the U.S. Treasury, stealing and scattering the public's money like crazed geese. The Crédit Mobilier scandal, historical basis for the novel, itself was a scheme premeditated to skin the public. The preposterous Subfluvial Tunnel Road in *Honest John Vane* is also conceived to enrich insiders at the expense of the American people. The high and mighty, senators in whose hands care of the nation is entrusted, are guilty. The novelist describes these public servants as corrupt, tainted with the rank sin of the knowledge of high finance: "Christian, Greatheart, and other reputed temples of righteousness were nothing but whited sepulchres, full of railroad bonds and all uncleanness." [10] Stocks and bonds, which forever hold the golden promise of ample wealth, breed corruption and moral failure not only in John Vane but in society as a whole. Washington in the novel is merely the microcosm of American society. As it is debased, Slowburgh, Vane's hometown in the country, is also contaminated, and the fiber of the entire nation is weakened.

Financial demonism in *Sevenoaks* wrecks society as well as individuals. Snuggled safely in the hills above the Connecticut River, Sevenoaks (modeled after Belchertown, Massachusetts, Holland's birthplace, which also provided the name of his central character), had been an edenic pocket of New England, free from the dark knowledge of investments and speculative gain. Robert Belcher disrupts the town's paradisiacal tranquillity when he promotes and sells stock in the wildcat Continental Petroleum Company. Whetted by Belcher's greed, the townsfolk themselves clamor and lust for a return on their Continental investment, as they turn from God and bow down to Moloch. Their anger when the speculative bubble bursts suggests the passion with which they plunged into the scheme in the first place. The financier leaves behind a town stirred up by dreams and fantasies of a great windfall, like Mark Twain's Hadleyburg. When Belcher repeats his swindles and bogus stock schemes on a grander scale in Wall Street, America is involved and corruption spreads unchecked.

> Not Sevenoaks alone, but the whole country was open to any scheme which connected them with the profits of these [oil] great discoveries, and when the excitement at Sevenoaks passed away at last, and men regained their senses, in the loss of their money, they had the company of a multitude of ruined sympathizers throughout the length and breadth of the land. Not only the simple and the impressible yielded to the wave of speculation that swept the country, but the shrewdest business men formed its crest and were thrown high and dry beyond all others, in the common wreck, when it reached the shore.[11]

5.

Stockbrokers to Strikebreakers

I

Wall Street during the boom years of the 1870s and 1880s attracted Mark Twain, Henry James, and William Dean Howells in different ways. In fact, these writers could not have been less alike in their treatment of high finance or the financial marketplace. Twain in his fiction displays a rollicking, good-humored taste for finance, accepting its comic upswings and tragic downswings with no more surprise than he himself would a sudden ticker-tape announcement that the human race is damned. James and Howells, on the other hand, remain aloof to the financial center, out of either diffidence or mistrust. Henry James's understanding of finance is blocked by a reserve that allows him to present it only in abstractions, never portraying the marketplace or the businessmen-financiers as they really are. Rather than with awe or respect, W. D. Howells's point of view toward Wall Street and its heroes is colored with mistrust and suspicion. He is philosophically opposed to high finance, on the grounds that it breeds the wrong system of values and brings out the worst in men.

Mark Twain may poke fun at high finance, but he never takes lightly the evil nature of mankind. Who can know the heart, for it is deceitful above all things and desperately wicked. What Twain does know is that money creates deceit and corrupts the heart. Money is found just about everywhere in his fiction, notably and most darkly in later works such as "The Man That Corrupted Hadleyburg" (1900) and "The Mysterious Stranger" (1916). Despite his theme of money's evil influence, Mark Twain yet falls outside the main scope of American financial fiction, principally because the nearest things to a financier he creates are Nigger Jim in *The Adventures of Huckleberry Finn* (1884), Electra Foster in "The $30,000 Bequest," or the Connecticut Yankee, who rearranges and modernizes medieval England in *A Connecticut Yankee in King Arthur's Court* (1889). He does provide a satirical perspective of Wall Street and the speculation mania rare in American fiction. In short, Twain offers comic relief.

Mark Twain felt the political and commercial morals of the United States were not merely food for laughter but an entire banquet. Speculation on the stock exchange was a particularly tempting source of amusement, as tempting, say, as silver mining in Virginia City or the moneymaking schemes of every greenhorn from Hawkeye to San Francisco and back again to Hartford. His treatment of the subject of high finance is parodistic, jocose, robust, funny, without the bitter and contemptuous edge revealed by Nathanael West, for example, another novelist who satirized Wall Street. Twain views the financial marketplace as an irresistible opportunity to poke fun at that queer and extraordinary exponent of the damned human race—the incorrigible speculator. Yet, while the novelist Mark Twain twits and jokes about financial matters, the man Samuel Clemens hides a deep hunger for riches of his own, a dream of fabulous wealth that led him into one entrepreneurial disaster after another. Fifteen years following his declaration of voluntary bankruptcy in 1894, he was still nurturing hopes for success of the Paige typesetter, a faulty invention that siphoned off huge pools of capital and yielded only nightmares of the poorhouse. "Get me out of business!" Clemens screamed when the panic of 1893 threatened his publishing house venture and put two and a half million men out of work. Seeking financial advice, he turned to the New York business world. H. H. Rogers (Henry Huttleston or "Hell Hound," as his enemies called him) of Standard Oil Company took Clemens under his wing. Rogers managed his affairs, selling assets, paying off indebtedness, and restoring solvency as if the humorist were a small business gone on the rocks.

Despite staggering financial losses and a reputation of being a sucker for every get-rich-quick scheme that came along, Mark Twain the novelist laughed at his own folly, if not the folly of the human race, for getting money quickly and in prodigious abundance, dishonestly if it could, honestly if it had to. Establishing himself as a sort of stock market sage or analyst, he uttered one wise dictum for stock market players that has never been refuted; namely, "October is one of the peculiarly dangerous months to speculate in stocks in." Other months in which to avoid stocks, according to his analysis, are "July, January, September, April, November, May, March, June, December, August and February."[1] Damnation is not a specific corollary of moneymaking in Mark Twain's fiction, as it is with so many American writers. Instead, Twain sees lust for financial gain and the stock market simply as further testimonies to man's already corrupt and fallen condition.

One foolish speculator who gets himself entangled in a terrible web is Huck Finn's loyal companion, Nigger Jim. Earlier, though, in *The Gilded Age* (1874), a novel written with Charles Dudley Warner, satirizing every form or type of speculation imaginable, Twain portrays the nincompoop trader-gambler-speculator in Colonel Beriah Sellers. Sellers has a moneymaking scheme for all occasions. On one such occasion he plans to corner the Negro market by buying up whole loads in Virginia, Delaware, and Tennessee for resale in Alabama, but not before he gets a law down stopping sale to the South after a specified day. The plot fails. Sellers loses his shirt. The same Colonel Sellers later disparages the gambling instincts of the "Niggro." In a conversation with Senator Abner Dilworthy, who pays a visit to Hawkeye, Missouri, he offers these tidbits after the senator asks about the local conditions of "the emancipated race."

> "You can't do much with 'em," interrupted Colonel Sellers. "They are a speculating race, sir, disinclined to work for white folks without security, planning how to

live by only working for themselves. Idle, sir, there's my
garden just a ruin of weeds. Nothing practical in 'em."

"There is some truth in your observation, Colonel, but
you must educate them."

"You educate the niggro and you make him more speculating then he was before. If he won't stick to any industry except for himself now, what will he do then?"

"But, Colonel, the negro when educated will be more
able to make his speculations fruitful."

"Never, sir, never. He would only have a wider scope
to injure himself. A niggro has no grasp, sir. Now a white
man can conceive great operations, and carry them out; a
niggro can't." [2]

Short on grasp himself, but long on greed and reluctance to work,
Colonel Sellers typifies Twain's gullible speculator, reembodied
later in Nigger Jim. Jim, like the Colonel, builds glittering pyramids of coins, but always returns home empty-handed.

A brief but entertaining interlude in *The Adventures of Huckleberry
Finn* reveals Twain's satire not only of the speculator but of three
sure ways in which he can lose all his money—the outright speculative plunge, participation in wildcat banking, and trust in an
investment broker. Huck plays the role of straight man in the
dialogue and leads Jim on. When he asks if Jim is rich, Jim replies:
"No, but I ben rich wunst, and gwyne to be rich ag'in. Wunst I
had foteen dollars, but I tuck to specalat'n, en got busted out." [3]
The stock that he put his money into turned out to be alive, at
least for a time, because the cow "up 'n' died" right after Jim
bought it. Jim didn't lose everything, however, but sold out at the
low bid,[4] a dollar and ten cents for the hide and tail. His next
financial venture was in a new bank that promised to pay a whop-
ping 400 percent rate of interest a year, a rate that Jim managed to
inveigle up to 700 percent before he made a deposit. The bank
went bust and Jim didn't recoup a single penny of his capital, but
Huck wants to know what he then did with his remaining ten
cents. Unaware of Huck's joke, the discombobulated investor goes
on, telling how he sought the services of an investment advisor
named Balum, "Balum's Ass dey call him for short." Balum apparently had a reputation for being lucky. "Well," Jim sadly laments,

"Balum he tuck de money, en when he wuz in church he hear de preacher say dat whoever give to de po' len' to de Lord, en boun' to git his money back a hund'd times. So Balum he tuck en give de ten cents to de po', en laid low to see what wuz gwyne to come of it."

"Well, what did come of it, Jim?"

"Nuffn never come of it. I couldn' manage to k'leck dat money no way; en Balum he couldn'. I ain' gwyne to len' no mo' money 'dout I see de security. Boun' to git yo' money back a hund'd times, de preacher says! Ef I could git de ten *cents* back, I'd call it squah, en be glad er de chanst." [5]

The remaining ten cents which he loses, not the fourteen dollars he began with, bothers Jim most. Besides satirizing the foolish speculator and ways in which he can get burned, Twain is commenting on phenomena common to the frontier in those days—speculation and wildcat banking. He is showing a primitive society that still thinks stock is cattle, and which is at the mercy of every bagman and highwayman who employs the deceptive methods of high finance to disguise his thievery.

The stock exchange figures prominently in other works by Twain. "Sold to Satan," a short piece written in 1904, proposes a financial scheme for incorporating and selling shares worldwide in Satan. This wild and grandiose plan is accidentally begotten on an occasion when the narrator, Twain himself, feels his spirits are as depressed as, well, the blue chip stocks on the exchange. Twain actually may have been disgruntled about some one of his own ill-timed speculative ventures that went awry and cost him a pile of dough, and thus this story about making a fabulous fortune was on his mind. At any rate, Twain feels a pact with the devil is just about the only thing that will halt his personal "bear" market and turn his luck around nicely for him.

It was at this time that I concluded to sell my soul to Satan. Steel was away down, so was St. Paul; it was the same with all the desirable stocks, in fact, and so, if I did not turn out to be away down myself, now was my time to raise a stake and make my fortune.[6]

A preliminary interview with Satan is subsequently arranged (through a broker named Mr. Blank, who receives a 2½ percent commission if the trade is consummated). When Twain sets eyes on Satan, who stands a shade over six feet and weighs 900 pounds of solid radium at $3,500,000 a pound, his mouth drools and his get-rich-quick instincts leap into full gear. Satan, however, reads Twain's mercenary mind and perceives the plot taking shape there to kidnap, incorporate, and issue stock in him, even to water the stock up to ten billions of dollars (only three times Satan's actual value) and market him around the world. Twain, a bit abashed when found out but mouth still agape, instead prods Satan to strike up a business partnership and form an energy company. The agreement duly made, Satan vanishes, and Twain is left awaiting the not yet made discovery of how to separate polonium from bismuth, which is essential to controlling radium. Twain's stock (already going down, remember, before he drummed up this deal) now plummets on the exchange. His last hope gone, he is forced into receivership and puts up a sign—"Stock for sale. Apply to Mark Twain."

In *The Innocents Abroad* (1869), the great slave marts of Turkey, where young girls once were publicly sold by auction, provide Twain with an opportunity to satirize Mohammedan morality—as well as that peculiarly American fetish and hunger for financial news. Sales are now conducted in private, sort of an "over-the-counter" market operation rather than the Big Board. A bull market in girls happens to be under way in Constantinople, the result of a combination of unusual economic factors that places excessive demand on available supply. The day's trading is described by Twain in the style of a stock or commodity report as it might appear in any American metropolitan newspaper.

SLAVE-GIRL MARKET REPORT

Best brands Circassians, crop of 1850, £200; 1852, £250; 1854; £300. Best brands Georgian, none in market; second quality, 1851, £180. Nineteen fair to middling Wallachian girls offered at £130 @150, but no takers; sixteen prime A 1 sold in small lots to close out—terms private.

> Sales of one lot Circassians, prime to good, 1852 to
> 1854, at £240 @ 242½, buyer 30; one forty-niner—dam-
> aged—at £23, seller ten, no deposit. Several Georgians,
> fancy brands, 1852, changed hands to fill orders. The
> Georgians now on hand are mostly last year's crop, which
> was unusually poor. The new crop is a little backward,
> but will be coming in shortly. As regards its quantity and
> quality, the accounts are most encouraging. In this con-
> nection we can safely say, also, that the new crop of Cir-
> cassians is looking extremely well. His Majesty the Sultan
> has already sent in large orders for his new harem, which
> will be finished within a fortnight, and this has naturally
> strengthened the market and given Circassian stock a
> strong upward tendency. Taking advantage of the in-
> flated market, many of our shrewdest operators are sell-
> ing short. There are hints of a "corner" on Wallachians.
>
> There is nothing new in Nubians. Slow sale.
>
> Eunuchs—none offering; however, large cargoes are ex-
> pected from Egypt to-day.[7]

Twain makes light not of the shameful practice of trading in
women, but of the lurid American appetite for stock market news
and love of a bull market, whatever the commodity happens to be.
Rising prices, prosperity, the American way! When prices for slave-
girls two or three years ago were low, parents in a starving condition could sell their young daughters for only twenty or thirty
dollars. "It is sad to think of so distressing a thing as this," Twain
says, "and I for one am sincerely glad the prices are up again." [8]

A clever young Harvard Business School type in *A Connecticut
Yankee in King Arthur's Court* rescues medieval England from economic ruin. He introduces a variety of economic measures to that
beleaguered sixth-century society in order to induce recovery. A
new currency, full-time employment as traveling salesmen for the
knights who previously had little to do other than ride around the
countryside—and a stock exchange—are a few of the drastic steps
taken. Sir Launcelot is made president of the stock board, and
seats at the Round Table where the daily volume of business is
transacted are apparently of such great value that the author
avoids stating the figure because no one would believe it. Sir Laun-

celot, as it turns out, is a chronic bear, and the great corner he pulls off in shares of the London, Canterbury, and Dover Railroad leads to the devastating war that breaks up King Arthur's realm. Launcelot had caught, among others, Sir Agravaine and Sir Mordred, nephews to the king, in a squeeze on their short positions and forced them to settle at an outrageous price. Embittered, the royal victims grudgefully inform Arthur about Launcelot's affair with the queen and proceed to lay a trap of their own for him. The knights of the kingdom split into factions over this issue, and many fall, including the Connecticut Yankee's handy right fielder and peerless shortstop, who are participants in another American pastime that had been introduced.

Mark Twain's viewpoint toward Wall Street and high finance is unique in American fiction. Unlike many writers who take money and its effects on the human soul seriously, Twain manages a humorous approach. William Faulkner, possibly influenced by Twain, brings this humor to life again in his satire of the confused speculator, Jason Compson, in *The Sound and the Fury*. Big Business and Eastern finance are held up to ridicule as well by Faulkner in his treatment of the Snopes family in the trilogy *The Hamlet, The Town,* and *The Mansion.*

II

A popular critical charge against Henry James is that he had no conception of the influences of economic fact upon men's lives. The novelist himself made admissions supporting that charge. James concedes in his preface to *The Reverberator* (1888), for example, that "before the American business-man, as I have been prompt to declare, I was absolutely and irredeemably helpless, with no fibre of my intelligence responding to the mystery." He goes on, "No approach I could make to him on his 'business side' really got near it." [9] Even though money is central in James's stories and novels, as it is in Balzac, Zola, or Turgenev, his treatment of the financial theme is shaped by those admitted difficulties he had in understanding business or penetrating the character of the businessman.

Henry James in his early stories evaded the task of characterizing the businessman, casting him instead as a minor or superfluous quantity who stays hidden in the background. Mr. Westgate is a New York lawyer busy with the Tennessee Central Railroad lawsuit as well as other matters downtown in *An International Episode* (1878). He remains in the city while his wife entertains at Newport, society's favorite watering spot. He is left behind again when she and her sister, Bessie Alden, trip off to merry England. "And what do you do with the American gentlemen?" Lord Lambeth innocently asks Mrs. Westgate in London, moved during conversation by her rather narrow definition of "society." Percy Beaumont interrupts, however. "She leaves them in America," he answers. Leaves them in America! Exactly what James himself does, especially if the gentlemen happen to be businessmen! Schenectady, Elmira, Utica, Poughkeepsie—drab nineteenth-century industrial and manufacturing cities in upstate New York—are favorite Jamesian dumping grounds. Mr. Ezra B. Miller is left home and safely out of sight in Schenectady while his family is off tooting in Europe in *Daisy Miller* (1878). "He's got a big business. My father's rich, you bet," [10] Randolph proudly informs Ralph Winterbourne in Vevey, the Swiss resort area, a reminder of Mr. Miller's token existence. Randolph, Daisy's brother, in fact is a nine-year-old extension of his prosperous and substantial father who is back "in that mysterious land of dollars." James evidently feels more comfortable with the boy as spokesman for the business side of the family than with Mr. Miller himself.

Henry James considered allegory unworthy of the realist in fiction, yet he reverted to that mode whenever he attempted the economic theme. The allegorical haze never lifts from his vision of the money world. The American air of moneymaking remains vague and clouded. In each tale or novel about the deplorable New York world of business lies a hint of the Fall of Man. Even when James allows the American businessman to walk out of the dim commercial wilderness and book passage aboard a steamer for Europe, he portrays him as a symbolic or allegoric figure. Christopher Newman in *The American* (1877) and Whitney Dosson in *The Reverberator* are two such businessmen, allegorical representations of American innocence. Of the two, Newman is less naive, with "an eye in which innocence and experience were singularly blended."

The trust that Christopher Newman, by his own good nature, continually ascribes and imputes to others stems from a sense of esteem in his own motives (if not too much a sense of power and self-confidence), yet still a natural basic decency. A quality of the prefallen or preindustrial man lingers about these businessmen, signaled by an eternal Arcadian optimism, a buoyant good faith, and a sense of conscience and morality. Authoritative and experienced in the world of American business as they were, both Newman and Dosson confront Europe like spoiled rich schoolboys on a class trip. Anything they want, they feel they can buy and stuff into their breeches' pockets.

Christopher Newman is the new American businessman of the last half of the nineteenth century who invented, then financed the industrial New World. He springs from the soil of the West, America's Garden, and penniless right after the Civil War, rises to become a successful capitalist. Compiling the bulk of his money in leather, washtubs, and copper, and the rest in railroads (he fizzled in oil), Newman is in the mold of a James J. Hill or E. H. Harriman. Rich though he is, he saves himself from the ruinous fall that haunts most heroes in the novel of high finance. Newman's sole aim in life had been to make money, yet at the very height of his financial powers he suddenly packs up and leaves the marketplace. Bent on revenge over a $60,000 sum at stake in a business affair for which he had traveled a long distance to Wall Street, the financier is abruptly made aware of the direction his life is taking. Rather than pursue his grim financial vendetta—as either Judge Jaffrey Pyncheon or Robert Belcher would have done with little regard for moral scruples—he quietly resolves to abandon the money game. He cares for moneymaking, but never particularly for the money. He gets out just in time, before he *does* care for the money.

> We pulled up in front of the place I was going to in Wall Street, but I sat still in the carriage, and at last the driver scrambled down off his seat to see whether his carriage had not turned into a hearse. I couldn't have got out, any more than if I had been a corpse. What was the matter with me? Momentary idiocy, you'll say. What I wanted to get out of was Wall Street.[11]

In an early story, "Guest's Confession," Edgar, the older of two brothers, forces a man who had defrauded him in a shady deal to kneel in public and confess his business sins. Revenge is a motive from which Christopher Newman instinctively recoils as he chooses to retain his virtue, his good conscience, and ultimately his large bank balance in this act of repudiation of the world of finance. These good qualities, preserved by Newman, do not go unnoticed later by Mrs. Tristram in Paris when she informs him, with her usual irony, "You are the great Western Barbarian, stepping forth in his innocence and might, gazing awhile at this poor effete Old World, and then swooping down on it." Resisting the dark forest of Wall Street, with all its sharp railroad men and stockbrokers, Christopher Newman moves on, still Adamic, to the dark forest of Europe and the temptations of its manners and traditions. Even there, although he has left behind "no monuments of his 'meanness' scattered about the world," he is rejected in part by the aristocratic Bellegardes as a "commercial person."

Another Jamesian example of the rich American financial innocent abroad is Whitney Dosson in *The Reverberator*. Dosson is "a man of the simplest composition, a character as cipherable as a sum of two figures." [12] One of the factors in his elementary total is his "genius for happy speculation, the quick, unerring instinct of a good thing"; the second factor is his attribute of being a pliable and docile father. Acute as his financial senses are, allowing him to hear the tune in the discord of the stock market or smell profits far downwind, he is dull and inept in Parisian social circles. Yet he remains as untainted by French morality as he did by American finance, blandly guiding two possessions, his daughters, through the thick and tangled way of the Paris *grand monde*.

Spencer Brydon in the story "The Jolly Corner" had renounced the world of American business for a life of leisure and culture in Europe. He had sold his commercial birthright for a bowl of meager pleasure. Curious, even a bit guilty, Brydon repatriates himself following a thirty-three-year absence. In so doing he falls victim to an obsession about how triumphant and successful he might have been in the vast world of figures and money had he never left. He wonders whether he would have discovered his genius for architecture and developed some new form or structure that would have produced a gold mine had he stayed home. Brydon tells Miss Staverton, an old friend and confidante, that he might have flowered in this New York environment if he had followed the course in business apparently set up for him by his father. Now, at the age of fifty-six, nagged by uncertainty at his original decision to defect, he says:

> I should have stuck here—if it had been possible; and I was too young, at twenty-three, to judge, *pour deux sous,* whether it *were* possible. If I had waited I might have seen it was, and then I might have been, by staying here, something nearer to one of these types who have been hammered so hard and made so keen by their conditions. It isn't that I admire them so much . . . it's only a question of what fantastic, yet perfectly possible, development of my own nature I mayn't have missed.[13]

Brydon pursues the vision or ghostlike figure of what he might have been, a grinning and unappeased aboriginal demon, through the bare rooms of his ancestral house in New York. That demon must be met and placated. As his obsession grows near to madness, he suddenly confronts this ghoul, a monstrous specter in evening dress, the consummate portrait of financial triumph. From one hand that shields its ghastly face, two fingers are missing, lost perhaps in some aggressive act of grasping or reaching for money! Brydon's denial of this deadly business world years earlier implies a curious prevision or precognition of such a hideous end. That repudiation, in effect, saved Brydon from a fate which the rank money passion would certainly have reserved for him. Despite his father's curse for leaving, he escapes the disintegrative influence of American business, but only by renouncing a life that would have blighted and misshaped his soul.

Not all businessmen in Henry James's fiction are the essence of innocence, types of Adam. Mr. Ruck in the short story "The Pension Beaurepas," or Frank Betterman and Abel Gaw in *The Ivory Tower* (1916), represent the countertype of financier, the fallen capitalist who has lost, if not his fortune, at least the humanity required by the necessities of the marketplace to be expended in order to get rich. Failing to turn his back on Wall Street, a decision that Christopher Newman happily makes, Mr. Ruck commits himself to a life of buying and selling until, in fact, he "knows how to do nothing else." Sickness and aging, symptoms of moral decay associated with money and the stock market, overtake the financier in this story and darken his last days. Ruck soon ends up "a broken-down man of business." Even in Switzerland, with his family to recover his health, he finds no escape or salvation from Wall Street. Ruck spends nearly all his time at the local bank reading correspondence from New York and poring over the daily financial news in the *New York Herald,* instead of forsaking business affairs. As economic conditions at home worsen and his own business, as a result, faces bankruptcy, Ruck's physical decline accelerates. Finally, alarmed by the severity of his financial reverses, he makes a sudden and perhaps fatal decision to return to New York and the marketplace. Ruck, so completely consumed by Wall Street, is unable to extricate himself from the endless cycle of moneymaking and spending.

Demonism and evil associated with the money man are hinted at by Henry James as early as 1881 in the novel *Washington Square,* a theme he was to develop later. The dark and alluring Morris Townsend threatens to upset the ordered world of Washington Square and make off in marriage with Catherine, only daughter of the rich Dr. Sloper. Townsend's character and reputation are based upon an abiding obsession with money, as Dr. Sloper's scorn is directed toward the young adventurer for chronic lack of it. After long years unemployed, he finally goes into business, a partnership with a commission merchant "downtown." Presumably Morris sets up shop as a broker, as easily and glibly as Melville's confidence man, for he speaks vaguely about buying some cotton in New Orleans for a six-thousand-dollar profit. Townsend's cousin, who married Catherine Sloper's own cousin, was also a broker, a profession with few connections in society but many pretensions and ambitions. At any rate, Dr. Sloper smells a fortune hunter in Townsend, or worse, a demon, hating him for his devilish tendencies. "He is not what I call a gentleman; he has not the soul of one," says Dr. Sloper. "He is extremely insinuating; but it's a vulgar nature. I saw through it in a minute. He is altogether familiar;—I hate familiarity."

Evil colors Henry James's final characterization of the American businessman in *The Ivory Tower*. As his means to wealth become more ferocious, his ends more ill-gotten, the businessman grows many shades darker. Primal qualities of newness and innocence originally ascribed in earlier portraits appear as corruption and sin by the time the novelist puts his finishing touches to the picture. Christopher Newman is metamorphosed into Abel Gaw and Frank Betterman. Adam, when finally drawn, looks unmistakably like Satan.

Abel Gaw, an abysmally rapacious Wall Street predator, is portrayed in *The Ivory Tower* as a vulture or hawk with talons and beak that have found many victims' hearts. He was an old business associate of Frank Betterman, who, like Gaw, rose out of the darkness of New York's financial history. But, because of unspecified differences that were so bad they became threatening, these allies parted ways and thereafter remained deadly enemies. While Betterman is awaiting death in his bedroom at Newport, Gaw fiendishly lurks nearby, seeking some last-minute advantage or triumph. Frank Betterman himself was a rich and ruthless operator on Wall Street. Having accumulated assets of more than $20 million, he epitomizes business and the world of finance. "I *was* business. I've *been* business and nothing else in the world," he tells his nephew, Graham Fielder, from his deathbed. "I'm business at this moment still—because I can't be anything else." [14] Unlike Gaw, Betterman is trying to redeem himself in his last hours from a life of terrible acquisition. Guilt-ridden, he hopes to escape damnation simply by divesting himself of his money. In one sweeping codicil that annihilates everything in the matter of precautions, usualisms, and provisions for trusteeship, he unconditionally passes his millions on to his nephew after he dies. First, however, the capitalist makes sure that Fielder is untainted by sin and evil of the financial marketplace, that his mind is an economic *tabula rasa*, innocent even of the ugliness of his inheritance. As if salvation could depend upon, or be minimized by, another's crown of righteousness. The nephew relates later how the dying millionaire wanted him to be "clear, to the last degree, not only of the financial brain, but of any sort of faint germ of the money-sense whatever—down to the very lack of power, if he might be so happy (or if I might) to count up to ten on my fingers. Satisfied of the limits of my arithmetic he passed away in bliss." [15]

Henry James rarely thinks as much about the corruptive effects of acquiring money as about the liberating effects of already possessing it without having worked for it. Money frees a character from the boring necessity of earning it or the deadening compulsion of acquiring more. Isabel Archer, for example, is loosed from economic necessity by an unexpected bequest in *The Portrait of a Lady* (1881), and Daisy Miller and Madame de Mauves are emancipated and unfettered by family fortunes. James's main interest as a novelist is in characters like these who pass beyond the money temptation and face more interesting kinds of temptations. The novelist, when free himself of the financial and economic theme, is able to focus more easily and effectively on the moral and cultural aspects of his characters' lives. He feels more comfortable in his fiction even with a man like Lambert Strether in *The Ambassadors* (1903), who has very little in the way of worldly riches and can say of himself, "And I, though with back quite as bent, have never made anything. I'm a perfectly equipped failure," [16] than he evidently does with such warriors of high finance as Christopher Newman and Frank Betterman during their salad days on Wall Street.

III

Wall Street was a stumbling block for William Dean Howells. He held the financial marketplace in low esteem, viewing it with distrust and condemnation. Centers of finance are regarded in his fiction as breeding grounds for social inequity and moral iniquity. The stock exchange itself stands openly as a symbol of what was wrong with the economic system. High finance and the exchange together epitomize the competitiveness that brings out the worst in men and distorts their values and ideals. They also represent the world of chance of modern business by which men, who foolishly misplace their hope and trust, are led astray.

Howellsian businessmen such as Silas Lapham, Jacob Dryfoos, and J. Milton Northwick are corrupted and defeated, as society is corrupted and defeated, by reliance on the stock market as the golden way to quick and certain riches. The greater tragedy of these men of affairs is that losses they suffer in the marketplace— whether financial or spiritual—go beyond their own lives and touch countless other people. Complicity, or the basic interdependence of men, a theme especially prominent in Howells's economic novels, illustrates the truth that no man sins or suffers alone. A man's errors afflict not only himself but everyone directly associated with him, as well as many others who, even in a most insignificant way, derive some economic, moral, or spiritual sustenance from his deeds. The effects of both good and evil, as Howells envisions them, spread outward like vast unseen ripples, influencing whole communities of men. Howells lived in an age when great fortunes were being assembled with little care for scruples as to the means, and with ideals that were low and vulgar. His apparent antipathy toward the individual businessman in his fiction was actually a more fundamental disavowal of economic individualism, for it was unsatisfactory to basic human needs and made a mockery of humanitarian brotherhood. He also disdained the economic system of free and open enterprise because it was built upon strife, forced to rely on chance, and fostered social inequality and inequity. Howells in his economic novels, particularly those written later, denies the efficacy of the competitive system and advocates the principles of socialism based on the doctrine of Christian brotherhood as the only path to reform. If only labor and capital could work together for mutual welfare, Howells hoped, instead of clinging to economic cross-purposes. He issued a sentimental plea in his novels to soften the capitalist's heart and feel a spirit of brotherly love for the laborer.

The typical capitalist in W. D. Howells's fiction, contrasted to Henry James's portrait of the unsullied and innocent businessman, is a good many shades darker. In *Their Wedding Journey* (1872), Howells's first novel, Basil March attests to the villainy of the breed, referring to them as "the shabby despots who govern New York, and the swindling railroad kings whose word is law to the whole land." [17] Mr. Peckham in *The Undiscovered Country* (1880),

Mr. Everton in *A Woman's Reason* (1882), and Mr. Gerish in *Annie Kilburn* (1888) are portraits of corrupt capitalists, and Royal Langbrith in *The Son of Royal Langbrith* (1904), already dead by the time the novel opens, leaves behind a ruinous aftermath of evil. The reverence for and pursuit of money, to which economic individualists such as these consecrate themselves, are spoken of contemptuously by Aristides Homos, the wayfaring man in *A Traveller from Altruria* (1894), as examples of the barbarity of American capitalism. Silas Lapham in *The Rise of Silas Lapham* (1885), Jacob Dryfoos in *A Hazard of New Fortunes* (1890), and J. Milton Northwick in *The Quality of Mercy* (1892) represent businessmen and financiers not inherently evil and corrupt but nevertheless unequipped to resist temptations of the stock market. They are natural or preindustrial men, sons of the soil and raised in the Garden, who are eventually corrupted by the world. With the exception of Dryfoos, who experiences a moral Fall without financial ruin, once these characters yield to the call of easy money, they plummet into financial disgrace and spiritual despair.

The Rise of Silas Lapham, published at the height of America's industrial expansion, pictures an era and personifies a type. The era is the Gilded Age. The type is the American businessman. He already had been shaped before the Civil War. H. G. Eastman founded a business school in Poughkeepsie in 1855, and by the end of the war had more than a thousand pupils. The Massachusetts Institute of Technology was established in 1861 and courses on industrial technology dominated its program. The Gilded Age merely blew its spirit into an array of businessmen and bred them unchecked, unmodified. Silas Laphams rose up by the dozens out of the bones of village peddlers and became manufacturers, industrialists, and financiers. Mr. Howells, as Owen Wister vouched in his foreword to *The Virginian*, saw many Silas Laphams with his own eyes.

William Dean Howells was a realist. If he saw many Silas Laphams, he felt it necessary to portray them as they were, true to life. Dedicated as he was to verisimilitude in observation and description, Howells, Edwin Cady points out, still wrote "a modern realistic version of a morality play." [18] Many American novels, not just *Silas Lapham,* become morality dramas whenever the hero contends with the stock exchange. *Silas Lapham,* the *locus classicus* Wall Street novel, sets forth themes and motifs, one of which is this struggle of man against a falling stock market, which are recapitulated in nearly every novel dealing with high finance. Good opposes Evil as the soul of the businessman or financier awaits the outcome of the struggle. Sickness or death result from direct involvement with stocks. Steady financial disintegration works like a chronic body disorder. Also, a fall into bankruptcy brings about a spiritual malaise, worse than death itself. Reconciliation and regeneration after the plunge into the evil of high finance, central in *Silas Lapham,* are further themes in the Wall Street novel. Businessmen like Silas, burned and bankrupted by speculation, accept responsibility for defeat. They emerge from the shadows of misfortune, repentant, freed from the bondage of the money lust, cleansed of the taint of financial corruption, and morally transformed. Like Silas, who withdraws to Vermont to take his "cure," they are allowed a new birth and a new life.

Silas Lapham is not really Everyman, whose soul hangs in the balance of the awesome war between good and evil, as found in the full-scope morality. But he is the embodiment of a particular American literary type, the beloved stock figure of the ingenious Yankee, hard-fisted, sensible, and God-fearing. Brought up on the principles of the Old Testament and Poor Richard's Almanac, he spends his boyhood years in the backwoods of Vermont. As a young man he serves the Union's cause in the Great War, for which he is promoted to captain and also wounded at Gettysburg. After the war he returns to his family paint business and slowly rises in the world as an unheroic, hard-working, and honest man. Lapham is the American businessman. He is commonplace, he is good, he is prosperous. When he moves his business to Boston, Silas retains the innocence of the Garden of rural America. He brings ideals and principles of the country with him to the city, center of commerce and finance. As one Howells commentator says, Silas Lapham is not of the mold or character of the contemporary robber baron, for whenever he is faced with making a decision in business, "he is firm, and ends with honor, if in poverty. Such a dilemma, so far as one can see, never disturbed for a moment even the more restrained generals of industry." [19]

Paints Lapham knows. But about money he is Adamically innocent. He displays a hopeful temperament and fondness for round instead of precise figures, which cause him to overestimate his actual worth. Also rather than real assets, Silas reckons his wealth on the basis of capital, some of which is borrowed. Unlike the businessman types in Henry James's earlier fiction, this innocence cannot last. The devil takes aim early, as if he has Lapham singled out and marked for an eventual target. During the war Silas's life is saved by Jim Millon, who stops a musket ball meant for him by an enemy sharpshooter. "He saw the devil takin' aim," recounts Lapham years later at a Corey dinner party, "and he jumped to warn me." [20] Another devil sharpshooter, Milton K. Rogers, draws a deadly bead on Silas and finds the mark. Lapham had to face him alone during this financial trial, with no loyal Jim Millon in the wings.

Rogers is the devil or tempter. His goal is to seduce Lapham in the greenness of prosperity, fulfilling a plan of revenge. In physical appearance Rogers is tall, thin, with a "dust-colored face, and a dead clerical air," yet he deceptively suggests "at once feebleness and tenacity." [21] Lapham's tempter recalls not only Darius Dorman in John W. De Forest's *Honest John Vane,* but also Roger Chillingworth, another pervasive figure of destruction in Hawthorne's *The Scarlet Letter.* The surname Rogers is an alias for Satan, or Old Roger. "Milton" suggests *Paradise Lost,* in which Satan invades the Garden and tempts Eve.[22] Howells incidentally uses the name Milton again in *The Quality of Mercy.* J. Milton Northwick, not quite the evil figure Milton K. Rogers is, but possessed nevertheless by a destructive lust for money, is a businessman who also is corrupted by high finance and falls into sin.

The business partnership that arises between Silas Lapham and Milton Rogers resembles a Faust-Mephistopheles relationship. A similar alliance is found earlier in *Honest John Vane,* as the congressman-businessman Vane becomes inextricably involved with the lobbyist-broker Dorman. It is Persis, Lapham's wife, who insists he take a partner into his business in the first place, "somebody with

capital." When Silas accepts the devil's money for expansion of his
paint works, he places himself under ominous financial as well as
moral obligations. The devil in this instance poses in the subtle
guise of a moneylender, who waits upon his victim to exact every
last penny of capital and interest. As the paint business prospers
and grows, however, Rogers is no longer of any use, so that after a
year and a half Silas pays him off and forces him out. Lapham's
move to get rid of a dead weight partner, sound Yankee business
instinct and practical sense, triggers Rogers's revenge plot.

The Devil, bent on destruction, again works through the
Adamic businessman's wife. Consequently, he is able to attain a
ruinous grip on Silas, ingeniously luring him into a less dissoluble
partnership or pact. Neither assuaged nor denied until his wicked
plan is finished in *Silas Lapham,* Rogers pops up suddenly on several occasions following his dismissal from the paint works. After
the first of these unexpected encounters, Persis reproaches and
badgers her husband for the unfair treatment he had shown his
former partner. When Lapham tells her it was a perfectly square
thing, that his conscience is not troubled by it, she answers ac-
cusingly, "And I can't look at him without feeling as if you'd
ruined him, Silas." [23] Because Lapham *had* forced Rogers out with
the foreknowledge that his paint was soon to double in value, Persis persecutes Silas for his business decision and ironically sees
Rogers as the victim, not the devil, while regarding her husband as
the real destroyer. She blindly reverses and muddles the actual
roles. Edwin Cady, one of the few critics to correctly evaluate Mrs.
Lapham's part in the drama, writes that "she might be taken as
the moral *raisonneur* of the novel, Howells' spokeswoman. . . . For a
long time she is Silas' conscience, unsparing, caustic, pessimistic.
But the country culture from which her Puritan hang-over comes
Howells had long seen to be riddled with dry rot." [24] Persis reveals
her shoddy double standard of morality when she insists Rogers
had saved Silas when he needed money. Yet her reaction is anger
and jealousy when she discovers Lapham had been financially
helping Zerilla Dewey and her mother, daughter and widow of
Jim Millon, the only man who ever did save him. Also, as Cady
observes, Mrs. Lapham becomes so caught up in her yearning for

social status with the Coreys that "consequently she falters and fails Silas completely when the crisis of his struggle for righteousness comes. In that crisis he is left entirely alone, deserted by the dry-rotted culture of his past as by the wife who embodies it." [25] Persis (an apt nickname for "persistence," for even Silas admits there is "no hang back about her") inadvertently is instrumental in Lapham's Fall. When Silas finally does relent and lends money to Rogers, she is relieved. "You've taken the one spot—the one speck—off you that was ever there, and I'm satisfied," [26] she informs her husband.

The devil keenly knows a victim's weaknesses. Reveal a chink in the defensive armor, and he is there, slipping a temptation through. With Silas Lapham, the weakness is not so much a yearning for money as for equality with his Brahmin neighbors, which he thinks money can buy. Rogers perfectly perceives this flaw and uses it as the fulcrum for his attack on Lapham. The handshake over the loan agreement thrusts the innocent businessman into a more deadly partnership with his former associate. Significantly, Lapham accepts stock certificates as collateral for the loan. Rogers borrows $20,000 in cash and puts up as "security" alluring low-priced stocks. The devil's deal with Silas is the perfect ruse. Cheap stocks always hold the promise of rising to high levels and yielding astronomical profits. And to the inexperienced and uninitiated investor, they always look like the golden way to riches. Actually, if Lapham had sold these issues at the current market value, they would have been worth only one fourth of the loan. By accepting them, therefore, he seals his fate and hastens his ruin. Suddenly, no longer satisfied with normal business profits, Silas craves the quick riches the stock market can provide. All his former Old Testament and Puritan values are swept aside like so much worthless impedimenta as he becomes immersed in the financial marketplace, addicted to the Ghost Dance religion, buying and selling stocks on his own.

Lapham's first stock market transaction is immensely profitable. In fact, Persis, who knows how opposed to investing Silas has always been, is puzzled by the extra money. Lapham is forced to explain.

"Oh, I've made a very good thing in stocks lately."

"In stocks? When did you take up gambling for a living?"

"Gambling? Stuff! What gambling? Who said it was gambling?"

"You have; many a time."

"Oh yes, buying and selling on a margin. But this was a *bona fide* transaction. I bought at forty-three for an investment, and I sold at a hundred and seven; and the money passed both times."

"Well, you better let stocks alone," said his wife, with the conservatism of her sex. "Next time you'll buy at a hundred and seven and sell at forty-three. Then where'll you be?"

"Left," admitted the Colonel.[27]

Despite the fact he tells Persis he made an "investment," Lapham actually turns the stock over for a quick speculative profit of almost 150 percent. Bewitched by this first flush and taste of success, he confidently believes even the cheap stocks he received from Rogers will go up in time. Meanwhile the devil fans Silas's financial fantasies white hot, as he dumps more worthless collateral on him from all sorts of wildcat stock schemes, patent rights, land speculations, and oil claims to secure additional cash loans. Then, just as certainly as the bedazzled businessman enjoyed initial triumphs in the market, the squall hits. He suffers some minor reverses. Losses mount. A short time later the seas burst and Lapham gambles away tens of thousands of dollars. Everybody had been taking in sail during a stormy economic period, selling what they could. Nobody was buying anything. Nobody except Silas. When financial losses reach a staggering figure and his ship nearly founders, Lapham confides to his daughter, Penelope, he is in trouble. Asked what he has been doing that is wrong, the beleaguered businessman laments, "I don't know as you'd call it wrong. It's what people do all the time. But I wish I'd let stocks alone. It's what I always promised your mother I would do. But there's no use cryin' over spilt milk; or watered stock, either." [28]

The fatal bargain with Rogers and stock market reverses cause

Lapham's Fall. His vanity and pride bring him lower, however, even to the edge of destruction's pit. Silas refuses to cut back production at his paint works at a time when supply is glutting the market. Time and chance also go against him. Competitors in West Virginia strike a vein of natural gas next to their factory, which cuts their fuel costs to one-tenth of Lapham's. Thus, unable to compete with lower paint prices, Silas is forced to shut down entirely—and his ruin is made complete. Brought low, he inveighs not against chance or financial misfortune. Rather, he lays bare his soul and makes confession of his sins of speculation to his wife:

> "I don't say it to make favor with you, because I don't want you to spare me, and I don't ask you; but I got into it through Milton K. Rogers."
>
> "Oh!" said Mrs. Lapham contemptuously.
>
> "I always felt the way I said about it—that it wan't any better than gambling, and I say so now. It's like betting on the turn of a card; and I give you my word of honour, Persis, that I never was in it at all till that scoundrel began to load me up with those wild-cat securities of his. Then it seemed to me as if I ought to try to do something to get somewhere even. I know it's no excuse; but watching the market to see what the infernal things were worth from day to day, and seeing it go up, and seeing it go down, was too much for me; and, to make a long story short, I began to buy and sell on a margin—just what I told you I never would do. I seemed to make something— I did make something; and I'd have stopped, I do believe, if I could have reached the figure I'd set in my own mind to start with; but I couldn't fetch it. I began to lose, and then I began to throw good money after bad, just as I always did with everything that Rogers ever came within a mile of. Well, what's the use? I lost the money that would have carried me out of this, and I shouldn't have had to shut down the Works, or sell the house, or . . ." [29]

Persis forgives him. "It's all right, Silas. I shan't ever bring it up against you." [30]

The Coreys, representative of the old Boston aristocracy, stay wisely and safely away from the stock market. They invest their money instead in paintings, which increase in value. Standing outside the periphery of this bear market drama in which Lapham is caught, they are well insulated from the financial struggles that take place on the stock exchange. Bromfield Corey, always aware of inherent values, provides a commentary on the investment situation that seems smug yet instructive:

> It's very odd that some values should have this peculiarity of shrinking. You never hear of values in a picture shrinking; but rents, stocks, real estate—all those values shrink abominably. Perhaps it might be argued that one should put all his values into pictures; I've got a good many of mine there.[31]

Like most new homeowners, Silas Lapham makes frequent stops on Beacon Street to view the progress while his house is under construction. He is struck on these visits by the pile-driving apparatus used to set the foundation of the house. In fact, he remarks to his wife, who accompanies him, "By gracious! there ain't anything like that in *this* world for *business,* Persis!" [32] But, although Silas admires one powerful machine, he is pounded by another—the stock market. He learns, too late, that there *is* something like that pile-driving machine in this world for business. The weight of a falling market in his stocks delivers heavy and portentous strokes, driving him financially into the ground. In contrast to the Coreys, therefore, the newly rich Colonel Lapham speculates with borrowed money to buy stocks on margin. Those stocks not only decline, they become totally worthless. Like his new house, which is consumed in a fire right after the builder's insurance policy expires, all Lapham's securities purchases end up in a useless heap, with nothing salvageable.

Ruin is formal—devil's work. Slipping is Crash's law. Silas Lapham's fall into the sin of speculation is prepared for, because the gods he has always worshiped are the wrong or false ones. Silas is a convert to success religion. His gods are merely idols of the marketplace. Reporter Bartley Hubbard, in a feature article about

Silas for *Events,* writes that this local businessman believes in mineral paint, "he makes it a religion; though we would not imply that it *is* his religion." [33] Lapham's wife, Persis, goes further, accusing him of actually making the paint his god and of being unwilling to let anyone share in its blessings. Silas does revere successful products, as he emulates successful men. During an inspection tour of his new house with Tom Corey, Lapham compares its architectural design to ordering a picture from an artist. "You pay him enough, and he can afford to paint you a first-class picture; and if you don't, he can't. That's all there is of it. Why, they tell me that A. T. Stewart gave one of those French fellows sixty thousand dollars for a little seven-by-nine picture the other day. Yes, sir, give an architect money enough, and he'll give you a nice house every time." [34] Alexander Turney Stewart, another of Lapham's gods, was a fabulous success story during the Gilded Age. An Irish immigrant, he rose from petty shopkeeper to famous dry-goods merchant and richest man in New York, save for an Astor and a Vanderbilt who inherited their wealth, accumulating a fortune estimated at between fifty and seventy-five million dollars. A crony of Ulysses S. Grant, whom he frequently entertained at his white marble palace on Fifth Avenue, Stewart was once considered by Grant for Secretary of the Treasury.[35] Thus, the mineral paint and successful businessmen like A. T. Stewart, along with the stock market, are the tutelary saints of Lapham's private world.

Cause and effect spin Silas Lapham headlong toward ruin. Commitment to the stock market clouds Silas's mind and drains his emotional reserves. The decision to keep the paint works running full blast in the face of a business recession comes from preoccupation with his investments as well as vanity and pride. Also, failure to buy an insurance policy after the builder's risk on the Beacon Street house expires results from the need to put all available money into his stock margin account, and it is a choice as adverse as the pure stroke of chance that destroys the house in a fire. Lapham's financial disintegration grips him "like the course of some chronic disorder, which has fastened itself upon the constitution, but advances with continual reliefs, with apparent amelioration, and at times seems not to advance at all, when it gives hope of final recovery not only to the sufferer, but to the eye of science itself." [36] As Lapham's mental and emotional health deteriorate, bankruptcy is imminent. Bankruptcy and financial ruin symbolize death in the novel of high finance. The fall of the House of Lapham is funereal and bears resemblance to the hushed atmosphere surrounding the house of the dead:

> The house of mourning is decorously darkened to the world, but within itself it is also the house of laughing. Bursts of gaiety, as heartfelt as its grief, relieve the gloom, and the stricken survivors have their jests together, in which the thought of the dead is tenderly involved, and a fond sense, not crazier than many others, of sympathy and enjoyment beyond the silence, justifies the sunnier mood before sorrow rushes back, deploring and despairing, and making it all up again with the conventional fitness of things. Lapham's adversity had this quality in common with bereavement. It was not always like the adversity we figure in allegory; it had its moments of being like prosperity, and if upon the whole it was continual, it was not incessant.[37]

When the bankruptcy is finally consummated, it brings relief and a "repose to Lapham and his family, rather than a fresh sense of calamity." [38]

Silas's salvation from the marketplace—not his success as a Boston businessman—symbolizes his real rise in *The Rise of Silas Lapham.* As he redeems only the finest grade of paint (the Persis brand) and purges his lower-grade products, he casts off and renounces his old self to emerge in "clean-handedness." The minister Sewall, a peripatetic character who appears in several Howells novels, visits the farm in Vermont to which Silas has repaired and finds the hero "shabby and slovenly in dress . . . fallen unkempt, after the country fashion, as to his hair and beard and boots." [39] Silas is the natural man once again, restored to his native surroundings in the Garden. When Sewall asks if he has any regrets, Lapham answers he would do it all over again in the same way. "All I know is," explains Silas, "that when it came to the point, although I could see that I'd got to go under unless I did it—that I couldn't sell out to those Englishmen, and I couldn't let any man put his money into my business without I told him just how things stood." [40] Good rises out of the darkness of high finance. After the fall into financial sin, there is redemption. Not every businessman or financier in American fiction entwined in the labyrinths of the stock market comes out as triumphantly.

The money temptation devours J. Milton Northwick in *The Quality of Mercy*. Lust for money simply germinates in his heart until this businessman-hero discovers himself far gone in financial sin.

Treasurer of the Ponkwasset Mills Company, Northwick has open access to company funds, but he fraudulently employs this resource for personal speculations in the stock market. A little cash taken here and a little taken there is enough to support his margin purchases. Blind to any wrongdoing, Northwick feels entitled to the money because the company owes its very success to his careful management over the years. Besides, he always restores money he borrows, neatly balancing ledgers and keeping stock market profits for himself. Only when an unexpected bad drop in railroad shares occurs on the stock exchange does he sense he is in error. Caught on the wrong side of a bear market, Northwick's losses balloon beyond the point where he can make good the company's money. Plunging deeper into error, he juggles the books to hide his borrowings. Northwick has little difficulty justifying this legerdemain to himself, even after the market has gone against him, for "in his long habit of making himself these loans and returning them he had come to have a vague feeling that the company was privy to them; that it was almost an understood thing." [41]

Both Northwick and Lapham, as they become immersed in speculation, shunt their business affairs to one side so that they may devote full attention to the stock market. Just as Silas buys stocks on margin, Northwick finances his equity purchases with embezzled funds. In each instance, because their wobbly operations are leveraged on borrowed money, losses are magnified when the market suddenly turns. Unable to dodge the debris of falling prices in a bear market, both are crushed on the stock exchange. Silas Lapham opts for bankruptcy rather than pull down anyone else, and atones for financial sins. Northwick, desperately weighing suicide or standing trial, chooses to skip out and abscond with a paltry few thousand dollars.

J. Milton Northwick, like fallen financiers later in Wall Street novels by Louis Auchincloss, becomes a self-exile. In Canada, refuge from extradition and prosecution, he slowly deteriorates, paralyzed by the enormity of his act. He fears particularly for his money, which he wears in a belt fastened so tightly it symbolically constricts him. Northwick dies before he can pay his debt. "His environment made him rich, and his environment made him a rogue," [42] says the embezzler's lawyer, trying to extract some meaning or moral from his wasted life.

Conditions rather than evil men are to blame for the economic disorders of the 1880s in *A Hazard of New Fortunes.* Yet Jacob Dryfoos, more than any in W. D. Howells's gallery of economic characters, represents individual corruption in the marketplace. As Edwin Cady observes: "Dryfoos is Silas Lapham reversed or turned upside down. The rise to power Silas declined to his soul's salvation Jacob Dryfoos has embraced—and paid his soul for success." [43]

Lapham, at least, was a manufacturer and a producer. Northwick, before he fell to temptation, was a capable businessman. But Dryfoos serves no useful function. The last effectual thing he does is buck the Standard Oil Company, which was taking over Ohio's natural gas fields farm by farm—until he is outvoted by his daughters to sell his own land. Then, stricken with boom fever, Dryfoos becomes a speculator in his own right. He embraces Wall Street and the New York Stock Exchange—and is damned. Dryfoos's one aim is to make money, pile it in a corner, and hurry back downtown for more. His only economic discipline is to arrive in the financial district in time to catch the market's opening, watch his favorite stock go up and down under the betting, then leave at the market's close. He has no more financial expertise than a boardroom habitué, one of those pilot fish who hangs on every flutter of a stock's price. Dryfoos effectively sells his soul to the "Street."

> He came where he could watch his money breed more
> money, and bring greater increase of its kind in an hour
> of luck than the toil of hundreds of men could earn in a

year. He called it speculation, stocks, the Street; and his
pride, his faith in himself, mounted with his luck.[44]

Dryfoos, in fact, is Howells's version of the contemporary robber
baron, that giant breed of capitalist thrust into the world by time
and chance and anointed by riches. While he plunders society for
thousands a day, more ordinary mortals in the labor class eke out
narrow existences on the fringe of poverty.

Moral and spiritual decay are not the only hazards of new fortunes portrayed in the novel. Beyond these, the costs for Dryfoos
are multitudinous. His eyes are blinded, his heart is hardened,
even his hands are bloodied. Conrad, his son, dies in a tragedy not
unrelated to Dryfoos's monomania with the stock market. The capitalist, disgruntled and evil-minded because he had made only a
few thousand dollars trading that day, is irritated further when he
has to return uptown during a streetcar strike. Enraged at his son's
sympathy for the strikers' cause, which includes a wage increase of
a few pennies a day, Dryfoos hits him in the face. Dazed, Conrad
wanders off and chances upon a protest in a West Side street where
strikers have massed. He is accidentally shot to death by a policeman while trying to intercede for a friend in the tumult.

Howells's plea to the capitalist to soften his heart and show
brotherly love for his fellow man strikes its deepest note in *A Hazard of New Fortunes*. The alternatives to humanitarian brotherhood
are all too clear. Evil, sown in Wall Street or anywhere, cuts a man
off. The money may keep pouring in. But the selfish and unregenerate capitalist reaps damnation.

6.

Romance and Adventure
on Wall Street

I

Booms always followed busts, peaks rose out of valleys, feasts
eventually relieved famines as America's economic history traced a
volatile path through the nineteenth century. Wall Street, once
only an arcane name, stirred the public's mind as omnipotent
trusts and monopolies, as well as kings such as J. Pierpont Morgan,
Sr., who reigned over them, lifted into view like pyramids. Aroused
by huge fortunes made overnight and epic hand-to-hand battles of
finance fought each day—whether read about on the front pages of
newspapers or in the pages of fiction—the public's fascination with
Wall Street steadily grew. The stock exchange and high finance, in
fact, became popular subjects in life as well as fiction. A boom year
in the stock market in 1899 saw the public participate heavily as
the number of stockholders reached an estimated 4,400,000. Also, a
flood of novels about business and finance formed a whole economic and literary *Weltanschauung* in the early 1900s. So widespread was the influence of Wall Street, it helped confer upon New
York an economic-literary ascendancy that resembled the preemi-

nence of Boston when life and literature were influenced by transcendentalism.

The ethos of prosperity created a modern Babylon or Rome out
of turn-of-the-century New York. Signs of wealth were abundantly
evident in the baronial and monarchial life styles, the splendorous
mansions erected along fashionable Fifth Avenue, the elegant gaslit drawing rooms with carved oak panels, tufted furniture, and
cut-glass chandeliers, the marble-paved halls and grand staircases,
and the carriage houses complete with clarences and four-in-hands.
Society thrived on commerce and business as banking institutions,
brokerage houses, and insurance companies grew into titular temples of the money religion. New York, however, instead of being
urbane and sedate, was wide open and rowdy. Despite a new
peerage postulated on wealth, it took on characteristics of a frontier boomtown, where the newest prospector could be the next
millionaire, and the next millionaire could be busted, bankrupt,
and back on the streets hoping to strike another bonanza. The
frontier itself, when the country underwent industrialization after
the War Between the States, was just as rapidly closing and disappearing. Wall Street reincarnated the legendary Old West, kept its
spirit alive, and brought it back East. In fact, Wall Street created a
new frontier—a frontier of high finance. Pioneers flocked in to
"stake claims" or set up businesses. The less hardy would hire out
an office on the ground floor in Broad or Pine Street, furnish it in
elaborate and showy style, nail up a sign in big letters, and wait for
customers. The more rugged and visionary—speculators, promoters, bankers, and investors—opened new lands, dug new mines,
built new railroads, and founded new industries to accommodate
nearly one and a half million people swelling the population each
year. Plundering these newly formed enterprises became a favorite
pastime. Piracy and theft reached such a grand scale that European investors beheld the looting in utter disbelief. They could
only ascribe the savagery on Wall Street to Red Indian influence.
The New York Stock Exchange had indeed become a vortex of
activity where ambushes and raids were hourly carried out. After
the Northern Pacific panic of 1901, railroad pioneer James J. Hill
likened scenes on the trading floor to "ghost-dancing" of the natives out in his Indian country.

> The Indians begin their dance and don't know why they
> are doing it. They whirl about until they are almost
> crazy. It is so when these Wall Street people get the spec-
> ulative fever.[1]

Not vast in the space it occupied, the financial district at the foot of Manhattan commanded a far-flung vista of the whole country, access to the hinterlands through shares in railroad and shipping companies, a grubstake in the oil, steel, and mining industries. Laws were few, people to enforce law and order were fewer, and money was the means by which an individual won respect. An uncivil world, its determining virtues were neither sophistication nor gentility, but sheer hardihood and combativeness, brute courage and selfishness, a keen sense of bluff and deception. Daring and bluster were more valuable in a dossier than the Groton-Harvard-Wall Street training expected of the power elite in the 1920s. Wall Street, a heartless place, never published lists of its dead and wounded.

Frontiersmen of the Old West, embodied in a legendary figure like Daniel Boone, were replaced in the popular mind by such black-suited, side-whiskered types as Daniel Drew. Backwoods demigods like Davy Crockett, who fought, hunted, and matched wits with all takers, were reborn in Jay Gould or Jim Fisk, men who used the ticker tape, stock certificate, and financial report as weapons rather than rifle or fowling piece. Even Wall Street language was frontier or country language. "Watering stock," originally a reference to the sly practice of allowing cattle no water until just before they were sold live-weight, then feeding them salt and letting them drink their fill, became the name for the nefarious scheme of watering stock certificates—printing up thousands of shares of worthless securities and foisting them upon a gullible and unsuspecting public. The term "bear" is believed to be an allusion to an Old West proverb about selling the bearskin before the bear is caught. In Exchange Alley, London's financial district in the eighteenth century, stock sold on such speculation was called a "bearskin" and the dealer a "bearskin-jobber." If the term "bear" is derived from American Western folklore by way of England, the origin of the expression "bear trap"—the ploy of luring short sellers into an illusory down market, then driving the price of the stock up and forcing settlement at higher levels—is more directly Western. The source of the term "bull" is not known, possibly originating from association with the sports of bullbaiting and bearbaiting. However, allusions to "wolves" and "coyotes," describing the less formidable but no less rapacious types on Wall Street who close in for the kill after the prey is fallen, stem from the predatory creatures that hungrily roamed the Western plains. A "stock corner" is merely a sophisticated variation of cattle or horse rustling, in which the buyer corrals someone else's stock on the exchange before the owner realizes it's gone. A "pool" is the posse hurriedly formed to chase down the manipulator and smash his corner.

Legends, anecdotes, stories, and epics of the type that circulated orally in the Old West were spawned in New York as well, as Wall Street developed its own mythology. For instance, the disreputable Erie Railroad, a highly speculative and manipulated stock whose control bounced back and forth among Drew, Gould, and Cornelius Vanderbilt, became known as the "Scarlet Woman of Wall Street," and itself accounted for hundreds of exaggerated tales. Jay Gould earned the menacing appellation "The Mephistopheles of Wall Street," as his reputation for destruction and deviltry grew into legend. There were also the incredible Jubilee Jim Fisk, otherwise known as the "Prince of Erie," the infamous James R. Keene, who was called "The Silver Fox of Wall Street," John W. "Bet-a-Million" Gates, "Sell 'em Ben" Smith, and such epic events as "Black Thursday" (October 24, 1929) or "Black Friday" (the day Gould and Fisk attempted to corner the nation's gold supply). A number of titans of the Street themselves hailed if not from the West, from rural areas. James J. Hill, the railroad baron mentioned earlier who became known as the "Prince of the Great Northern," arrived in St. Paul, Minnesota from Canada in 1856 with aspirations of working as a trapper. Uncle Dan'l Drew, although a country boy from upstate New York, started with his military bonus as a drover and moved cattle (watered) from Ohio and Pennsylvania to New York markets. Son of a Vermont tinware peddler, Jim Fisk held odd jobs in a traveling circus, where he learned at first hand the art of spotting an easy mark and boldly taking his money. John Warne "Bet-a-Million" Gates brought from the Illinois frontier a readiness to gamble on anything from faro and euchre to raindrops running down a Pullman car window. And James Keene had a speckled background as hostler, mule-puncher, prospector, curbstone broker, and speculator in California during the silver mining stock heydays of the Comstock Lode before hauling his millions east to conquer the jackals on Wall Street. The rawboned physical prowess, crude ethics, and shrewd intelligence of the frontiersman or country boy, therefore, found their way into New York through the men who migrated there and molded the basic character of the Wall Street financier. Scratch a little beneath the surface and, lo, there was a Western adventurer with red bandanna and revolver. Backwoods virtues were popularized even further by the rough-and-tumble public image of the president of the United States, whose terms of office spanned these early years of the 1900s. Teddy Roosevelt (author of the six-volume *The Winning of the West,* which also helped keep the nearly vanished frontier alive) himself played the role of the great sheriff who bravely rode up to the Wall Street canyon hideouts and flushed out such trust-making "outlaws" and "robbers" as J. P. Morgan, Sr. and John D. Rockefeller, Sr.

Wall Street fiction in the early 1900s, like Wall Street life, also retained many characteristics of the literature and mythology about the Old West. The financier in the Wall Street novel is portrayed as both heroic and picaresque. As a hero he is a development of the legendary frontier character, boasting the epic dimensions of Paul Bunyan, the prowess and resourcefulness of Natty Bumppo, and the unmatchable wilderness skills of Mike Fink. As a picaro he is an extension of Owen Wister's famous Virginian of the plains, an unlettered rogue who comes from the soil, rises in station, and enters big-time business. The fictional financier of this period also borrows many qualities from a wholly non-Wild West source, Napoleon Bonaparte. The vainglorious figure of Napoleon curiously was a hero par excellence during the Gilded Age. Napoleon-like figures were the heroes in much of the popular success literature. Also, a number of biographies about Napoleon appeared between 1890 and 1905, testimony to his widespread revival. One "eminent man of middle age" quoted in Tilley's *Masters of the Situation, or Some Secrets of Success and Power* (1887) admitted, "If

I had read the life of Napoleon when I was a boy, my own life might have been different. It would have filled me with the ambition to make the most of myself. . . ." Two biographies published in 1894—*The Life of Napoleon Bonaparte* by William Mulligan Sloane, and *A Life of Napoleon Bonaparte* by Ida Tarbell—were such bestsellers they went through several editions. The publisher Samuel S. McClure had persuaded Ida Tarbell to write her biography of the Corsican. After completing it, she joined the staff at *McClure's* and tackled the industrial Napoleons, writing "The History of Standard Oil Company" series, which appeared regularly in that magazine from 1902 to 1904. Earlier in 1893, *McClure's* had capitalized on the first wave of the Napoleon vogue by publishing a collection of pictures of him that drove circulation up by thirty thousand copies in a month. The popularity of Napoleon may have contributed to American financial fiction the image of the financier as general, whose legions were syndicates or rings, whose battles and campaigns were carefully mapped-out bear raids and whose armies were moved from an office high above Wall Street that served as the remote command post. Financiers such as Curtis Jadwin in *The Pit* by Frank Norris, John Dumont in D. G. Phillips's *The Cost*, E. V. Harrington in Robert Herrick's *The Memoirs of an American Citizen*, and Sampson Rock in *Sampson Rock of Wall Street* by Edwin LeFèvre all are described as Napoleonic, as men who acted as if they were a part of God's destiny.

The popularization of Western frontier culture influences other aspects of the Wall Street novel besides characterization of the financier hero. Even the minor figures in these novels of high finance are colorful reproductions of striking and memorable frontier types. The hunter, trader, and gambler are recast into the characters of the boardroom habitué, stockbroker, and stock manipulator. The land-grabbing, livestock-rustling hunger of the frontier is transferred into the stock-buying hunger of the Street and becomes the master passion of the financier. Also, the element of the morality drama, a recurrent and often veiled feature found in most financial fiction, may have been carried on and restimulated by the universal appeal in the "dime Western" of good struggling with evil. In this respect, the financier is reminiscent of the stock Western hero who contends with evil, but nevertheless is victorious in the end over the lawless forces in society. Not only do the literary characteristics of regionalism and local color, exhibited in the styles of Owen Wister or Bret Harte, among others, survive in the blend of romance and realism that typifies the Wall Street novel of this period, but some of the real-life characteristics of the frontier, themselves, linger on in the actual customs of Wall Street at the turn of the century. In his essay "The Frontier Gone at Last," Frank Norris marks how the practices of "competition and conquest" are interchangeable with the concepts of "capturing" businesses, "seizing" opportunities, and "killing" industries. He concludes from observing the contemporary economic scene that "perhaps we have not lost the Frontier, after all."

Two opposing viewpoints toward business and high finance developed in economic fiction of the early 1900s. One, a fundamental skepticism about the economic order, is a view that grew out of the populist-progressive and utopian-socialist reform movements of the previous decade. Economic skepticism characterizes the Wall Street novels of David Graham Phillips, Upton Sinclair, Jack London, and Winston Churchill. The other, a view of the romance of business, originates from converging late nineteenth-century literary traditions of sentimentality, romance, naturalism, and native American realism. Financial novels of Frank Norris and the less-known Will Payne and Edwin LeFèvre portray the adventure and chivalry of the struggle in the economic marketplace.

"Fancy a good romance about Wall Street,—so written that the public could understand it!" wrote Lafcadio Hearn just before the turn of the century.[2] Like Hearn, Frank Norris sensed the possibilities of Wall Street in fiction and sought to understand its mystery and machinery. He realized that, if the artist only chose, "he could find romance and adventure in Wall Street or Bond Street." But Norris knew as well that "romance there does not wear the gay clothes and the showy accoutrements, and to discover it—the real romance of it—means hard work and close study, not of books, but of people and actualities."[3] *The Pit* (1902), the action of which takes place in Chicago's financial district, not New York's, is a blend of romance and business without the local color that Norris always thought superficial and steadfastly opposed. Will Payne's novels of high finance, lacking the atmospheric and thematic richness of Norris, are by comparison a bland mixture of romance and sentimentality. A common pattern in Payne's fiction is the mawkish love subplot, which involves the principal characters who had been at odds all along in a life-and-death economic struggle. Usually, the son of the victorious financier falls in love with the daughter of the ruined victim and, despite her reduced economic circumstances, still wishes to marry her. Edwin LeFèvre is a local colorist, a period writer who never penetrates the surface realism of New York's financial district. He staunchly defends and glorifies high finance, carrying Wall Street chauvinism to its most extreme conservative posture.

II

What are the fickle principles and puny techniques of the financial marketplace, the Chicago Board of Trade, in the face of the great flow of wheat that moves "resistless, along its ordered and predetermined courses from West to East, like a vast Titanic flood"? Natural law ultimately proves more powerful than human or economic law in *The Pit,* second novel in Frank Norris's unfinished wheat trilogy. Norris, no disciple of the contemporary gospel of wealth who preaches the false doctrine that underlying forces of economic law are natural and therefore benevolent, instead views these forces as corrupt, evil, and controlled by man's selfish purposes. By contrast, the laws of nature, he believes, are pure and incorruptible. The novelist rose above the orthodox progressivist clamor of the 1890s and the muckraking concerns that sprang up in the early 1900s, despite his abiding care for political, economic, and social problems. Norris's vision of the injustices and wrongs of the current order is more cosmic and universal, his artistic response more poetic and romantic.

Economic law clashes with natural law in *The Pit.* Financiers and speculators who tamper with the natural order of the whole wheat cycle are crushed and obliterated. Helmick, Hargus, Charles Cressler, Dave Scannel, Crookes and his ring, and Curtis Jadwin, all of whom have power to manipulate wheat prices and influence crop production, meddle with the natural order through the devilish instrument of the commodity market. So foreboding is the Helmick episode, for example, talked over in hushed voices by operagoers during intermission, it lays a thick pall over the La Salle Street atmosphere at the beginning of the novel and presages worse failures. Helmick dared attempt to singlehandedly swing a wheat corner, but had failed that very afternoon. Another financier, Hargus, had earlier tripled his fortune by cornering September wheat, then lost it all within a year. Now a decrepit old man draped in threadbare and filthy garments, wretched and broken, Hargus is a fearful reminder of the fate of the Pit speculator. Cressler, yet another dark and portentous figure, also attempted a wheat corner and failed. Utterly ruined, he falls sick and commits suicide. Finally, Curtis Jadwin, whose desperate cry, "Give a dollar for July—give a dollar for July!" goes unheard in the frenzied climax of his failure, numbers among those fallen financiers who attempt a wheat corner and are punished for interfering with nature.

Curtis Jadwin's beginnings are humble and impecunious. Like Silas Lapham, he originates in the backwoods. His family all are farmers, close to the soil. Innocent and inexperienced, Jadwin comes to Chicago quite by chance when offered property as payment for a debt. He then parlays this piece of city land into a spectacular real estate empire. Rising to commercial success and prominence, he is a man whose opinions are respected, whose friendship is sought by businessmen and promoters, and whose "name on the board of directors of a company is an all-sufficing endorsement." An esteemed and established bulwark of society, business, and church, Curtis Jadwin is the stock figure of the good man in the financial novel.

Although charitable and pure of heart, Jadwin at bottom is a man of business who respects and admires power. His wonder at the mechanical organ he installs in his art gallery recalls Silas Lapham's awe of the pile driver on the construction site of his Beacon Street house. Like Lapham, his awe of another powerful machine—the commodity exchange—turns out to be almost fatal. Though he deplores speculation, Jadwin does occasionally hazard a few "small operations." Sam Gretry, a commodities broker and consummate master of pit tactics, has the businessman on his list of hot prospects. He gradually breaks down Jadwin's resistance to speculating and convinces him he should make his first trade in futures. From a despatch that Gretry receives from sources in France, the broker learns the French government will introduce a bill within a month levying onerous import duties on all foreign grains. Gretry draws the obvious conclusion that domestic grain exports will fall sharply, lowering the demand for and consequently the price of wheat. The La Salle Street broker, who suggests a parallel to Milton K. Rogers, the tempter in *Silas Lapham*, obscures his real motive from his client—vengeance against the Porteous gang, a bull consortium that has held sway in the pit since long before the Helmick bust. Gretry intends to use Jadwin as a tool in his own scheme of revenge. The innocent businessman balks at first when the broker dangles before him this speculative opportunity to sell wheat short before the bad news hits the market.

> "But to tell the truth, Sam, I had sort of made up my mind to keep out of speculation, since my last little deal. A man gets into this game, and into it, and into it, and before you know he can't pull out—and he don't want to." [4]

Gretry, the tempter, persists, entreating his client to understand his viewpoint:

> "But lord love you, J.," objected the other, "this ain't speculation. You can see for yourself how sure it is. I'm not a baby at this business, am I? You'll let me know something of this game, won't you? And I tell you, J., it's found money. The man that sells wheat short on the strength of this has as good as got the money in his vest pocket already." [5]

Jadwin, like a shy maiden whose better judgment struggles against desire, resists the tempter's argument:

"*I* know, Sam," answered Jadwin, "and the trouble is, not that I don't want to speculate, but that I *do*—too much. That's why I said I'd keep out of it. It isn't so much the money as the fun of playing the game. With half a show, I would get in a little more and a little more, till by and by I'd try to throw a big thing, and instead, the big thing would throw me. Why, Sam, when you told me that that wreck out there mumbling a sandwich was Hargus, it made me turn cold." [6]

Finally, his willpower so broken down that he lets the toss of a coin decide, Jadwin gives Gretry the order to sell short a million bushels of wheat and draws a check to cover margin costs. Signing his name, the businessman-turned-financier seals the pact. He is committed to the sin of speculation. The fall is complete.

What Jadwin's lusts and desires of the heart conceive are brought forth in the sin of speculation. Speculation in the novel of high finance, when it is finished, brings forth death. Evolving into a bold financial captain, Jadwin becomes "blooded to the game" and plunges into one venture after another until caught up in the biggest deal of all—a corner in May wheat. The ruinous path downward into the pit yawns and beckons. When he buys a seat on the Board of Trade, Jadwin significantly is "no longer an outsider" but becomes a fraternal member of the Order of the Pit, a fellow demon in the underworld. The Adamic financier is metamorphosed into a "merchant prince," like the figure of the prince of Tyre in Ezekiel, who lifts his heart up in pride and says, "I am a God, I sit in the seat of God" (Ezekiel 28:2). "The Unknown Bull," as Curtis Jadwin is called by the public, blasphemously acts as though he were a god, omnipotent and all-ruling. His hand is upon the indicator of the wheat dial of the pit, "and he moved it through as many or as few of the degrees of the circle as he chose." [7] Jadwin is

as completely master of the market as of his own right hand. Everything stopped when he raised a finger; everything leaped to life with the fury of obsession when he nodded his head. His wealth increased with such stupefying rapidity, that at no time was he able to even approximate the gains that accrued to him because of his corner. It was more than twenty million, and less than fifty million. That was all he knew. Nor were the everlasting hills more secure than he from the attack of any human enemy. Out of the ranks of the conquered there issued not so much as a whisper of hostility. Within his own sphere no Czar, no satrap, no Caesar ever wielded power more resistless.[8]

When Jadwin boasts that he has the new wheat crop all figured out, Gretry's only reply is, "Well, then you're the Lord Almighty himself." [9] Jadwin, like Lucifer, the morning star, aspires to be God, to rule in heaven rather than serve. The corner fails, however, and the merchant prince is cast out of heaven and brought down to hell, to the sides of the pit. His voice rings out "like a trumpet call: 'Into the Pit,' " as he symbolically descends to the trading floor of the exchange. Saint John the Divine's vision seems suddenly brought to pass, like an eerie fulfillment of biblical prophecy:

And the fifth angel sounded, and I saw a star fall from heaven unto the earth: and to him was given the key of the bottomless pit (Revelation 9:1).

Jadwin's association in the novel with Lucifer, the Prince of Light, is striking. Always pushing buttons to create light, he is awed by electric power and electric lights, false light, invented light. His great electric organ, with its mighty pipes built into the two-story art gallery, bathes "in the dulled incandescence of the electrics." As Jadwin enters the rotunda, "electrics all over the gallery flashed out in sudden blaze." Laura and Sheldon Corthell, the artist, shade their eyes from the glare. "Oh, I didn't mean to blind you," apologizes Jadwin. Cast down into the pit at the end, a dazed and ruined fallen angel, the financier whispers almost inaudibly, "It's dark, it's dark. Something happened. . . . I don't remember." [10]

Shakespeare's Macbeth had been an angel of light, favored in the king's sight, until he sinned. Forcibly reaching for a throne that would have been his anyway, he went too far into evil. Jadwin's becoming "blooded to the game" recalls Macbeth's awareness that "I am in blood / Stepped in so far that, should I wade no more / Returning were as tedious as go o'er." Nature, roused like an angry titan in *The Pit* by Jadwin's puny tampering with her laws, resembles the natural disorder and chaos that follows Duncan's murder. Jadwin's wife in fact memorizes and rehearses the role of Lady Macbeth, even entertains the notion of Corthell painting her portrait as Macbeth's wife. Despite these similarities to *Macbeth*, *The Pit* more closely draws from William Dean Howells's *The Rise of Silas Lapham*, the *locus classicus* novel of high finance. Frank Norris does not hide his admiration for Howells in the novel, repayment no doubt for support the Dean had given him in publishing *McTeague* and, later, for a favorable review of it. Jadwin says of Howells, whom he included in a list of favorite authors, "Come, this chap knows what he's writing about—not like that Middleton [George Meredith] ass, with his 'Dianas' and 'Amazing Marriages.' " [11] Even while reading *Silas Lapham*, Jadwin forms a particular affection for Howells's unfortunate hero, a feeling of kinship.

> He never could rid himself of a surreptitious admiration for Bartley Hubbard. He, too, was "smart" and "alive." He had the "get there" to him. "Why," he would say, "I know fifty boys just like him down there in La Salle Street." Lapham he loved as a brother. Never a point in the development of his character that he missed or failed to chuckle over. Bromfield Corey was poohed and boshed quite out of consideration as a "loafer," and a "dilletanty," but Lapham had all his sympathy.

The moral lesson provided by Lapham's catastrophe is, however, completely lost on Norris's financier. " 'Yes, sir,' he would exclaim, interrupting the narrative, 'that's just it. That's just what I would have done if I had been in his place.' " [12] Jadwin ultimately makes the same mistakes, commits the same sin. He is in effect a reproduction of the Adamic Lapham.

Norris's Sheldon Corthell, on the other hand, suggests Bromfield Corey in *Silas Lapham.* Jadwin's dismissal of Howells's rich old Brahmin as a "loafer" and "dilletanty" also reveals his attitude toward Corthell, whose intellectual and artistic interests parallel Corey's. Jadwin and Lapham, both men of business and affairs downtown, are deeply antipathetic toward the Corthells and Coreys of the world, men of the arts. The investment advice Jadwin gives Corthell is a direct reply to old Bromfield's smug comment about putting money into paintings rather than stocks.[13] "Corthell," Jadwin declares, "take my advice. Buy May wheat. It'll beat art all hollow." [14]

Written in the period between publication of *The Octopus* and *The Pit,* Frank Norris's story, "A Deal in Wheat," is important primarily as a prelude to *The Pit.* One critic, though, believes any similarities are superficial. He argues that the shift of viewpoint away from the cosmic optimism of *The Octopus* to a more coldly analytic assessment of the effects of financial dealings in "A Deal in Wheat" bears no similarity to *The Pit.*[15] Actually, the story is closer in detail and point of view to a piece previously unpublished that Norris wrote during this same period, entitled "The Great Corner in Hannibal & St Jo."[16] Both "A Deal in Wheat" and "The Great Corner," predecessors of *The Pit,* are accounts of massive financial frauds, crowded by the novelist into extremely short narrative spans.

Norris's biographer, Franklin D. Walker, reported that the novelist had difficulty mastering technical aspects of the commodity market, especially the details of "short selling." [17] A short sale takes place when a speculator sells stock that he does not own in the hopes he can cover (buy it back) at a later date and at a lower price. A profit is realized if the covering price is lower than the short sale price. But, when a short seller has to pay more to cover than he received as proceeds from the short sale, a loss is sustained. Short selling is a trading technique essential to understanding the exploit of a corner, a superhuman financial feat that continually fascinated Norris. In *The Pit* alone, there are four separate corners, including Jadwin's, each of which crashes in ruins. Another corner is pulled off in "A Deal in Wheat," but the maneuver is finally foiled with a subterfuge. The real victim of this chicanery of high finance is the small man, the innocent public that always gets caught in the middle of the eternal war waged on the exchange between bull and bear. The motif of the sabotaged corner is repeated in "The Great Corner." [18] William J. Hutchinson, a member of the New York Stock Exchange, organizes a syndicate to buy up all the shares of the Hannibal & St Jo. Railroad. They bull the stock from its normal level in the 40s into the high 200s, manipulating it along the way to suck in the public and trap short sellers. When the syndicate effectually masters the market, it chooses to squeeze its victims further by driving the price of the stock higher. Meanwhile, in a dire act of treachery and betrayal (not unlike Scannel's desertion of Hargus, or Crookes's of Cressler, when both Hargus and Cressler were attempting a corner in *The Pit*), Hutchinson secretly sells out as the syndicate keeps buying. The corner quickly collapses, and Hutchinson is the only survivor. Honor, even among thieves, is violated. Duff, one member of the ring "who had lost every penny of his vast fortune, died after the collapse of the corner of a broken heart." [19] Money must have been his first love. Another member "seven months later threw down an empty bottle of cyanide of potassium and sank back upon an unmade bed in an obscure boarding house to die in poverty, unheard of and already forgotten." [20] Death's shadow falls over the exchange as well, as the sharp decline in the stock of Hannibal & St Jo. is described as an "expiring death struggle." The exchange itself, in both "The Great Corner" and "A Deal in Wheat," is a machine of destruction, a naturalistic symbol of death. As the syndicate in "The Great Corner" "tighter and tighter turned the screw," pressure on the victims, or short sellers, becomes so intense that the machine finally releases and crushes the operators in their own device. Similarly in "A Deal in Wheat," the small man who is represented by the farmer, "caught once in the cogs and wheel of a great and terrible engine," had seen none better.

The populist anti-Wall Street attitude, which embraces the theory that insiders rule and conspire against the public, can be traced in Norris's financial fiction. The public, innocent pawns in the chess game of corners, raids, and takeovers, is the sacrificial victim of the willful and immoral legerdemain that takes place behind the scenes. Frank Norris's attitude toward Wall and La Salle Streets is, at bottom, reproachful and condemnatory, and it foreshadows the anti-Wall Street virulence and muckraking fervor in the financial novels of David Graham Phillips and Upton Sinclair.

III

Will Payne (1865-1954), a minor Chicago realist and forgotten figure in American fiction, wrote several stories and novels about high finance. Born in the Midwest, Payne was a journalist, financial reporter, and editor for a number of years, six of which were spent with the *Chicago Daily News*. He also wrote for *The Saturday Evening Post,* contributing articles and biographical sketches about well-known contemporary financiers like Thomas Fortune Ryan. Payne published fiction about the wheat market around the same time Norris did, and although there is no evidence of any influencing of one by the other, striking similarities appear. Both novelists choose Chicago's La Salle Street as the setting for their financial fiction. The hell-like murkiness and gloom of Payne's *The Money Captain* (1898) in fact anticipates Norris's description of the atmosphere around La Salle Street in *The Pit.* Both are also fond of employing the double plot, with the motif of the business story overlapped by the sentimental love episode. Ultimately, Payne and Norris both portray the romance of the economic struggle. Yet, despite surface elements of romance, both novelists present action that is basically naturalistic, depicting the life-and-death conflict in the financial marketplace, or the tooth-and-claw battle of finance between bull and bear.

Two stories in Payne's *On Fortune's Road* (1902) coincidentally offer a number of points of comparison with Norris's *The Pit,* published in the same year. Lester Wells, hero in "The End of the Deal," almost exactly parallels Curtis Jadwin as his preoccupation with speculating in wheat futures turns into madness. He is clawed by the villainous bear Bowles and buried under oceans of wheat when he fails to hold up its price on the exchange. In "A Day in Wheat," the financier Thatcher is yet another facsimile of Jadwin. Seduced by the broker Peter Gund, a more evil figure than Sam

Gretry, he falls when his bull clique is smashed, the climax of which is remarkably close in detail to the wild scene in *The Pit* when Jadwin's mad campaign collapses.

Payne turns to comedy several years later in *The Automatic Capitalists* (1909). The romance of business in effect gives way to light-hearted burlesque. Apparently he was trying to cash in on the popular anti-Wall Street appeal of the populist-progressivist novel of the early 1900s, a type of fiction that exposed corruption and chicanery in high places of finance. *The Automatic Capitalists* actually is a madcap situation comedy of confidence, the absurdity of which squelches any tone of exposure or social protest that may have been intended.

Barrington & Benton is a brokerage firm in Chicago's La Salle Street. Barrington, the more polished and smooth-tongued of the partners, is a dissimulator and fake in the mold of Herman Melville's trickster in *The Confidence Man*. Unlike Melville's villain, though, both these rascals are benign and humorous, comic versions of the figure of broker as devil in the novel of high finance. Messrs. Barrington and Benton are simultaneously their own tempters and victims, as they talk and entice themselves into a fraudulent scheme that leads straight to bankruptcy. Originally, when these rogues formed their partnership, they conned and duped one another, each believing the other had fifty thousand dollars and a sizeable clientele. The discovery that between them they did not have a cent hoists the devil in this novel by his own petard of the stock market. Tomfoolery and sleight of hand conducted with bundles of bonds evolves into an elaborate financial shell game as these capitalists strive for instant riches. A comic account of La Salle Street tactics and insider dealings, as well as a parody of the public's gullibility and the "confidence" upon which business relationships are based, *The Automatic Capitalists* is a rare example of satire in the novel of high finance. These two brokerage-office picaros are not held responsible for their sins, nor is the financial ruin they suffer suggestive of the moral Fall that struck Silas Lapham or Curtis Jadwin. Payne's rascally pair could very well come out on stage after the curtain and take a bow for their antics. So rare is the satirical approach to the subject of money and Wall Street in American fiction, in fact, that only

Mark Twain, Nathanael West in *A Cool Million,* and William Faulkner in *The Sound and the Fury* as well as the Snopes trilogy treat the stock market with similar humor and irony.

A steadfast champion of the American success myth was Edwin LeFèvre (1871-1943). LeFèvre wrote a number of popular stories and novels about business around the turn of the century. He offered a unique pro-capitalism, pro-establishment, and pro-Wall Street point of view. The American corporation was portrayed as the perfect medium for productivity and profit, where dividends were the symbol of health and a rising stock the emblem of success. Financial failure was always possible in America, but unthinkable. Opportunity needed only to be recognized. Capital provided only brains. Ironically, LeFèvre appealed to the same reading public that fed on the anti-Wall Street muckraking series in *McClure's,* and thirsted after financial exposés in *Everybody's,* like Thomas W. Lawson's "Frenzied Finance," as well as the stories in *Success* and *Collier's* that pried into stock market skulduggery from the perspective of the small investor.

Historically, Edwin LeFèvre is the founder of the genre of popular Wall Street fiction, a species of literature that stirs the public periodically, especially in boom economic times. A stockbroker and newspaperman as well as novelist, he is at the head of a pop cult tradition that couples Wall Street with just about any topic imaginable, such as love, romance, adventure, courage, and sex. LeFèvre's collection of tales called *Wall Street Stories* (1901) appeared separately in *McClure's* and *Munsey's.* The main characters are drawn from well-known financial figures. Samuel Sharpe is really James R. Keene, John F. Greener is Jay Gould, and Silas Shaw is the treacherous bear Daniel Drew. His novels of high finance include *The Golden Flood* (1905), *Sampson Rock of Wall Street* (1906), and *The Plunderers* (1916). *Reminiscences of a Stock Operator* (1923), based on the career of Wall Street trader Jesse Livermore, is actually a semifictionalized textbook on stock market trading techniques. LeFèvre's *The Making of a Stockbroker* (1925), a spurious autobiography of one John K. Wing, who is typically Wall Street and typically American, is the father of the popular insider exposé of stockbrokers (customers' men) and clients. *50 Wall Street* (1968) and *The Dinosaur Fund* (1972), by newspaper financial writer Vartanig G. Vartan, as well as *The Confessions of a Stockbroker* (1971), by the pseudonymous "Brutus," fall into this bestseller category.

LeFèvre essentially is a local colorist with a journalist's eye for realism and a novelist's penchant for romance. The Street's surface realism, such as its jargon and colloquialisms and its casual relationships, catch his journalistic fancy. The novelist's imagination is stirred by great schemes of financial captains, born in offices overlooking Pine and Nassau Streets, which reshape the face of America. LeFèvre particularly glorifies the mechanics and details of high finance. The stock ticker (first used in 1867), for example, clatters incessantly in the background of LeFèvre's Wall Street fiction. A small machine with a bubble dome, the ticker printed out abbreviated letters and figures of all stocks traded on the Exchange on an endless paper tape that passed through it. A million shares of stock traded, New York Stock Exchange officials would have confirmed, required 500 miles of ribbon to roll over the spindles of the ticker. The novelist sees in only a half inch of ribbon a story of sudden disaster or a fairy tale of riches, in a foot a whole epic, in a yard a history. Characters and figures of the tape are soldier ants carrying tiny nuggets of gold to a thousand stockholders. LeFèvre wonders if these ticker-ticks are not actually recordings of the heartbeats of anxious traders and speculators who rarely move their eyes from the tape. Overall, Edwin LeFèvre's fiction, in which Wall Street is so highly romanticized, fits into the local color tradition of the popular Van Bibber stories by Richard Harding Davis, and the New York tales of Henry Cuyler Bunner, as well as magazine pieces such as "Wall St. Wooing" (1896) by Brander Matthews, or "The Romance of a Busy Broker" and other Manhattan stories by O. Henry. Together, these writers form a small school of regionalists who employ New York and its financial district as the setting for their fiction.

Sampson Rock of Wall Street was published in 1906, at the peak of the public's hunger for Wall Street stories and novels. This novel is a characteristically chauvinistic defense by LeFèvre of methods used by the reigning captains of industry. LeFèvre represents the ultraconservative viewpoint in fiction about Wall Street, almost as if the genus robber baron exchanges roles for a time with the sub-genus artist to publish its own apologia. Echoes of Henry Clews's *The Wall Street Point of View* (1900) also sound in *Sampson Rock*. Clews, a veteran stockbroker often remembered as the "Pepys of Wall Street," felt that the stock exchange was indispensable to America. He pictured it as a great economic mother that provides the national increase. He also praised the mighty financiers as "pioneers of development," and especially extolled the virtues of the railroad barons who boldly opened up the fertile American West. Enmity toward Wall Street was folly, Clews fervently held.

John D. Rockefeller, Sr. sat for his portrait as LeFèvre's hero, Samspon Rock, a character whose first name implies the oil baron's crushing strength and last name an all-too obvious abbreviation. The novelist saw in the Croesus-like magnate the rigid piety of an evangelist, the morals of a saint, the ideals of a nobleman. A type and shadow of Rockefeller, Rock is the great American businessman who creates the nation's prosperity. His character and integrity are solid as his name implies. His business methods are the right methods. He has faith and hope in America, which, in effect, are LeFèvre's own faith and hope. A vehicle for the novelist's pro-business, pro-capitalist, pro-Rockefeller philosophies, Sampson Rock is the apotheosis or glorification of success in a benign and egalitarian world.

Blessed with a miraculous ability to turn water into gold rather than gold—or stock certificates—into worthless water, Sampson Rock is the good man in this morality drama of high finance. Unlike those real-life Wall Street villains and succubi such as Cornelius "Commodore" Vanderbilt, Jay Gould, and J. Pierpont Morgan, Sr. (Morgan the financial Gorgon), all of whom conducted business with one eye forever on the stock market and issued stock, manipulated it, watered it, and cornered it at every opportunity, Rock is not a robber baron. His desire to control the diluted Roanoke & Western Railroad in the novel, for instance, is a desire to promulgate economic growth and make the nearly defunct railroad the dividend-paying company of tomorrow. Sampson Rock's pronouncement that "money is made by the people who have faith in this country, by upbuilding and not by pulling down," echoes Rockefeller and represents LeFèvre's reply to the popular notion that only self-interest and personal gain motivated the titans. Sampson Rock, also a figure of Adam, is the primal economic man, whose acts and deeds on the stock exchange are translated into fruits for the common people. Without this financial Adam, there would be no jobs, no money, no life. Like his real-life prototype, Sampson Rock *is* the beginning, the ancestral father of American industry and commerce. He surveys and subdivides the undeveloped land, sets up a corporate "trust," and turns the Garden into a profitable, moneymaking region.

Capitalism is anathema to Sampson Rock, Jr., the hero's son. Rock the younger views his father not as a builder, but as a panic maker, and rebels against those repeated bear raids used to establish control of companies. He rejects his father's platitudes and explanations, such as, "I don't want to wreck the road in order to get it for practically nothing. I'm after the control of it because I tell you, my boy, that the possible welfare of an individual [president of the Virginia Central Railroad] must not be allowed to stand in the way of the actual welfare of hundreds of thousands of people." [21] Young Rock, however, in a sudden turnabout, betrays privileged information involving one of his father's imminent bear raids, not to cancel out but to rival Rock *père* with some speculative trading of his own. Had his father not interceded, Rock II would surely have brought financial ruin down upon his own head.

John D. Rockefeller, Sr., who trained his sons and instructed them in the principles and methods of business, owned,

> I cheat my boys every chance I get, I want to make 'em sharp. I trade with the boys and skin 'em and I just beat 'em every time I can. I want to make 'em sharp.[22]

Sampson Rock I's ruse of allowing the stock exchange to panic on rumor of his death is a hard but necessary lesson in high finance for his son. Tempted by financial sin, Sampson Rock, Jr. confesses his aberrant ways and is forgiven. Baptized now with his father's philosophy, he is reborn through the gospel of honest wealth. Young Rock in the end espouses the stock market and bear raid as necessary tools of finance, realizing that it is "the man at work, improving railroads, establishing efficiency, the fighter of the modern battle of business, the man who commanded thousands of other men," [23] who is the real savior of the country. John D. Rockefeller, Jr., incidentally, underwent a similar baptism and rebirth when trader David Lamar, "The Wolf of Wall Street," duped him of nearly $1 million. He abjectly approached his father, who told him, "All right, John, don't worry. I will see you through." Young Rockefeller, too, realized that speculation was just about the poorest occupation any man could give himself to, and just as sure a way to financial ruin as could be devised.

7.

Wall Street in the Muck

I

Beneath the outward atmosphere of gaiety in the 1890s, the zenith of America's Gilded Age, social discontent with the accepted order of life was growing. Agitation and unrest were the developing moods. The economic system and materialistic philosophies that promoted the system were breeding distrust. Individualism and freedom, long valued and cherished as the cornerstones of American life, fell under question. America, after a quarter century of rapid industrialization, was beginning to sober up and assess itself.

Andrew Carnegie's gospel of wealth was the popular philosophy of America's industrialism. Like other millionaire barons and kings of the period, Carnegie preached that inequality of wealth was inevitable in a successful economic system, and that the law of competition was essential to the progress of society. The steel magnate promulgated the idea that economic struggle was necessary to ensure advancement of the race, and must not be impeded by governmental interference. Carnegie, a kind of Messiah of capitalism, first introduced the gospel in a two-part article in the *North American Review* in 1889, which appeared in book form a year later. Three, perhaps four prophets whose theories were incorporated into his gospel of wealth were precursors of Carnegie. John Locke, seventeenth-century English philosopher, proclaimed the sociopolitical preeminence of the individual. He asserted that man had a right to self-preservation, which included the privilege of accumulating as much money as possible, possessing private property, and of owning material goods in general. Americans accepted Lockean theory, intended originally to sanction the rise of the English middle class, because it recognized the primacy of the individual. Individualism, economic as well as social, was, of course, cherished as a basic American freedom. Adam Smith, nineteenth-century British economist, introduced the classical economic doctrine of laissez faire, along with the theory that natural law was benevolent. Economic phenomena, according to Smith, were manifestations of underlying natural law and, consequently, were also benevolent. To preserve the economic system and allow it to function at its most efficient, a system of natural liberty was required. Government regulation, for example, corrupted that natural system. Under Smith's laissez faire doctrine, man must remain autonomous, bound only by natural law to compete and pursue his self-interest. Other "prophetic" voices were heard in the background as Carnegie preached and defended his gospel of capitalism. Charles Darwin's theories of evolution and natural selection, tailored by another Englishman, Herbert Spencer, to fit individuals in economic society as well as beasts in the wild, gave rise to the philosophy of Social Darwinism. Social Darwinism allowed the economically fit to survive and the rich to get richer. Wealth was, in fact, a sign of fitness. Struggle in the commercial and financial marketplace was still tooth and claw, albeit economic, and only the fit and powerful deserved to succeed.

Unrest and discontent in the 1890s were founded on the suspicion that wealth was becoming too concentrated, business and industry were getting excessively institutionalized, and the individual was no longer free and unhindered. The progressive movement, with roots in the decades following the Civil War, sprang into view during this period. The movement was a many-sided attack or reaction against the evils of an oligarchic society, particularly the despotism of the business community, which stifled individual initiative and opportunity. Philosophically, progressivism was an attempt by the people to recapture the ideals of an earlier day, when the individual rather than the institution was the mainstay of American life. Always advocates of competition, progressives fought instead the practices of "unfair" competition, which eliminated not only the fundamental rules of equity, but the legal clout to enforce these rules. Overall, progressives believed the business ethic of the country was doing more harm than good to the greatest number of people.

Many Americans were in sympathy with progressive ideals. During the last quarter of the nineteenth century, momentum for the movement was provided particularly by Henry George and Henry Demarest Lloyd. These men feared the abuses of unequal distribution of wealth in the United States and saw the need for reform. Henry George, in *Progress and Poverty,* introduced a number of innovative ideas, including his single tax proposal, to counter land speculation and monopolization. Henry Demarest Lloyd, as early as 1881, attacked unfair business methods in his exposé of Standard Oil entitled "The Story of a Great Monopoly," which appeared in the *Atlantic Monthly.* Lloyd's *Wealth Against Commonwealth* (1894) became a guidebook for muckrakers after the turn of the century. Progressive complaints against the abuses of capitalism rose in volume in the first decade of the 1900s as muckrakers joined in the chorus. Novelists David Graham Phillips, Upton Sinclair, and Jack London seemed to unite in the common purpose of exposing to public view the causes of society's economic and political ills. Although these writers did uncover corruption and injustice, they went further, using the muckrake to advance a particular social or economic system, even converting the muckraking novel into a platform for propagating Marxism. Wall Street, the symbolic heart of American capitalism, stood out in these novels as a specific target of attack. The progressivist-socialist attitude toward Wall Street that developed was condemnatory and served to intensify public distrust, already prevalent since the 1870s, when pools, cliques, and syndicates dominated high finance. Such heinous current events as the panic in May 1901 (otherwise known as the

"Northern Pacific Corner" and one of the worst stock market disturbances in history), the 1905 New York insurance scandal revealed by the Armstrong investigation, the multifarious accounts of corporate corruption such as Ida Tarbell's *"History of the Standard Oil,"* or municipal corruption such as Lincoln Steffens's *The Shame of the Cities* (1902), and the Panic of 1907 also fueled liberal unrest and contributed to the general ill will.

A triad of frothy financial novels by David Graham Phillips—*The Master-Rogue* (1903), *The Cost* (1904), and *The Deluge* (1905)—as well as Upton Sinclair's group of novels about high finance—*A Captain of Industry* (1906), *The Metropolis* (1908), and *The Moneychangers* (1908)—aroused the popular muckraking fervor, animating it with an undisguised abhorrence of the economic system as a whole and of money masters in particular who ruled by their own code of ethics. Phillips tempered the movement, however, by optimistically believing that plutocracy was only a passing phase in history, a mania or malaise from which America would soon recover and return to its original democratic ideals. Sinclair, adhering to Marxist ideology, thought America had gone beyond the high point of its capitalistic development and would devolve into a more socialistic system and order. Jack London, though chastening his own mood after an earlier assault on capitalism in *The Iron Heel* (1907), continued to picture in *Burning Daylight* (1910) the greed, selfishness, and evil that the economic system breeds.

II

The Master-Rogue. The Confessions of a Croesus acts as a prologue in the trilogy of "novels of purpose" by David Graham Phillips, novels intended to examine underlying corruption of the plutocracy and expose unethical methods employed by the robber barons. Compared with *The Cost* or *The Deluge,* both of which followed, *The Master-Rogue* is less interesting as a novel, thin in substance, dull in characterization. Yet it introduces ideas important not only in demonstrating Phillips's attitudes toward money and its power to rule, but themes and motifs fundamental in the American financial novel. *The Master-Rogue* also is proof that the morality pattern indigenous to Wall Street fiction provides a handy vehicle for the muckraker by which to present moral and social issues. Somehow the "good guys," symbolized by underdog individuals repressed by the system, are always pitted against the "bad guys," those who control the system, in a formula situation reminiscent of the dime Western.

David Graham Phillips never showed much sympathy in his fiction for Wall Street types. Invariably he portrays the plutocrat as the "bad guy," a satanic financier innately evil and beyond regeneration. The fiend of finance in *The Master-Rogue* is James Galloway, who reappears in *The Deluge* as a powerful and fearsome Wall Street baron. Galloway's sinister beginnings recall Robert Belcher in J. G. Holland's *Sevenoaks.* Like Belcher, he forces a weak employer out of his dry goods business without the faintest twinge of conscience. Absolutely certain that he will be a millionaire some day, and dead set on that goal, Galloway rises from small business-man to railroad titan. His assuredness that he will be wealthy echoes a remark said to have been made by J. Pierpont Morgan, Sr.: "I knew I'd be rich. I knew I'd be rich." Galloway's philosophy of success—one of hating and grabbing—also is reminiscent of Morgan as well as Andrew Carnegie, both notoriously unforgiving.

> To get what you want in this world you must be a good hater. The best haters make the best grabbers, and this is a world of grab, not of "By your leave," or "If you'll permit me, sir." You can't get what you want away from the man who's got it unless you hate him. Gentle feelings paralyze the conquering arm.[1]

Proceeding from evil to evil, Galloway's rise to power enables him to "steer" lawmakers in Washington through a lackey senator who looks after his corporate interests. The financier also is able to exert a Godlike control over the stock market in New York by manip-ulating prices on the exchange.

Evil corrupts not only the robber baron Galloway but his family as well, like pollution that seeps through cracks in the foundation and fouls the whole house. Once established as an industrial lord or king, Galloway harbors a secret ambition to see his huge fortune and personal fame perpetuated through his family line. He envisions the Galloway clan continuing on as royalty. Inevitable fruits from a life of hating and grabbing are made manifest, however, in his sons' hearts. Tyranny, where love should have ruled, turns his sons against him. As a way to free themselves from the yoke of their father's bondage, they rebel and attempt to overthrow him as the financial authority figure in the family. Dreams for a royal family dynasty are therefore shattered when the master rogue dispossesses one son and reduces the other's inheritance. Heaping up riches, Galloway knows not who will gather them. No sooner is his family line established than it is left to disintegrate and vanish. The purport of *The Master-Rogue*, in the father-son rivalry theme, is that the tenure of industrial royalty in America is brief; the dream of creating a nobility founded on money and power is unrealizable. Phillips demonstrates this viewpoint again in *The Reign of Gilt* (1905) by averring that money rules for the moment, but it cannot reign for long.

The master rogue's sins as an operator on Wall Street come back to haunt him in other ways. Galloway catches sight of his face in the shaving glass one morning, and he, like Hawthorne's veiled Puritan minister who sees his image in a looking-glass, is overwhelmed with horror. The ghastly figure who stares back recalls as well Spencer Brydon's monstrous alter ego in Henry James's "The Jolly Corner," which Brydon confronted face-to-face one evening in his empty New York house. Galloway, unlike Brydon, views the man he had *actually become*, not the man he would have been had he pursued a business career.

> I saw my face—suddenly, with startling clearness, and when my mind was on the subject of faces. The sight gave me a shock—not because my expression was sardonic and—yes, I shall confess it—cruel and bitterly unhappy. That shock came in that, before I recognised myself, I had said, "Who is this *old* man?" [2]

The reflection of his face a second time in the mirror of a brougham recalls thoughts of "the end" he had when he first noticed his twisted image. Death stalks this financier for hellish sins on Wall Street. Galloway reaps his reward as he is brought to the edge of the pit of doom.

Decrepitude and death as products of the money pursuit are evident not only in Wall Street fiction, but in real life. Curtis Jadwin and old Hargus in Frank Norris's *The Pit,* Dan Waterman in Upton Sinclair's *The Moneychangers,* and Eldon Parr in Winston Churchill's *The Inside of the Cup* are among those in fiction whose foolish lust for riches withers them away. Money and death figures in D. G. Phillips's novels alone are numerous. In real life, many of the nineteenth-century robber barons themselves were sickly, gaunt, and fierce in countenance, unpleasant or hideous to the eye. Jay Gould, with more than $100 million accumulated at age forty-five, was described by historian Gustavus Myers as "prematurely old, his beard was streaked with gray, his hair thin, and his swarthy, bilious, glowering face was rigid with hard, deep lines. His form had shrunk so that he looked more insignificant than ever before." [3] After his partner Charles Leupp committed suicide when a joint scheme failed, it became legendary that Gould's touch brought death. Shipping and railroad magnate Cornelius Vanderbilt, the Old Commodore, ostensibly energetic, robust, and physically hale, was actually an ailing man, dyspeptic most of his life, and suffering from a variety of intestinal, heart, kidney, and stomach disorders. Vanderbilt was known to have consulted clairvoyant Victoria Woodhull, like Saul seeking out the witch of Endor in the Old Testament, evidence of an even deeper psychological and spiritual malaise. E. H. Harriman, the "Little Wizard of Wall Street," was semi-invalid, frail and feverish already by the time he engaged in an abortive struggle for control of the Northern Pacific Railroad from 1901 to 1907. That struggle further weakened him, and he died two years later. Daniel Drew and Russell Sage took to their beds under the shock of believing they were ruined men.

If money and the means to wealth were the sole worries of these financiers, what importance had mental, emotional, or physical problems, let alone moral or spiritual? "I am not on Wall Street for my health," snapped the elder Pierpont Morgan, a favorite reply whenever queried about the ethics of his latest stock deal or financial transaction; or Henry H. Rogers, partner of John D. Rockefeller, Sr., responded when asked why Standard Oil had not

lowered prices for crude despite higher volume and reduced costs:
"We are not in business for our health, but are out for the dollar."
Chauncey M. DePew, president of the New York Central Railroad, who for years hobnobbed with the high and mighty, summed
it up in his memoirs:

> I think the reason why I am in excellent health and vigor
> in my eighty-eighth year is largely due to the fact that the
> points or suggestions of great financiers never interested
> me. I have known thousands who were ruined by them.

If *The Master-Rogue* is the prologue or warmup for David
Graham Phillips's trio of Jeremiads against plutocracy and corruption, *The Cost* and *The Deluge* are the main performance. Like most
American financial novels, *The Cost* is an amalgam of allegory and
morality drama. A new epic element is introduced into financial
fiction, however. *The Cost* becomes a Miltonic account of the old
struggle for preeminence among the masters of finance.

Jack Dumont, a type of Satan, is a ruthless speculator and
monopolist in *The Cost*. He steals or merges many woolens manufacturers, seventeen companies in all, into one monolithic corporation. Controlling this huge trust (parentally named National
Woolens Company), Dumont has absolute and unyielding power
over the entire wool clothing market. A Bunyanesque Mr. Badman
figure, who grinds the poor with high prices and usury in the manner of a medieval friar, he advances costs on all products in the
midst of one of the worst winters on record. The public outcry that
follows is loud but useless, because the plutocracy is unmoved.
Dumont's stranglehold on the industry as well as the public is
strengthened by his buying off judges, legislators, and others in
high places. His minions, Messrs. Larkin, Culver, and Merriweather lurk in the shadows with hands always full of mischief and
bribes. Culver, who occupies an exalted position in Satan's legions,
sits beside the master "at the inner-most wheels, deep at the very
heart of the intricate mechanism." [4] Evil holds sway in *The Cost*
until the novel's hero, Hampden Scarborough, opposes Dumont.
Scarborough, symbol of virtue, threatens the devil's very omnipotence. "There's no way we can get our hooks in him. He don't give

a damn for money," [5] Merriweather informs his master. The devil's kingdom then divides against itself. One of Dumont's acolytes cites him as corespondent in a divorce suit, and the evil monopolist's name is impugned by the yellow press. Dumont's enemies swiftly follow up with Wall Street rumors that a raid on National Woolens is taking place. His end is imminent. National Woolens stock then dives into a dizzying tailspin when rumors turn into fact, and the whole stock market, awash in this bearish tidal wave, threatens to crash. Order is eventually restored, but not before catastrophe has had occasion to purge the investment community. King Melville, president of the National Industrial Bank—"the huge barometer to which both speculative and investing Wall Street looks for guidance" [6]—divinely intervenes. Melville, a fanatically religious man who abhors any form of moral deviation, calls in Dumont's loans and casts the archangel out of power in the Woolens Trust.

The Cost evolves into a modern financial *Paradise Lost,* a melodramatic Miltonic epic. Dumont's vow to grind King Melville into the gutter within six months is followed by a final assault on Wall Street, like Satan's revenge in the Garden. The fallen financier summons his legions to attack the ancestral family of the Fanning-Smiths. James Fanning-Smith, grandson of the baron who founded the family empire, is an innocent Adam of finance, a third-generation business-neglecting plutocrat guilty of "cupidity and conceit." Having speculated his patrimony away on Wall Street, James is already weakened by the taste of original sin. Unwittingly he had sold short more shares in the family railroad than he owned. Dumont, aware of this vulnerability, wages a vicious battle on the floor of the New York Stock Exchange, and succeeds in destroying the ancestral family. Revenge is gained on King Melville. Judgment, however, is reserved for Dumont. In the climactic moment of victory, Dumont is found lying dead on the floor of his hotel room—the command post far removed from the battle's noise and confusion—strangled by stock market ticker tape.

> In his struggles the tape had wound round and round his
> legs, his arms, his neck. It lay in a curling, coiling mat,

like a serpent's head, upon his throat, where his hands
clutched the collar of his pajamas.[7]

The financier as devil is symbolically bound and cast into the
bottomless reaches of hell.

The Deluge, David Graham Phillips's most devastating exposure
of corrupt and venal capitalism, is a sequel to *The Cost.* After John
Dumont dies in *The Cost,* control of his textile trust passes on to
"The Seven," an omnipotent gang of Wall Street financiers, bankers, and industrialists in *The Deluge.* "The Seven" is based upon the
"System," comprised of the rulers of the Standard Oil Company
and National City Bank of New York. Matthew Blacklock, who
apparently is transformed from villain into good man in the novel,
is modeled after the historical Wall Street iconoclast, Thomas W.
Lawson.

Tom Lawson's background as a stock market operator and lone
guerilla fighter during the late 1890s and early 1900s was well
known. Worth a fortune of $50 million by 1900, he amassed a large
portion from an enormous public who followed his full-page newspaper ads on the market. Lawson's bare statement that a stock
would go up or down was enough to make it do so. Frequently he
could be found on the opposite side of the market, plucking profits
out of his loyal readers' pockets like a common cutpurse. Lawson at
the crest of his popularity was named by Standard Oil to head up
a new company, Amalgamated Copper, created as a holding vehicle for copper properties. When Amalgamated stock was issued in
May 1899, Lawson discovered that not only was he being used by
oil chieftains Henry H. Rogers and William Rockefeller as well as
James Stillman, president of the National City Bank, but worse,
the "copper crazy" public was being taken advantage of. After the
turn of the century, when Amalgamated was suddenly pulled
down, Lawson was so incensed that he declared open war on the
whole "System." He denounced its tactic of incubating wealth
with funds entrusted by the public to banks and insurance companies. Its ethics, he alleged, were not just self-serving but "tigerishly
cruel," "an eye for eye, a tooth for a tooth." Lawson broke with
Rogers & Co., accusing them of a voracious financial double-cross

of his Amalgamated Copper enterprise. A master of epithet, he further accused these men of knowing no Sabbath, knowing no Him, of immunity to every human or spiritual feeling, and of knowing only dollars. Lawson eventually became regarded by the financial community as a kind of quack, an expedient type or con man. One Wall Street veteran, James R. Keene, disgustedly told Clarence W. Barron, "Lying is an art and you will yet be erecting a monument to Lawson." Barron himself complained that when Lawson has told you something, what do you really know? After his crusade to shine light into the darker regions of the Street, Lawson went back to touting stocks and get-rich-quick schemes, finally dying in near poverty. At any rate his articles, which revealed the heinous corruption of the "System," were serialized in *Everybody's* for almost two years under the title "Frenzied Finance: The Story of Amalgamated." [8] The first installment in July 1904, which instantly sent the magazine's circulation soaring from 150,000 to 950,000, appeared one year before publication of *The Deluge*. Himself angered by Lawson's popular cause célèbre and insider revelations, David Graham Phillips focused his own exposure in the novel on the plutocracy. Phillips's *The Deluge* therefore stands with Upton Sinclair's financial novels as extreme examples of Wall Street muckraking.

Like Lawson, Matthew Blacklock is a Wall Street insider in *The Deluge*. Aspiring to a seat among the powerful kings of finance, he uses the system to rob the public. Blacklock's stock market tool is an investment advisory letter. By turning insider tips into bull market profits and keeping Wall Street rumors from becoming bear market facts, he gains a huge following. "Black Matt" also secretly manipulates stock prices for the big powers on the street by furnishing a ready army of buyers and sellers from among his readers. Some clients make money, but most get wiped out. Blacklock's justification is that it is business: "it was—and is—right under the code, the private and real Wall Street code." [9] That code proves the neophyte's undoing. "The Seven," a facsimile of the Standard Oil crowd, turns against Blacklock and conducts a relentless campaign to wreck him. "A band united by a common interest to control finance, commerce and therefore politics; a band united by a common purpose, to keep that control in as few hands as possible," [10] the syndicate determines that whenever a financier or businessman is getting too powerful, he is cut off. Roebuck, one of the ring's chief figures, feeds Blacklock a tip to buy stock in National Coal. Blacklock then blithely plunges into a false bull market, for, as he buys up National Coal, the ring quietly unloads. Enraged when he finds he is duped, the financier singlemindedly "bears" National Coal in a series of articles in his advisory letter entitled "History of National Coal Company," details of which are dead ringers for Thomas Lawson's "Amalgamated" series in *Everybody's*. The whole stock market topples in the ensuing panic. Roebuck dies, and the rest of the syndicate capitulates. The Augean stables of Wall Street are given a good cleaning, at least in the novel. Lawson lamented how the National City Bank continued on unscathed at its old stand and Rogers, Rockefeller, and Stillman walked the streets twelve months after his charges against the "System" were made public.

Unresolved in *The Deluge* is the issue of Matt Blacklock's own redemption—as it was also ambiguous with the real-life Tom Lawson. Was "Black Matt's" scourge of Wall Street motivated by lust for revenge, or by desire to purge this hellish realm of its satanic powers? Fired by a self-righteousness that only pride in victory over evil can bring, Blacklock himself goes on to replace those principalities he overthrew. After all, evil and darkness on Wall Street abhor a vacuum. Undelivered from the financial marketplace, he says at the novel's end, "I think I shall, in due season, go into action again—profiting by my experience in the futility of trying to hasten evolution by revolution." Silas Lapham, Curtis Jadwin, and Jack London's hero Burning Daylight knew better. They forever abandoned speculation and high finance.

As a muckraker of Wall Street, novelist David Graham Phillips's tone and attitude are almost indistinguishable from those of Gustavus Myers. Myers had worked early in his career as a research assistant under Phillips, when they were on the staff at *Cosmopolitan*. Something of the pupil rubbed off on the master, apparently, for Phillips often sounds more like a historian than a writer of fiction. He thinly veils real-life characters and events, at times changing little else than names. In *The Deluge,* the author, with muckraking zeal, describes the public as a great cow milked, sent out to grass, then milked again by Wall Street financiers. With the righteous yet ironic "Frenzied Finance" voice of Thomas W. Lawson, Blacklock in the novel rhetorically asks:

> Does not the cow produce milk not for her own use but for the use of him who looks after her, provides her with pasturage and shelter and saves her from the calamities in which her lack of foresight and of other intelligence would involve her, were she not looked after? And is not the fact that the public—beg pardon, the cow—meekly and even cheerfully submits to the milking proof that God intended her to be the servant of the Roebucks—beg pardon, again, of man? [11]

Or earlier, in a more indignant tone, Blacklock, like Lawson, says:

> You can't establish a railway or a great industrial system by rose-water morality. But I shall show, before I finish, that Roebuck and his gang of so-called "organizers of industry" bear about the same relation to industry that the boll weevil bears to the cotton crop.[12]

Phillips's Bible-toting capitalist Roebuck is a scarcely concealed portrayal of John D. Rockefeller, Sr. Blacklock compares Roebuck to a robber of the lowest species, just as Lawson assailed Rockefeller, Rogers, and the entire Standard Oil crowd in "Frenzied Finance." Phillips's representation of Roebuck-Rockefeller, heavily biased by Thomas Lawson's maledictions, is many shades darker than Edwin LeFèvre's glossy black-and-white reproduction in *Sampson Rock of Wall Street*. Not only Lawson's but others' revelations about Rockefeller and Standard Oil came to light early in the 1900s. Such unspeakable acts as railroad rebates, drawbacks, systems of discriminations, and monopolies shocked the public. Each new discovery of graft and greed metamorphosed the redoubtable image of Standard Oil Company into the "Standard Oil Gang," and venerable John D. himself was viciously caricatured as an emaciated death's head, clutching bags of the public's money with bony claws.

The Galloway-Roebuck feud in the novel is a dead look-alike for the famed Carnegie-Rockefeller enmity that cropped up over founding of the Steel Trust in 1901. Rockefeller tried early to buy the Carnegie Steel Company for $250 million, an offer the Scottish-born magnate summarily rejected because Rockefeller refused to pay cash. The oil king thereafter seethed with pique and bitterness. Carnegie, in negotiating sale of his company, assumed with all parties an infuriating "you-buy-me-to-save-your-own-hide" attitude, for he seemed bent on driving both Rockefeller and J. P. Morgan, Sr., out of the steel business altogether. After open war between these rivals threatened, Carnegie sold out to Morgan for a "settlement" of more than $447 million. Carnegie, the story goes, met Morgan some time later aboard ship and told him he should have asked more. Morgan replied that he would have paid it if only to be rid of him. The giant United States Steel Corporation, which included not only the Carnegie Steel Company but 70 percent of the steel manufacturers in the country, was born. Gustavus Myers describes it: "Not with a rhythmic placidity did the Steel Trust come into being. An embittered contest, tinged with much personal animus, among certain of the great magnates preceded, and in some degree precipitated, its formation." [13] Also, Phillips draws upon the historic coal strike of 1902 as the basis for the national coal strike threatened in the novel by the Roebuck-Langdon-Melville ring.

David Graham Phillips wrote for leading circulation magazines during his early career. He was trained primarily by George Horace Lorimer of *The Saturday Evening Post* to conform to current literary standards. Perhaps his magazine background explains why *The Deluge*, besides being a roman à clef or fictionalized version of "Frenzied Finance," is a mélange of popular literary genres. There is the formularized romance or sentimental love tale, which was the vogue of business-romance novels in the early 1900s. Also, the novel is hard-core journalistic realism, the patent style of the muckraking novel or essay. Conventional characteristics of the dime Western novel are in evidence as well in *The Deluge*. Owen Wister, whose popular Western novel *The Virginian* was published in 1902, was a fellow contributor of Phillips to *The Saturday Evening Post*. Possibly envious of its sales and rapid climb to fame, Phillips may have decided to incorporate some of the same motifs into *The Deluge* that proved so commercially successful for Wister. At any rate, the financiers in the novel are renegade outlaws who operate in bands or pools and plunder corporations and industries, not lonely banks. Blacklock is the gambler-hero, in the same tradition as Bret Harte's John Oakhurst, who adapts to the code of the frontier. Blacklock learns "never to sleep except with the sword and gun in hand, and one eye open." Overall, David Graham Phillips's chief interest is in portraying the cutthroat American business ethics of the late nineteenth century rather than in matters of literary form or style. Like that of Upton Sinclair, his art is the art of expedience as well as purpose.

III

Upton Sinclair takes aim at a wide range of targets in his dozens of novels about America and her institutions. On the one hand, *The Jungle* is a powerful study of working conditions in Chicago's stockyards, the shocking realism of which aided passage of the Pure Food Laws. On the other hand, *The Metropolis* and *The Moneychangers*, both financial novels, are revelations of the "conditions" of high society in New York, where a barnyard ethos of greed and selfishness prevailed. Whatever his target, Sinclair writes with an investigative reporter's zeal for facts, a social philosopher's eye for the future, and most important, a reformer's courage to stand for what he believes. Facing a mountain of controversy, he refused to cut any of the horribly realistic sections out of *The Jungle*. Risking denouncement and uncertain recrimination, he fearlessly attacked J. Pierpont Morgan, Sr., in *The Moneychangers* as the perpetrator of the panic of 1907. At that time Morgan was one of, if not the most powerful businessman in the country. He appeared to tens of thousands of anxious depositors during the panic as the shepherd on Wall Street who rescued lost banking souls when their poorly managed and undercapitalized institutions faced insolvency because of mass runs. Queued up in long lines waiting for bank doors to open at ten o'clock so that they could withdraw money, people read this notice:

TO OUR DEPOSITORS

WE HAVE RECEIVED THE FINANCIAL SUPPORT

OF J. PIERPONT MORGAN AND CAN ASSURE YOU

THAT YOUR MONEY IS NOW SAFE IN THIS BANK

Later, Sinclair braved a possible score of criminal libels as well as countless civil suits in publishing *The Brass Check,* in which he accused the American press of compromise and prostitution with powerful financial interests. If there was wrong, Sinclair wanted to right it; if injustice, he sought fairness and equity; if corruption, he resorted to exposure. The novelist attacked press, church, universities and schools, government, big business—and he muckraked Wall Street.

Upton Sinclair himself owned that *A Captain of Industry* (1906)— ironically subtitled "The Story of a Civilized Man"—is his most ferocious novel.[14] He also lays claim in its preface to the first American novel of exposure, stating the book had been written five years earlier. Exposure with ferocity is the only characteristic of the novel, which otherwise presents a lifeless stereotype of the Wall Street financier. Years later in *Money Writes!* the author reveals the simple reason it took so long to get *A Captain of Industry* into print. He said forty or fifty magazine and publishing houses rejected the manuscript because all were directly under Wall Street control. If true, Wall Street understandably wanted no part of an incriminating book. Upton Sinclair, however, was obsessed most of his life with Wall Street's influence and control over nearly every aspect of American society. The picture of a fascist America held down under the thumb of a dozen or so money masters dominates his fiction, even as late as the Lanny Budd series published in the 1940s. To understand Sinclair's attitude toward Wall Street, therefore, is to first recognize this lifelong obsession.

Robert van Renssalaer, the captain of industry, is the personification of Wall Street's money power as well as one of Sinclair's priapic cartoons of a financier. A master of high finance, he is portrayed in the novel as thoroughly evil, a devil figure. Lust for gain atrophies all his generous instincts and human sympathies. Van Renssalaer is unmoved when he finds his mistress is his illegitimate daughter, and she kills herself after making this discovery. His exploits on Wall Street are equally hideous and perverse. He corners stock, smashes bear syndicates, unmercifully destroys his victims, and rains general chaos down on the marketplace. Poetic justice, however, bears a hard decree for van Renssalaer. His life ends as violently as it was lived. The financier is pounded to death on the rocks off the Maine coast when the lifeboat from his capsized pleasure yacht is caught in the surf. Breakers beat him all day until his battered corpse is washed ashore. There birds of prey symbolically gorge themselves on it, as van Renssalaer himself had feasted on the dead in Wall Street. Fishermen find the remains, which include a wallet full of money and identification. "You've never heard of him?" asks one. "Why, he's the richest man in the country." "He smells like the devil, anyhow," answers his companion as he steps back in horror. This early muckraking novel by Sinclair, with its jejune melodrama and sensationalism, presents the Wall Street morality in its most banal form.

Sinclair relies on anecdotes and gossip provided him by people intimately aware of goings-on in New York for his novel *The Metropolis* (1908). Admittedly a poor book, it is primarily an exposé of fashionable and moneyed Manhattan society. Published in the wake of the shocking New York life insurance scandal of 1905, however, *The Metropolis* seemed, if not to the public at least to Sinclair himself, "the biggest news story ever sprung in America."

As the story unfolds, the old stock morality character types reappear, as the edenic theme of Adam struggling against temptation on Wall Street comes out. The young and innocent Allan Montague, hero of an earlier novel, *Manassas* (1904), and a cardboard character who in many ways depicts Sinclair's own naiveté, comes to New York fresh off a rural Mississippi plantation. Money makes itself acquainted early when Montague receives a large sum for services as a lawyer. Suddenly he is thrust into the strange role of capitalist and financier. Oliver, his brother, already successful and established in the bosom of New York society, is the novel's tempter or devil figure. He makes Allan privy to inside information about how a stock listed on the exchange is going to behave: "I want you to take every dollar you have, or that you can lay your hands on this morning, and turn it over to me to buy stocks with," Oliver urges his brother. "To buy on margin, you mean?" is Allan's startled reply. The Adamic hero, however, finds refusal difficult as he withdraws money from the bank, hands it over to Oliver, and takes the plunge, buying 6,000 shares of Transcontinental Common on a 10 percent margin. The mathematics of the deal appall Montague and make him realize the "wild game" his brother had planned for him. Standing in the visitors' gallery of the exchange later, he is unable to feel the excitement on the floor below because he realizes "he had sold his own soul to the enchanter, and the spell was upon him." [15]

Like Silas Lapham, who also reaped a harvest on his very first venture into stocks, Montague shows a gain at the end of the day of almost nineteen full points, or a profit of more than $100,000.[16] Unlike the typical financier in the Wall Street novel, however, he is not lured by success into further speculations. Allan is neither bewitched by money nor transfixed by the stock market. Rather, his growing awareness of the inner workings of Wall Street and New York society darkens his attitude and offends his high sense of morality. At this point in the novel, Sinclair, almost as if he feels his hero is safely beyond the temptation of speculation and sufficiently conscious of corruption in society downtown as well as uptown, abandons the lightfooted allegory for the heavier muckrake. The artist becomes the voracious and resolute novelist of purpose. Sinclair transforms Allan Montague into a moral crusader, as well as a mouthpiece or spokesman character, against the idleness, degeneracy, venality, and graft New York is transmitting to the whole country like a virulent disease. The crusader-hero shuns society and, instead, spends weeks investigating the affairs of the Fidelity Company, which is ridden with dry rot and corruption. Shocked at how deplorable Fidelity's financial condition is, Montague wonders how it could have been concealed so long and so

well from public view. Sinclair's white knight finally files suit
against Fidelity on behalf of millions of policyholders who were
being betrayed, a direct strike at big business and the plutocracy.

Actually, in January 1905, three years before publication of *The
Metropolis*, there were faint rumors about management troubles at
the Equitable Life Assurance Society in New York. Those rumors
soon rose in volume above the murmur of a quiet internal struggle,
as the powerful outside director interests of J. P. Morgan, Sr. were
maneuvering in the boardroom against those led by E. H. Harriman for control over the Equitable's assets. Later that year the
Equitable went on trial in Albany before the Armstrong Committee, which unearthed during the hearings a vast network of corruption, misuse of policyholders' premiums, bribes to state legislators
and judges, and illegal political campaign pools. Fidelity Company in the novel is based on the Equitable Life Assurance Society.
Charles Evans Hughes, a highly respectable New York lawyer who
acted as counsel for the Armstrong investigation, is the model for
Sinclair's lawyer-hero. Like Hughes, Montague is morally idealis-
tic and a determined crusader for the public's rights. Sinclair's
hero impassionately conveys his moralistic resolve to his brother,
Oliver, who represents all he detests about the ruling class of New
York:

> You've shown me New York as you see it. I don't believe
> it's the truth—I don't believe it for one single moment!
> But let me tell you this, I shall stay here and defy those
> people! I shall stay and fight them till the day I die! They
> may ruin me—I'll go and live in a garret if I have to,—but
> as sure as there's a God that made me, I'll never stop till
> I've opened the eyes of the people to what they're do-
> ing.[17]

Like the revelations in the insurance scandal of 1905—which tarred
not only the Equitable but every major New York-based life insur-
ace company—Upton Sinclair's exposé of American business and
plutocracy in *The Metropolis* is devastating and complete.

The theme of society's decline and fall, found throughout Wall
Street fiction, is strongly implicit in *The Metropolis*. The picture

Sinclair creates is of a New York whose luxury and opulence rival that of ancient commercial Rome, Babylon, or Tyre, and a spectacle of vice and debauchery paralleling Petronius's mordant description of decadence in *The Satyricon.* So venal are the ways of New York they spread to every corner of the country, infecting society as a whole. Wealth—gaudy, vulgar, vice-ridden wealth—is the culture of the metropolis. Bribery, license, fraud, and thievery are the accepted customs. The great merchants, financiers, bankers, and businessmen who figure there constitute the ruling class and foster nepotism and plutocracy. Their multi-million-dollar mansions sit like mausoleums on a block and a half of Fifth Avenue, more dismal than tombs of Roman financial magnates along the Appian Way. Years later, Sinclair said he was never proud of *The Metropolis* as a work of art. The novel's tone is heavily didactic, almost defiant, the language captious and hyperbolic. It is, however, an exemplary novel of condemnation of late nineteenth-, early twentieth-century America, when capitalism threatened to topple the structure of society.

Upton Sinclair's *The Moneychangers,* dedicated to Jack London and published in the same year as a sequel to *The Metropolis,* is about the Great Panic of 1907. The "Roosevelt panic" or the "rich man's panic," as historians call it, essentially was the culmination of a growing money shortage amid a business boom. Someone asked for a dollar and everybody ran scared, was the common joke. Precipitating that money shortage were the outrageous shenanigans of F. Augustus Heinze and Charles W. Morse. These financier-gamblers formed an alliance to buy up a chain of banks, employing stock of one enterprise as collateral on which to borrow money for purchase of another. When Heinze's attempted corner in United Copper failed after somebody in the pool secretly sold out, the smash shook his banking pyramid and put his brother's brokerage firm, Otto Heinze & Co., under. Banks involved in the copper scheme felt the blow and scrambled for money. Panic gathered force. Stock prices, which had forecast bad weather early in the year by turning bearish, broke in October. Call money shot up to 125 percent, then became scarce at any price. Numerous other banks fell with appalling swiftness, like helpless dominoes. When the fashionable Knickerbocker Trust Company, solid as a fort, closed its doors, all-out disaster was triggered. The public created mass runs on nearly every New York City bank, which then sank the nation into a full-scale money scare.

Upton Sinclair tells in *The Brass Check* (1920) how he got the "inside story" of the scheme by which the New York banking masters, led by J. P. Morgan the elder, deliberately brought on that panic as a means of putting the independent trust companies out of business. The fact was that Morgan did permit some of these smaller trust companies, which he regarded as financial freebooters, to go to the wall. There is, however, no evidence that he precipitated the panic or had anything to do with the money crisis that speeded it along. Conversely, it was widely known that Morgan headed a hurriedly formed rescue operation that loaned huge sums to keep the big New York banks afloat after the Knickerbocker Trust "went over the dam." Ten million dollars was first raised to shore up the Trust Company of America, still solvent although its surplus had been wiped out, then another $25 million on top of that. Sinclair provocatively argues that the great banking baron was forced to do this because the panic had gotten out of control and only by desperate efforts stopped it. Mark Twain, on the other hand, who lost money when the Knickerbocker Trust failed, resignedly took the popular view of "The Panic." In a diary entry dated November 1, 1907, he assessed President Roosevelt, not the money masters, as the "author of it." [18]

The Moneychangers is a fictional account of the Great Panic of 1907, although Upton Sinclair also telescopes historical material from the panic of 1901. Dan Waterman, colossus of finance, Croesus of Wall Street, is a repulsive caricature of J. Pierpont Morgan, Sr. Emaciated, white-haired, eighty years old, with a hawk's face and unquenchable lusts, the banker is a human predator who feeds on money and sex. Simultaneously conjoining money and death, Waterman represents the figure of financier as devil. "How many trusts had Waterman organised! And how many puns had been made upon that name of his!" [19] The background episode early in the novel of the struggle for the Northern Mississippi Railroad, which evolves into the main plot, is based on the six-year-long battle for control of the Northern Pacific Railroad begun in 1901 by J. P. Morgan, Sr., James J. Hill, and James R. Keene in one armed camp, against E. H. Harriman and Jacob Schiff of Kuhn, Loeb & Company in the other. This epic confrontation unexpectedly resulted in a corner of Northern Pacific, in which the Street's two greatest banking houses had bought up all the available stock. Shares of Northern Pacific rose under the bidding to figures that meant doom to unnumbered men, foolish bears who sold the stock short as the big buyers were gobbling it up. Northern Pacific rocketed to 160 a share, then in an hour 100 shares were traded at 700, 300 more shares exchanged hands at 1,000. The market as a whole began to collapse in fear that Morgan and Kuhn, Loeb & Co. would exact blood from the short sellers (actually, Morgan permitted shorts to settle at 150 a share). Waterman in the novel (supposedly like Morgan) carefully lays plans to create panic in the financial community. A secret meeting in an obscure hotel is called by the master, as the half-dozen most powerful men in New York convene. Sinclair here is reproducing a meeting that did take place, the famous conclave of bankers and financiers summoned to Morgan's East Thirty-sixth Street library, where the real-life master locked his doors, allowing nobody to depart until funds were pledged to stem the 1907 panic. "This country needs a lesson," says Waterman. "If the people get a little taste of hard times, they'll have something else to think about besides abusing those who have made the prosperity of the country." [20] When the Gotham Trust (in reality the Knickerbocker Trust Company) is smashed according to plan, Wall Street reels under the financial tremors. Stocks fall, banks fail, and the little fish are eaten by the bigger in the panic. Waterman (like Morgan) emerges as king of finance, with control over nearly every bank in the city.

Death as well as destruction follow Dan Waterman's path, just as those powers of darkness stalked Robert van Renssalaer in Sinclair's *A Captain of Industry*. Lucy Dupree, the besieged heroine, gives herself up to the evil capitalist to spare the man she loves from financial ruin. Horrified at her own debasement and unsuccessful in saving her doomed lover, Stanley Ryder, she poisons herself. Ryder, suggestive of Charles T. Barney, president of the Knickerbocker Trust Company who, mixed up in the Heinze-Morse chain banking deals, took his own life a year after the panic, also commits suicide when his bank, Gotham Trust, is wrecked by

Waterman. Innocent businessmen, laborers, widows, and orphans—"the vast public which furnished all the money for the game"—are ruined when their savings are swept away in the hysteria.

International economics, Wall Street, and the downfall of capitalist America are the subjects several decades later, when Upton Sinclair writes his "Lanny Budd" novels. Sinclair had just lived through the Great Depression, an agonizing period during which he sharpened his view of as well as solutions to America's ills, many of which found their way into this sextet of novels. Back in 1913, Sinclair had prophesized socialism for America, doubting that capitalism could bring about a truly free and democratic society. But for years, while always emphasizing social and political rather than economic answers, he was a critic without a cure, a diagnostician short of a remedy, until his EPIC campaign. End Poverty in California, slogan for his 1934 run for governor of California, encompassed a wide range of reform principles, not the least of which prescribed taking management away from the capitalist class and setting up self-help cooperatives in which the people themselves produced and exchanged goods for their own use. Capitalism, a system based on pig ethics, he felt created distortions in supply and demand, unfair prices, and "hard times." Wall Street, arch-symbol of capitalism founded upon profits and dividends, encouraged pig ethics. Sinclair during his campaign repeatedly asked, in demagogic fashion, who needs the capitalist class? Who needs mismanagement? Who needs scarcities, high prices, hard times?

The Lanny Budd novels, a series of six published between 1940 and 1945, provide a Marxist view of historical events dated from the eve of World War I through the middle of World War II. The hero, Lanny Budd, an effete playboy heir of the vast Budd Gunmakers fortune, epitomizes the weaknesses and infirmities of the American capitalist system. A Connecticut Yankee in Adolph Hitler's court during the prewar years of the Third Reich, Budd is politically impotent, although still motivated by financial profit. His role as a political and economic force, in Europe as well as the United States, steadily diminishes.

Dragon's Teeth (1943), fourth in the series, is a socioeconomic study of the post-1929 Crash era in America as well as the rise to power of Nazi Germany. Sinclair draws an implicit parallel between economic conditions in the United States and in Germany during the dark 1930s. Franklin D. Roosevelt's New Deal program, in many ways, resembles Hitler's convulsive efforts to lift want from the German people and provide prosperity. In both countries, as economic depression grows more severe, the governments gain in centralization of power. In fact, the novelist pictures a fascist state in the United States during the depression, endowed with authority to regulate, control, and even confiscate industry. Sinclair in the novel compares the tactics of Wall Street syndicates—myrmidons of Washington who freely raid and pillage American business—to methods used by the Nazis in seizing control of Jewish-owned commercial enterprises. The group of Wall Street financiers that suddenly grabs controlling interest in the stock of the Budd munitions company is as ruthless and maniacal as Minister-President Hermann Göring, who arrests and imprisons a business partner of Lanny Budd's father when he tries to leave Germany with as much capital as he can salvage.

The Great Depression in the 1930s, as Sinclair portrays it, has a devastating effect on America, not because of the economic paralysis it produces, but because it gives the free enterprise system an opportunity to show its real ugliness and tyranny. That mean and shabby capitalistic face, only partially hidden from public view since the early days of the robber barons, is fully unmasked. Banks close in waves of failures, municipalities default on bond interest, corporations omit dividends, and the stock market falls unrelentingly lower as Sinclair grimly portrays in *Dragon's Teeth* a country having reached and gone beyond its apogee of capitalism.

IV

One of the reasons Jack London wrote the novel *Burning Daylight* (1910) was to cash in on the popular craze in the early 1900s for Wall Street fiction, as well as regain some of his lost readership.

Competitive capitalism was still high on London's list of enemies. Could he have had his way, he would have boarded up Wall Street and converted the Big Board and Curb into food exchanges, with stockbrokers and financiers pushing produce carts through the narrow streets side by side with the Wobblies. Like Upton Sinclair, he believed competitive capitalism was soulless and defeated any system of altruism. Rockefeller, Carnegie, and Morgan all locked the door against opportunity, while thousands of young men were forced to stop at the placard: NO THOROUGHFARE. London, though, apparently had lost some interest in the Marxist-socialist bias against oligarchy and capitalism seen three years earlier in *The Iron Heel*, because he replaces the novel of ideas with his old formula of raw naturalism. Competitive capitalism, rather than a specific target for criticism, provides a perfect naturalistic environment for London's stock atavistic hero to be tried and tested in. Wall Street, symbol of vice, evil, and moral corruption in the novels of D. G. Phillips and Upton Sinclair, in *Burning Daylight* is a realm absolutely amoral and lawless.

The Wall Street setting in *Burning Daylight* is no less malign or tooth-and-claw than the Arctic wasteland where Elam Harnish, King of the Klondike, learns to survive. Harnish was the living legend who had met the giants Al Mayo and Jack McQuestion, the man who raced the mail from Circle to Salt Water and back again in sixty days, the hero who saved the whole Tanana tribe from perishing in the winter of '91. The game of life that Harnish (Burning Daylight, as the Alaskans call him) has a strong instinct for playing in the wild makes him naturally fit for the game of speculation in the stock market. Survival and victory in both games require playing a lone hand as well as holding contempt for the enemy. Although Burning Daylight has deep respect for the wilderness, he reckons Wall Street no more fearsome than a hotel casino and the stock market the biggest gaming table in the world. Also, he judges the masters of finance and captains of industry as weak, frightened animals of prey who only pretend to be predatory. "They're a lot of little cottontail rabbits making believe they're big rip-snorting timber wolves. They set out to everlastingly eat up some proposition, but at the first sign of trouble they

turn tail and stampede for the brush," [21] he contemptuously
mutters.

Jack London's model for the character Burning Daylight is the
historical financier James R. Keene, who more than thirty years
earlier earned for his exploits the sobriquet "The Silver Fox of
Wall Street." In fact, Daylight is a dead ringer for Keene. His
fictional history as a miner turned capitalist is an almost exact
reproduction of the famed buccaneer's. As James Keene was staked
to his first speculative mining profits during the 1856 Comstock
Lode silver rush, Burning Daylight discovers gold later in 1897
prospecting on the Yukon. Both the historical and fictional capitalists cut their stock market teeth on the San Francisco and Nevada
exchanges, parlaying earlier mining profits into gambling fortunes.
Meanwhile, legends about their daring and brilliance as freelance
operators swiftly grow up on the Pacific Coast. After the Comstock
bubble burst in mid-1875, Keene packed his gambling earnings
and headed across the country for New York, where big-time financier Jay Gould seemed waiting to strip his millions from him.
Similarly in the novel, the king of the Klondike also leaves San
Francisco for the East, flush with cash, where a group of Wall
Street wizards skin him as well.

Historically, Jim Keene stopped off on Wall Street with a fortune variously estimated at $4 million or $6 million. Railroad
stocks, gold, the New York Stock Exchange, and Newport provided
many attractions for him, but the mechanics of Jay Gould's financial operations particularly mesmerized him. The story on the
Street had gone that when someone pointed out the stooped,
shrunken figure of Gould, Keene remarked he had a few millions
with him and would stay a while to take the "Wizard's" scalp.
Gould subsequently invited the eager Westerner to join a stock
pool organized to "break" the Western Union Telegraph Company and take possession of the whole enterprise away from
William H. Vanderbilt. During the ensuing bear campaign, Gould
forced down the price of Western Union by relentless short selling,
but then betrayed Keene, who had gone mad over his gains, and
quietly began buying. Keene was caught red-handed in the "sell-
out"—a common practice whenever a cagey operator seized the

opportunity to turn a large and quick profit at the expense of his unsuspecting collaborators. Believing himself infallible, Jim Keene was instead shorn like the veriest lamb, "euchred" of his millions, and turned adrift a bankrupt. An embittered Keene, discovering the "double-cross," is reported to have confronted Gould in Russell Sage's office. The Californian brandished a pistol in Gould's face before Mr. Sage could calm him down. The only compensation Keene could claim from this meeting was some soothed pride and vanity, but certainly not his pilfered millions.

Even if this story about Jim Keene's Wall Street plucking in the late 1870s by Jay Gould were apocryphal, Jack London reproduced it in *Burning Daylight* almost down to the last detail. Daylight, recruited as a pawn to play the big game on Wall Street, brings his $11 million in Yukon gold and Western stock market booty to the New York Stock Exchange. The Wall Street financiers in the novel, John Dowsett, Nathaniel Letton, and Leon Guggenhammer urge him to "buy, buy, buy, and keep on buying to the last stroke" in Ward Valley Copper, while they secretly plan to unload. Daylight is led to believe the company's directors are about to declare a double dividend, which, he is told, will make the price of the stock "rush heavenward." He buys heavily, until the thunderbolt falls—the directors levy an assessment on the stockholders rather than pay out a dividend. BURNING DAYLIGHT CLEANED OUT, the next day's headlines read. DAYLIGHT GETS HIS. ANOTHER WESTERNER FAILS TO FIND EASY MONEY. Not to be outsmarted by these lesser creatures who cower in Wall Street offices, however, London's hero bursts into their lair with a Colt's .44 and reclaims his money at gunpoint. Like Keene, he meets Wall Street dead on its own terms.

Attempting to create an authentic and convincing Wall Street atmosphere in the novel, Jack London portrays not only his hero but also the financiers who bunko the Klondike gambler as recognizable New York Stock Exchange personalities. Nathaniel Letton is a reproduction of real-life operator Jay Gould. Gould, of course, was famous for his bold campaigns to corner the nation's gold, which created financial panic on Black Friday, September 1869, wrest control of the Erie Railroad from Cornelius Vanderbilt, or corner the stock of the Union Pacific Railroad. Feared as the

"Mephistopheles of Wall Street," Gould was the trickiest of all the tricksters on the exchange. After his Western Union debacle, Keene even called Gould "the worst man on earth since the beginning of the Christian era." Newcomer Burning Daylight had seen Letton's face "a score of times in the magazines and newspapers, and read about his standing in the financial world." [22] Letton, almost exactly like Gould, was "thin to emaciation . . . a cold flame of a man" with a "glacier-like exterior" and eyes that blazed out from what was "almost a death's-head." [23] Besides suffering from chronically poor health, Gould was also an ascetic, untrusting, skeptical, and parsimonious in his personal life. Meanwhile his âme damnée, Jim Fisk, represented in the novel by financier John Dowsett, was just the opposite, a sybarite who loved life and consorted with several mistresses, spent money lavishly, and lived in high style.

The contrast in fact was as complete as it was startling, according to Robert H. Fuller, who wrote the biographical novel *Jubilee Jim.* Jim was florid and fond of the table, a weakness that showed forth in his figure; Gould was abstemious. Jim was loud and self-confident; Gould was silent and seemed diffident. Jim was bold; Gould was cautious. Jim said what he thought; Gould kept his mouth shut. Although Jack London portrays Letton as the inscrutable plotter and cold manipulator, Dowsett is the warm, hale fellow well met. Daylight is struck by the contrast between the two men, "puzzled in that he could find no likeness in Dowsett. . . . Nathaniel Letton was unlike the other in every particular." [24]

London takes poetic license with the third member in the group of financiers that hornswoggles Daylight, Leon Guggenhammer. The novelist may actually have had Russell Sage in mind, who *was* with Gould when Keene fell victim to the Western Union double-cross, but probably wanted to include a Jewish financier to add a touch of usury and greed to the scheme. Guggenhammer, "one of the great Guggenhammer family; a younger one, but nevertheless one of the crowd with which he had locked grapples in the North," [25] suggests one of the wealthy Guggenheim sons. Patriarch Meyer Guggenheim was a Swiss-Jewish immigrant who amassed a fortune in Canadian and Colorado mining ventures before establishing his family empire on Wall Street. The seven Guggenheim sons went on to become famous as the "silver princes," then the "smelter overlords," and finally the "copper kings" by the time Jack London wrote *Burning Daylight*. Because the name Guggenheim was synonymous with honesty and fair dealing in the business world, London miscasts "Guggenhammer" as a robber baron and freebooter of the ilk of Gould and Fisk, much less an associate with them. Incidentally, while taking license with Guggenhammer, London also freely places John Dowsett (Jim Fisk) together with Nathaniel Letton (Jay Gould) at the time of the Ward Valley Copper smash. Fisk and Gould *were* collaborators, but if the Ward Valley swindle of Burning Daylight is based on James R. Keene's Western Union betrayal in 1877, Fisk would have been dead five years, shot and killed by a former business associate. London takes no poetic freedom, though, when his miner turned capitalist hero sizes up the circumspect threesome who are about to pluck him of his millions.

> These men were big players. They were powers. True, as
> he knew himself, they were not the real inner circle. They
> did not rank with the Morgans and Harrimans. And yet
> they were in touch with those giants and were themselves
> lesser giants.[26]

Jay Gould and Jim Fisk were jackals on Wall Street rather than titans, natural enemies of J. Pierpont Morgan, Sr., E. H. Harriman, or the Vanderbilts. London, therefore, offers true-to-life portraits of these robber barons, men who toiled only to exploit, bleed, water, and destroy.

The historical James R. Keene never left New York to go back to the Pacific Coast. The last quarter of the nineteenth century saw him rise in fame as one of the greatest stock manipulators who ever lived, the financier who managed pools for H. H. Rogers and William Rockefeller of Standard Oil and J. P. Morgan, Sr., the "Silver Fox" who cornered the stock of the Northern Pacific Railroad. Jack London's financier, however, returns to San Francisco with cash intact to become a veritable pirate of the West Coast financial main. "Ware Daylight" is the watchword as he takes control of Panama Mail or sees the California & Altamont Trust

Company hopelessly wrecked and Charles Klinkner, its president, a suicide in a felon's cell (more shades of Jim Keene, whose short selling helped trigger the collapse of the Bank of California in the mid-1870s, which led to the suicide of bank president William C. Ralston).

Metamorphosed from popular Alaskan hero into stock market bully, gambler, plunger, desperado, and all-round bad man, Jack London's Burning Daylight is gradually overtaken by the same dehumanizing that afflicts businessmen-financiers Silas Lapham, Curtis Jadwin, James Galloway, and John Dumont, for example. Money and death also work their effects on Daylight's health, as the destructive process began back in Dawson with his first stock market successes. He steadily loses physical strength and energy, and sees signs of rapid aging while his speculative riches increase. Fortunately, love and marriage redeem the hero before money destroys him. Burning Daylight forsakes high finance and returns to the land as a farmer. The temptation of easy money is laid before him one final time when he discovers a piece of quartz laden with gold, and the enchanting vision of a whole mining operation spreads itself in front of his eyes. As testimony of his regeneration and restoration, Daylight buries the rock and walks home to his wife "through the fires of sunset with a milk pail on his arm." [27] Financier James R. Keene's end was neither romantic nor idyllic. Refusing to vanish from the financial firmament, he returned again and again like a burnt-out comet to do weary battle on the exchange. After the collapse of the ill-fated Columbus & Hocking pool in January 1910, the last one he ever managed, Keene's health slowly faded until he died in New York in 1913.

8.

Debt in the Genteel Garden

I

The new hybrid class of industrialists and capitalists in the latter half of the nineteenth century were the makers and promoters of America. A self-made moneyed breed, they molded a new aristocracy out of the old order. Racing, hunting, and yachting may have filled their idle hours, but moneymaking and empire building were their most serious pursuits. Ironically, those same "old order" values which the makers and promoters had toiled to overturn were incarnated anew, when second- and third-generation descendants began inheriting their wealth after the turn of the century. Nonetheless, business and commerce were sacrosanct for these mighty shapers of industrial society. Money was a god, and life meant and depended upon a bull market.

The rise of capitalism and the capitalist class brought many social inequities into existence. The plutocracy, blamed for these ills, particularly came under attack from the political left. Liberals found sympathetic voices in the muckrake and progressive novelists of the early 1900s. D. G. Phillips, Upton Sinclair, and Jack

London, considered earlier, represent the liberal or "macroeco-
nomic-literary" point of view, if such a coinage has any currency.
These novelists assessed how the public and country as a whole are
affected by concentrations of vast capital and surplus. Writers of
social protest, they believed the costs of wealth and power were too
great a burden on the public, which inevitably had to pay the
price for every excess. Other novelists, antagonized by the rise of
the plutocracy, were more concerned with the individual effects
money had on manners, morals, and cultural values than the
broader social, economic or political effects. Robert Grant and
Edith Wharton, for example, in novels written after 1900, conversely took the "microeconomic-literary" viewpoint, which ana-
lyzed the relationship between the costs of wealth and the moral
and spiritual price the individual had to pay to obtain it. Later on,
F. Scott Fitzgerald and John P. Marquand also wrote about the
costs and effects of money on individual lives. Fitzgerald described
in the 1920s the dangers and pitfalls of aspiring to be rich, and
Marquand in his novels of manners in the 1930s and 1940s pictured the penalties and hazards of already being rich.

The genteel novel of high finance is about microeconomics, or
about individuals whose lives are influenced and determined by
economic factors. The genteel hero, even though he may dream, is
not a mighty robber baron who creates economic destiny for thousands, nor is his own conflict in life an epic struggle on the exchange over control of railroads. Far less imposing, he fails to
master even his own economic fate. And his struggle is merely for
survival. He is usually the scion of wealth, a descendant of either
old or new money, who glories in the name as well as speculates
with the fortune his father or grandfather made on Wall Street.
Originating not from the backwoods, the genteel financial hero is
raised in fashionable city districts such as the sunny side of Commonwealth Avenue and water side of Beacon Street in Boston, or
the upper ends of Madison and Fifth Avenue in New York. Rather
than naked and innocent, the young naïf comes into the world
financially well adorned. Money so weakens this upper-class species, however, that when adverse winds do blow and financial catastrophe occurs, moral or spiritual strength to endure loss of
fortune is found wanting. Ruin becomes a permanent condition for

the old order. Wall Street in the genteel novel of high finance, like the devil himself, respects no social distinctions or class lines, devouring whomever it will devour. The stock exchange usually is the means by which the old aristocracy, in pursuit of speculative riches, is broken down and dissolved, just as it is the agent that lifts the new moneyed class into existence.

Robert Grant (1852-1940) was well known during his lifetime, but is now a forgotten novelist. Lawyer, probate court judge, and writer, he shared a long friendship with Chicago novelist Robert Herrick, with whom he often exchanged novels. Also, Grant's chronicles of the Chippendales and his naturalistic novel *Unleavened Bread* (1900) drew the admiration of Edith Wharton. His father was a well-to-do merchant in mid-nineteenth-century Boston, so that Grant as a young man observed and knew the Brahmin class intimately. In fact, in *The Chippendales* (1909), he brings out the Bromfield Corey types—those Brahmins encountered in Howells's *Silas Lapham*—from the protected shadows into the sharp glare of the financial marketplace to portray how this old aristocratic order ineptly flounders in competitive society.

Boston, up until this time, had been free from the mushroom variety of millionaires who had sprung up overnight in such abundance in New York and Philadelphia. Its ruling class consisted of the old-line merchant and shipping families, like the Chippendales in Grant's fiction, who represent the *vieux riches,* the last members of the old order able to live off income from inherited wealth. Old Harrison Chippendale, a senior member of the clan, believes himself wealthy beyond the most vulgar dreams of avarice, and, much like John P. Marquand's rich Boston scion, George Apley, he is free to devote time not to moneymaking but to clipping bond coupons and developing cultural interests. Unlike Howells's Coreys, who considered paintings the only sensible investment, the Chippendales tie their money up primarily in "gilt-edged" securities. Old Harrison, keeping regular tabs on his portfolio, "was a familiar and dignified figure on his walks to and from State Street." [1] The companies in which he owns bonds and stocks, however, are losing ground in the competitive world and begin passing on dividends.

While everyone else is becoming richer, Harrison Chippendale is steadily growing poorer.

Chauncey Chippendale, Harrison's son, opposes his father's staid old Boston conservatism, hoping he will see the investment opportunities of the future rather than stay wedded to the defunct possibilities of the past. Young Chauncey sees no moral distinction between buying common stocks on margin and borrowing on bills of lading, as the old-fashioned merchants did, including both his grandfathers. Harrison, though, scoffs at Chauncey's advice that the surest way to make money quickly is in the stock market. The elder Chippendale, to whose sense of tradition and decorum the whole commercial trend of society is repugnant, and who regards syndicates, underwritings, and reorganizations as new and dangerous forms of gambling, complains that "an aristocracy of stockholders is an anomaly." [2] Elegant, dilettantish, and shallow, Chauncey Chippendale represents a new breed of Brahmin, an inferior species fundamentally weakened rather than strengthened by expectations of a large inheritance. With the Chippendale income rapidly tapering off and the family's social status dwindling into insignificance, Chauncey is more certainly lured by the siren's call of high finance. Susceptible to the money temptation and poised for the Fall, he dives headlong into speculation in the stock market.

The devil figure in the novel is a stockbroker who intrudes into the genteel Garden and reaps a living off its fruits. An outsider, Hugh Blaisdell comes to Boston to seek his fortune. Like Chauncey, he graduates from Harvard, yet he finds his application for a bank position turned down, the job given instead by social preferment to young Chippendale. Blaisdell rises in the Boston world of finance anyway, as if in defiance of being cast out of the Chippendale heaven. He masters the complex machinery of the financial marketplace, subtle tool of the devil in the Wall Street novel, and gains an incredible reputation for making money. In fact, Chauncey, overwhelmed by Blaisdell's brilliance, informs his father, "He's one of the rising luminaries on the State Street horizon; some people say *the* rising luminary." [3] Buying into companies such as the nearly defunct Warrior Mills—one of Harrison Chippendale's floundering investments—Blaisdell seems to revitalize these businesses with a Midas touch. He represents, however, a rebellion against Chippendale ideals and principles; namely, "never speculate, only invest, and never change your investments." The emerging class of makers and promoters, the new plutocracy that spoils the genteel preserve, therefore, is embodied in this devil-as-stockbroker figure.

Chauncey Chippendale's enchantment with the stock market seals his Fall. His sin is more than just an involvement with speculation, it is his willful betrayal of the godly Brahmin values by which he had been reared. He panders his genteel innocence, however outmoded, for lowly membership in the plutocratic class; he sells his natural birthright for the empty values of Philistia. No sooner does he set foot on State Street than Chauncey is outmaneuvered by the clever Blaisdell, who buys a bank out from under him, forcing Chauncey to give up the family-held shares with "feelings akin to those which a traveller experiences when ordered to hand over his valuables by a gentlemanly highwayman." [4] The showdown between banker and broker occurs over control of Electric Coke, a speculative issue that promises millions in profits. Chauncey, expecting a sizeable inheritance from his uncle who has just died, buys heavily. Blaisdell's fears that "his rival on State Street might spread his wings on the strength of his large nest egg and indulge in fresh financial flights" [5] are confirmed. But, as in everything else connected with money, the aristocracy fails again. Chauncey's rich uncle, a senile octogenarian, had secretly wedded his secretary and gotten her with child, invalidating his will and dashing his nephew's hopes of a huge legacy. Chauncey Chippendale, the aristocratic Adam who only pretended to be a financier, remains an obscure Boston banker, "a power down-town largely by reflected light." [6] The now rich and powerful Blaisdell marries into the Chippendale family, with no less than Chauncey's sister, making the adulteration of the species complete.

The old aristocracy is an endangered order, but withal worthy of respect as an American way of life of the past. The new moneyed class, which rises from the ashes of the old by worshiping the stock market as a tutelary saint of the same holy order as athletics and cocktail parties, is the object of Robert Grant's antipathy. A similar animus is also evident in fiction by Edith Wharton, when she portrays the *nouveaux riches* as a vulgar bunch whose only real intent is to social climb. Grant along with Wharton would surely have confirmed Jonathan Swift's observation that the attitude in climbing is the same as in crawling, particularly in parvenu circles in America around the turn of the century.

II

Wall Street's growing preeminence in American life made it a popular subject for fiction at the beginning of the new century. The stock market boomed in 1899, driving up securities prices as well as the number of stockholders in domestic companies to record highs. Four and a half million Americans owned shares of stock, a figure that, according to New York Stock Exchange data, only doubled over the next fifty years. Wall Street thwarted Teddy Roosevelt, reelected president in 1904, when he tried to curb growth of the industrial "trusts." The insurance scandal that blew wide open in late 1905, involving the four giant New York life insurance companies, was Wall Street related. Wall Street even played hero when it came to President Roosevelt's rescue, and supported the stock market during the disastrous panic of 1907. Wall Street seemed to be everywhere, in newspaper headlines, magazine features *(Everybody's* ran Thomas W. Lawson's "Frenzied Finance. The Story of Amalgamated" nearly two years, 1904-6), stories, poems, and novels.

In the opening decade of the 1900s, New York was fast in the grip of a Wall Street craze. Novels about business and economics flooded the market, mirroring the public's fascination with high finance. The influence of Wall Street was so compelling that it helped confer upon New York a long-term economic as well as literary ascendancy. Financial fiction published during these turbulent years appeared in various forms. Censures of speculation, diatribes against the New York Stock Exchange, insider exposés about Wall Street, even chauvinistic defenses of capitalism and the free enterprise system were the rule.

Although Wall Street and the aura of high finance dominated many of these novels, they also exerted an omnipresent, almost premonitory influence over Edith Wharton's fiction, particularly *The House of Mirth* (1905) and *The Custom of the Country* (1913). Mrs. Wharton in these novels portrays *fin de siècle* New York society, a time when "uptown" Fifth Avenue culture and fashion, already in a final phase of decline, are giving way to "downtown" business and finance. The New York Stock Exchange "downtown," in fact, may have been a dominating factor when the novelist created the character and situation of Lily Bart in *The House of Mirth*. The social circles through which the unfortunate heroine descends, for example, take on the characteristics of impersonal human stock exchanges, each no longer willing to "list" her. As friendships and alliances are strategically made on these "social exchanges," or as marriages are negotiated and transacted, reputations (not to mention family fortunes) usually are strengthened. Lily, however, suffering an unsteady fluctuation in her fortunes and unable to make an alliance or marriage, sees her reputation weakened.

Lily Bart's days as a teenager, filled with "grey interludes of economy and brilliant reactions of expense," had always paralleled the stock market. In a desultory yet agitated fashion, life traced "a zig zag broken course down which the family craft glided on a rapid current of amusement, tugged at by the underflow of a perpetual need—the need of more money." Eleven years after her debut, Lily by herself, separated from the financial vicissitudes of her family, is like the shares of a corporation's common stock that falter under heavy selling and slip in price on the stock exchange. The highs and lows of her life, still uncertainly zigging and zagging, resemble the downward trading pattern of a stock that, after a season of popularity and demand, runs out of investment appeal and falls into disfavor with the buying public. With the New York Stock Exchange itself suffering a prolonged selloff in the background of the novel, the decline in Lily's value that is accelerated in her last few months could be viewed as an allegory of yet another bear market on Wall Street.

A place in the New York aristocracy is always tentative at best for Lily Bart. She well knows her father's fortune will not endure investigation. When Hudson Bart suddenly announces his financial ruin, Lily's veneer as a blue chip social equity just as suddenly drops away. After his death a short time later, her association with monetary and exchange value is unmistakably established by Mrs. Bart, who finds consolation in her daughter's beauty, regarding it as "the last asset in their fortunes, the nucleus around which their life was to be rebuilt." She takes over management of the portfolio of Lily's beauty "as though it were her own property and Lily its mere custodian," and displays the same selfishness and social ambition with which she always managed the family money. Mrs. Bart, spoken of by friends as a "wonderful manager," was known for producing unlimited effects with limited means. "You'll get it all back—you'll get it all back with your face," she tells Lily after the Bart money is swept away by an unlucky turn in the stock market. Had Mrs. Bart also not died soon after, she might have guided her daughter into a comfortable and secure marriage—as did Mrs. Van Osburgh with her daughters or Mrs. Light with daughter Christina in Henry James's *Roderick Hudson*—selling off Lily's assets to the highest bidder. Left alone in the world to handle her own affairs, however, Lily flounders. Beyond the tender debutante age at twenty-nine years old, and without any immediate family fortune to underwrite her, Lily's social or intrinsic "book" value nevertheless does remain high. She *is* beautiful, charming, and intelligent—qualities that attract premium prices in any market. Lily no doubt often reminds herself of this fact, like those women whom French novelist Paul Bourget classifies as "Beauties" in his collection of impressions about America entitled *Outre-Mer* (1896). " 'I know my social value,' said one girl. She spoke of herself as of a certificate of New York Central, or Chicago, Burlington, and Quincy stock."

Lily Bart's first "buyer" in the marketplace is Lawrence Selden. He recognizes her real value, considering her almost as if she were a tangible product, a precious commodity with a justifiably high price tag. Selden has "a confused sense that she must have cost a great deal to make, that a great many dull and ugly people must, in some mysterious way, have been sacrificed to produce her." Of all the men who bid for her, he probably knows better than any Lily's worth. Yet Selden knows too that "there must be plenty of capital on the lookout for such an investment." He is an extremely cautious investor, with an innate fear of taking risks. Perhaps the influence of his parents, whose purchasing habits were characterized by restraint and discrimination, always remained strong. Nevertheless he is willing to take the plunge into the market. Accordingly, his is the fairest offer she is to receive. Selden offers Lily love. She does warn him that a marriage with her "would be a great risk, certainly—and I have never concealed from you how great." Only after she actually rejects his offer does Selden's fundamental conservatism again take control, forbidding him to make another later on, even when her price has substantially fallen.

The next buyer in the market for Lily Bart contemplates a deal that presumably is in no way a measure of her real worth or book value. Unlike Selden, who is unable to afford a risk, Percy Gryce is extremely rich. His income alone is rumored to be $800,000 a year. Gryce, though, is interested in investment and ownership, not love. Aware of both his passion and ability to pay for rare things like his Americana collection, Lily tries a bluff. She wonders what the largest price is that she could exact from him. Yet in so doing, Lily lacks her mother's instinct to set the current market quotation fairly and accurately, and instead creates an unreasonable "spread" between her own asking price and Gryce's bid. She clings persistently to values and ideals Mrs. Bart would have dismissed as silly. Measuring Gryce's limitations, such as his dullness and power to bore, she thinks of him as "a merchant whose warehouses are crammed with an unmarketable commodity." Meanwhile, as she deliberately sets an added premium on her worth and thereby prices herself out of the market, Lily's prospective buyer is brokered off into another marriage transaction with a less glamorous but more solidly financed issue of preferred society stock in one of the Van Osburgh daughters.

Like a stock reacting to rumors of impending bad news, Lily Bart plummets on the social exchange. Her long-term investment prospects suddenly look dim. Lily, however, "had learned the value of contrast in throwing her charms into relief." Against a background of dull and lifeless issues listed on the "Big Board" or social register of the elect—such as the sluggish Gerty Farish, the inactive Grace Stepney, the laggard Van Osburgh girls, or the volatile Carry Fisher—she looks like a bargain at almost any bid.

Gus Trenor, a stockbroker on Wall Street who has a greedy eye for the short term, is the next buyer. Trenor sees an opportunity for a quick turnover with Lily, so he provides thin buying support at a price well under the current market. He tells her that "a man has got to keep his eyes open and pick up all the tips he can." Further, he says, "At the pace we go now, I don't know where I should be if it weren't for taking a flyer now and then." Trenor's interest in Lily Bart is the trader's interest in an occasional high flyer, a glamor stock that has sold off but holds the potential for a rebound and short-term profits.

Gus Trenor is the devil as moneyman, a type in the American novel of high finance whose dark history proceeds from Melville's trickster aboard the *Fidèle* in *The Confidence Man* to Louis Auchincloss's coldly ambitious banker, Rex Geer, in *The Embezzler*. Trenor's devilish crimson-hued mien causes Lily no small uneasiness. Florid and massive, with small dull eyes and a heavy carnivorous head, he preys upon Miss Bart as he did upon a jellied plover at one of the Bellomont dinners. The information Trenor receives on his short-term stock speculations all comes from Simon Rosedale, a dazzling and fast-rising newcomer to the New York financial scene. Rosedale in fact is the Great Giver of Stock Market Tips. When one is as eager to enter society as Sim is, one must be prepared to strew such bits of information about. He had already been served up and rejected at the "social board" a dozen times within Lily's memory. Rosedale saw Lily leaving his apartment building, The Benedict, and wrongly surmised she was having an affair with a tenant. Presumably he also passes this "tip" on to Trenor, which, by implication, makes Lily one of Rosedale's stock "buys" or "flyers." The stockbroker therefore tries to pick her up on the market for a bargain—nine thousand dollars, to be exact. He had been systematically making loans to Lily under the guise of "investments," expecting repayment of capital *and* interest when he suddenly "called" them. Trenor's attempted rape on the basis of her obligation to him for the amount represents a new low bid on the exchange for Lily Bart.

After the Trenor move in the market, selling pressures on Lily increase in the absence of new bids. Finally the shrewd investor Sim Rosedale, with an unerring sense of market timing, steps forward when all other buying interest seems to have scurried to the sidelines. One of the few men on the right side of the bear market currently in progress on Wall Street, he is said to have doubled his fortune. Rosedale's timely move to purchase a Fifth Avenue mansion at depreciated prices from one of the stock market's recent victims adumbrates his attempt to also add Lily to his portfolio. He has "his race's accuracy in the appraisal of values, and to be seen walking down the platform at the crowded afternoon hour in the company of Miss Lily Bart would have been money in his pocket, as he might himself have phrased it." Rosedale first approaches Lily with all the tact and grace of an exchange floor broker bidding for a block of blue chip stock that is sunk in the doldrums. The financier comes right to the point, without bothering about social amenities, telling her, "if I want a thing I'm willing to pay: I don't go up to the counter, and then wonder if the article's worth the price." He goes on to inform her, "I've got the money, and what I want is the woman—and I mean to have her too." The deal he offers Lily is to pay off all her outstanding debts and support a long-term recovery in her market value, if she will marry him. But, perceiving his motive to dress up his own list of investments, which would give him an aura of respectability and open doors into fashionable New York society, Lily hesitates to jump at the deal.

Lily Bart's financial situation worsens after the Rosedale offer. She is further weakened by debt spending as well as loss of anticipated future cash flow when her rich aunt, Mrs. Peniston, disinherits her. Approached again by Sim Rosedale, who now senses an even cheaper bargain, Lily is eager to consummate a deal. She hopes he will propose the same offer, and reminds herself that to put up with him temporarily "was the price she must pay for her ultimate power over him." Accordingly she tries "to calculate the exact point at which concession must turn to resistance, and the price *he* would have to pay be made equally clear to him." Lily now is the aggressor, the corporation with a block of stock for immediate sale yet at a guarded discount, Rosedale the wary buyer. She is surprised to find, however, that the financier has drastically lowered his original bid, almost as if news of impending bankruptcy had somehow leaked to the Street. More important than her financial condition, though, Rosedale is worried by stories circulating about Lily, rumors started by Bertha Dorset. And rumors of a shaky situation always scare a prudent investor. Only Bertha Dorset rivals Lily Bart in glamor and appeal on the New York social exchange. Despite stronger annual earnings and a triple A credit rating based on her "impregnable bank-account," Bertha is distressed by the market's lower evaluation of her and, thus wages a constant campaign to bear Lily's stock. As a result of this negative factor in Lily's long-term investment outlook, Rosedale's new offer includes an entirely different set of terms. The deal now is that Lily use Bertha's love letters to Selden that she has in her possession as blackmail in order to squelch her ruinous gossip. Lily *must* regain her former prestige on the social exchange before Rosedale will consider marrying her. Rosedale sounds like a big-time conglomerateur advising a prospective subsidiary to get tough with the competition, or call off the merger talks!

> It's one thing to get Bertha Dorset into line—but what you want is to keep her there. You can frighten her fast enough—but how are you going to keep her frightened? By showing her that you're as powerful as she is. All the letters in the world won't do that for you as you are now; but with a big backing behind you, you'll keep her just where you want her to be. That's *my* share in the business—that's what I'm offering you. You can't put the thing through without me—don't run away with any idea that you can. In six months you'd be back again among your old worries, or worse ones; and here I am, ready to lift you out of 'em tomorrow if you say so. *Do* you say so, Miss Lily? [7]

Sim Rosedale is prepared to back Lily and infuse new funds into her red ink operation, if she can first check the decline in her own market value. Lily's flat rejection of these terms, however, eliminates any hope of a turnaround situation for her and ensures Rosedale's withdrawal from the market.

The falling action in the last months of Lily Bart's life coincides with the bear market Wall Street had been experiencing (and which earlier may have accounted for Hudson Bart's failure). The

New York Stock Exchange is omnipresently felt in the background of *The House of Mirth,* like a great unseen force weighing on individual lives.

> It had been a bad autumn in Wall Street, where prices fell in accordance with that peculiar law which proves railway stocks and bales of cotton to be more sensitive to the allotment of executive power than many estimable citizens trained to all the advantages of self-government. Even fortunes supposed to be independent of the market either betrayed a secret dependence on it, or suffered from a sympathetic affection: fashion sulked in its country-houses, or came to town incognito, general entertainments were discountenanced, and informality and short dinners became the fashion.
>
> But society, amused for a while at playing Cinderella, soon wearied of the hearthside role, and welcomed the Fairy God-mother in the shape of any magician powerful enough to turn the shrunken pumpkin back again into the golden coach.[8]

So pervasive is the spirit of Wall Street in the novel that society and Wall Street are almost one. Life "uptown" on Fifth Avenue is described by or aptly translatable into terminology of the "downtown" world of the financial district. Several times Miss Bart had been in love with fortunes or careers, but only once with a man. When she first comes out she has a romantic passion for one Herbert Melson, who possesses no other "negotiable securities" than his blue eyes and wavy hair. After Lily skips a few weekends at the Trenors, she feels "the reckoning she had thus contrived to evade had rolled up interest in the interval." The fact that "she must trade on his [Selden's] name, and profit by a secret of his past, chilled her blood with shame" when she hesitates outside Selden's apartment building with the packet of Bertha Dorset's letters. Carry Fisher's efforts at finding a position for Lily when she is in need of a job are described in terms of manipulating the market, because her "inexhaustible good-nature made her an adept at creating artificial demands in response to an actual supply." The surname, Bart, itself suggests the practice of bartering, or even the auction that takes place in the "crowd" around any trading post on the stock exchange floor. Overall, Edith Wharton describes in the novel a society that *is* a trading arena for those with something to sell and those eager to buy, a social exchange where marriages are negotiated and transacted.

A look at *The House of Mirth* as a stock market allegory or Wall Street parable may focus too closely on the downward fluctuations and fall of the heroine, Lily Bart. If so, a naturalistic view of the novel is persuaded, which sees the central character as a doomed and predestined failure. There *is* growth, however, in Lily Bart—moral growth. The one element in her makeup that grows stronger than her need for security is her sense of morality. In a way there is a double plot in the novel parallel to the bankruptcy and ethical-rise plots in William Dean Howells's *The Rise of Silas Lapham.* As with Silas Lapham, an earlier American financial innocent, the depth to which Lily falls into debt and despair is a measure of her moral rise. Although she never fully understands the financial code of ethics that governs her social world, Lily Bart does not succumb to its amorality, making her at the end of this genteel novel of high finance more tragic than pathetic.

Wall Street may not only have influenced character and action in *The House of Mirth,* it may also have provided impetus for the book's surprisingly rapid sales.[9] Mrs. Wharton herself refers to its "prosperous career" in *A Backward Glance.* The novel was first se-rialized in *Scribner's Magazine* in twelve monthly installments that began in January 1905. When published in book form in October of that year, the novel became an immediate national bestseller. The phrase "house of mirth" coincidentally had already become well known to the public. It had been popularized by the press during coverage of the enormous New York insurance scandal that, when fully disclosed in the final quarter of 1905, shook the nation. Commercial sales of *The House of Mirth* surged during this same period, most certainly benefiting from the colossal Wall Street-related swindle.

Indecisive about an appropriate title, Mrs. Wharton had changed the original *A Moment's Ornament* to *The Year of the Rose* in the typescript, then luckily struck that out in longhand and wrote in *The House of Mirth*. If the phrase the "house of mirth" found in Ecclesiastes—"The heart of the wise is in the house of mourning; but the heart of fools is in the house of mirth"—is the source of the title, critics are thereby justified in focusing on the Ecclesiastical themes of "vanity" and "vexation" implicit in the novel, even to the point of speculating on how the scriptural reference suggests a sermon on a text.[10] Whatever the title's source, however, its choice could not have been a more fortunate one. Overlooked has been the effect of newspaper editorials—full of the insurance scandal—on the novel's success. Mrs. Wharton just happened to capitalize on a phrase that suddenly had burst into popular currency. The slogan the "house of mirth" was immediately associated by the reading public with the current legerdemain of Wall Street and the New York insurance industry.

Throughout the spring and summer of 1905, hints of scandal in the highest financial circles of New York—the large New York-based life insurance companies—began circulating. In Joseph Pulitzer's newspaper *The World*, for example, the public read a flabbergasting series of editorials, all published under the same scathing heading—"Equitable Corruption." Cautious at first, the editorials became more factual and bold as accusations were made by one faction against the other in the battle for control of the Equitable Life Assurance Society. The Equitable's troubles all began when its founder, Henry Baldwin Hyde, died in 1899, and the executive control passed to his son. James Hyde, the heir, was a young dandy and aesthete caricatured in *Puck* and satirized as the pitiful character Freddie Vandam in Upton Sinclair's *The Metropolis*. The sharp banking and promoting crowd in New York assiduously cultivated young Hyde, with an eye only for the $400 million in assets over which he was chief custodian. Lured into a web of high finance about which he hadn't the faintest knowledge, Hyde freely opened up access to the Equitable's treasury. However, the Alexander family, cofounders of the company, tried to rescue the Equitable as well as safeguard their own interests from exploitation by this outside group of financiers. James Hyde finally was forced to surrender control in February 1905, which left the field wide open for contest over the Equitable's assets between the Alex-

anders on the one hand and the bankers and promoters, such as
J. P. Morgan, Sr., E. H. Harriman, and J. J. Hill, on the other.

The New York Times fanned the fires of scandal further by publishing accounts of mysterious loans made by insurance companies,
such as the Equitable's loan of $250,000 to the Depew Improve-
ment Company. Chauncey Depew, a United States Senator at the
time who simultaneously held seventy-two corporate directorships,
was also a member of the Equitable's executive committee, which
not only voted the loan but understated its value on the insurance
company's books at $150,000. More serious was the $685,000 loan
made to the Equitable through the Mercantile Trust Company,
for which no record on the insurer's books was ever found. Then
there was the question of the Equitable's illegal involvement with
the Union Pacific preferred stock underwriting syndicate. E. H.
Harriman, chairman of the board of Union Pacific, was also a
director of the Equitable, which had purchased $50 million of the
railroad's new preferred stock issue. Rather than a legitimate investment, the purchase presumably was made for the purpose of
protecting control of Union Pacific for the Harriman interests.
Public suspicion, therefore, was slowly aroused in the summer of
1905 by the shocking prospect that the large number of policyholders of the Equitable, as well as the Prudential Life Insurance
Company, the New York Life Insurance Company, and the Mutual Life Insurance Company, were being defrauded.

A sweeping investigation into the dubious practices of insurance
companies finally was launched in September 1905, intensive in-
quiries and hearings that were concluded a few months later in
December. The Armstrong Committee, chaired by state senator
William Armstrong but directed by its astute chief counsel and
examiner, a young lawyer named Charles Evans Hughes, was
formed by the New York legislature. This committee scrutinized
the records and books of the four major life insurance companies,
excavating from the dry rot around the foundations of these institutions the existence of the so-called yellow dog funds. These
funds were set aside for "legal expenses" or for contributions to
political campaigns, payments to judges and legislative agents, and
for lobbying at the state capital in Albany.

The name of Andrew C. Fields figured prominently in the investigation, although Fields himself disappeared soon after the hearings began. Long engaged by the Mutual Life Insurance Company to influence legislation at Albany, he was one of the many lobbyists employed by the big insurance companies to get laws on the statute books under which they could carry on their mammoth frauds. The Mutual alone expended more than $2 million in "legal expenses" from 1898 to 1904.[11] Fields, before he mysteriously vanished, testified to the committee that although he received money from the Mutual, he never bribed anyone or committed a dishonest act. The Mutual, together with the Equitable, maintained a house in Albany that was discovered to be the headquarters for Andrew Fields and his lucrative lobbying operation. The name that the press derisively dubbed this residence was the "House of Mirth," and "Andy" Fields became disdainfully known as "the host in the house of mirth." The investigative hearings by the Armstrong Committee eventually produced widespread reform in the insurance industry, the most significant of which was the mutualization of these New York goliaths from stock-held to mutual life insurance companies. The policyholders, who had seen their premiums so flagrantly misused, were now the owners, replacing the inside stockholders and Wall Street financiers.

The insurance scandal made a sensation when it was disclosed in New York magazines and newspapers in 1905. Blown up to a national disgrace, the corruption caught the attention of the literary world as well as the public. Less than two years later, the scandal and Armstrong investigation became the basis of David Graham Phillips's novel *Light-Fingered Gentry* (1907). Charles Evans Hughes, who conducted the committee hearings, was the model for the honest and intractable lawyer-hero, Allan Montague, in Upton Sinclair's novel based on the scandal, *The Metropolis* (1908). And Mark Twain, also attracted by the scandal, entitled a journal entry on the subject, dated February 16, 1906, "The Teaching of Jay Gould." [12]

Appearing in book form at the high point of national obloquy, shock, and outrage, *The House of Mirth* created an immediate sensation. The public gobbled up the first printing in two weeks, not just because Edith Wharton was a name novelist, but because the title phrase had become synonymous with money and its power to persuade and suggested scandal. The theme in the novel of the grip that the "downtown" financial world has over society, and over individual lives, partially fulfilled what the title promised. The public knew that those many New York insurance secrets were Wall Street secrets. They also knew that Wall Street was gaining too great an influence on American culture and society at the turn of the century. Mrs. Wharton seemed to be aware of the same things. The accidental marriage between novel and public scandal, therefore, was a happy one. The public was grateful that such economic rot found a ready voice of exposure even in literary circles, and the novelist reaped a financial windfall. Edith Wharton truly seemed to have made the epithet the "house of mirth" catchwords for greed, materialism, and the power of money to corrupt.

III

The role of the financial marketplace gains increasing visibility in Wharton's fiction after *The House of Mirth*. The relationships and dealings between people in society uptown become openly and directly explicable in terms of the commercial world downtown. For instance, the customs of Fifth Avenue take on the crass characteristics of Wall Street, not the country, in *The Custom of the Country* (1913). A New York society marriage is less an occasion of royal nuptials than a stock deal on a straight cash basis. Ralph Marvell, a scion of New York's Four Hundred, in the novel sums up the whole matrimonial situation: "The daughters of his own race sold themselves to the Invaders; the daughters of the Invaders bought their husbands as they bought on opera-box. It ought all to have been transacted on the Stock Exchange." [13] Himself acquired like a blue chip equity, Marvell marries Undine Spragg, daughter of a newly rich Western millionaire.

The Spragg family from Apex City in *The Custom of the Country*, like Sim Rosedale in *The House of Mirth*, represents the invaders who began infiltrating New York in the 1880s. Undine, in her marriage transaction, picks up a social title in the manner of a robber baron raiding the stock of a nearly defunct railroad. In gaining control of Ralph Marvell, she proves an even more forcible and astute buyer than Rosedale, who tried but failed to swing a big investment deal for Lily Bart. The acquisition is short term, however, for Undine soon after her child's birth goes off to Europe and seeks a divorce. To understand this millionaire's daughter, "the answer would have been obtained by observing her father's business life. From the moment he set foot in Wall Street Mr. Spragg became another man." Undine's behavior in New York society, including her marriage, parallels her father's Wall Street speculative habits. Like him, she cares only for the quick-turnover profit, the short-term gain that comes from being on the "right side" of the market. Besides his investment objectives, Undine shares Spragg's determined Wall Street manner and code of ethics. Running off with Peter Van Degen, she thinks later that she acted "from a motive that seemed, at the time, as clear, as logical, as free from the distorting mists of sentimentality, as any of her father's financial enterprises." Her flight "had been as carefully calculated as the happiest Wall Street 'stroke.'" When she is back on the social market following her divorce, Undine assesses her own value as a purchasable commodity. She is motivated only by a desire "to get back an equivalent of the precise value she had lost in ceasing to be Ralph Marvell's wife. Her new visiting-card, bearing her Christian name in place of her husband's, was like the coin of a debased currency testifying to her diminished trading capacity." Again, like her father, she makes an attempt in the market to recoup her losses.

The aristocratic innocent in the genteel Garden, prelapsarian man who becomes involved in high finance and falls, is Ralph Marvell. Marvell's downfall is predestined by his fatal association with the outsiders, or by his mingling the holy seed with a strange wife. Chauncey Chippendale and Lily Bart are innocents contaminated merely through a business or money relationship with the *arrivistes.* Money needs doubly adulterate Ralph Marvell, forcing him into unaccustomed circumstances and speeding up his ruin. He renounces law and enters into a partnership in a real estate firm, a step down from the professional to the crass commercial world, to make enough money for his wife. Failing in this venture as well, Ralph finds himself in deeper financial trouble when Undine sues for divorce and seeks custody of the child. Soon after, as his cousin's guess proves true, Undine indicates she would settle for money in return for custody. Thus, Marvell resorts to Wall Street and the stock market. He naively believes "the sum his wife demanded could be acquired only by 'a quick turn'. . . . The market, moreover, happened to be booming, and it seemed not unlikely that so experienced a speculator might have a 'good thing' up his sleeve." The "experienced speculator" is Elmer Moffatt, a man involved in scandal even in his Apex City days, who since then had come to New York and carved out an even more erratic and questionable financial career.

Elmer Moffatt is the tempter or devil figure, the moneyman associated with Wall Street, who lures Ralph Marvell to his doom. Moffatt's "redness, his glossiness, his baldness," and a habit of twisting his moustache between his fingers like some melodramatic villain, give him the same sickening and evil mien conveyed by Gus Trenor, the stockbroker in *The House of Mirth*. Another moneyman in the novel, Harry Lipscomb, whose surname in one word reminds you of lips that are too red and hair that is pomaded, is a stockbroker who gets suspended from the stock exchange for shady dealings. Needing $100,000 within three weeks, Ralph is told by Moffatt to put up half that amount in order to double it in the stock market. Marvell raises the sum by deducting from his share in an estate and by borrowing the remainder. The broker then plows the whole amount into Apex Consolidation, whose stock he believes will soar when the company gets its expected land charter. Apex's scheme fails, however, the charter is vetoed, and Ralph's original investment melts away into thin air. "Well, you've got to lean over to see it" is Moffatt's unfeeling reply, when Marvell weakly asks if Apex common has dropped much. Despite the stockbroker's assurances that his investment is safe and he must have patience, the dazed speculator returns uptown from the financial district to kill himself with a revolver.

The Adamic financier falls in the marketplace of high finance, but the wicked seem to prosper. Undine reaps a windfall when the Apex land scheme turns out successfully after all, and Moffatt himself comes out with a huge fortune, becoming one of the wealthiest men in the East. Satan's victory over the ancestral family in the genteel Garden is complete when the old conspirators, Moffatt and Undine Spragg, remarry in Paris (they had been husband and wife earlier in Apex City). Money and its power to destroy dismay Edith Wharton. She, like so many American novelists, for that reason portrays the dark side of Wall Street and the evil types who inhabit the region.

Scattered throughout Edith Wharton's fiction are references and allusions to the link between money and manners, between the stock exchange on Wall Street and the drawing rooms of Fifth Avenue. In *The House of Mirth,* for example, Simon Rosedale's accumulation of wealth and his masterly use of it places "Wall Street under obligations which only Fifth Avenue could repay." Undine Spragg in *The Custom of the Country* never had time "to follow the perturbations of Wall Street save as they affected the hospitality of Fifth Avenue." If the details and technicalities of the arcane language escaped her, Undine certainly knew how to translate those occult phrases into success, because "every Wall Street term had its equivalent in the language of Fifth Avenue, and while he [Moffatt] talked of building up railways she was building up palaces." Ralph Marvell, impressed how the architecture at one end of Fifth Avenue differs widely from the other, thinks to himself that "society was really just like the houses it lived in: a muddle of misapplied ornament over a thin steel shell of utility. The steel shell was built up in Wall Street, the social trimmings were hastily added in Fifth Avenue; and the union between them was monstrous and factitious, as unlike the gradual homogeneous growth which flowers into what other countries know as society." The topics of the financial marketplace and drawing room are even debated in Wharton's fiction by the august personages Mrs. Fairford and Charles Bowen in *The Custom of the Country.* Bowen's opinion, the more dominant in the discussion, is that the relationship between men and women in America is materialistic rather than ideal or romantic, that business is the emotional center of gravity. He argues that "in America the real *crime passionel* is a 'big steal'—there's more excitement in wrecking railways than homes." Mrs. St George in the unfinished novel *The Buccaneers* also knows the connection between the stock exchange and uptown. She is aware that "a gentleman's financial

situation might at any moment necessitate compromises and con-
cessions. All the ladies of her acquaintance were inured to them;
up one day, down the next, as the secret gods of Wall Street de-
creed." Disappointed that her own daughters aren't launched in
society, Mrs. St George is less philosophical and blames her husband for being "too free-and-easy, too much disposed to behave as
if Fifth Avenue and Wall Street were one." Fifth Avenue and Wall
Street *are* one in Edith Wharton's fiction, because she clearly perceives they are governed by the same principles, operated by the
same codes, and subject to the same fluctuations.

IV

Money and prosperity were the substance of the American
Dream that F. Scott Fitzgerald knew to be futile and empty. The
dream falls into dissolution in Fitzgerald's fiction and ends up as
meaningless as the story in "Babylon Revisited," about a man who
found his life filled to the full, then drained to the dregs by the
stock market Crash of 1929. The dream is as illusory and unbeliev-
able as the anecdote in *The Beautiful and Damned* about an assistant
secretary in a brokerage office who invested all his savings in Beth-
lehem Steel, hung on patiently, and built a triumphal palace in
California. Anthony Patch, in that novel, although lured and victimized by this dream, saw through its golden aura, viewing it as a
"fruitless circumambient striving toward an incomprehensible
goal, tangibly evidenced only by the rival mansions of Mr. Frick
and Mr. Carnegie on Fifth Avenue." The only time it did seem
romantic was when he was under the kindliness of intoxication,
"And Wall Street, the crass, the banal—again it was the triumph of
gold, a gorgeous sentient spectacle; it was where the great kings
kept the money for their wars." The dream to Jay Gatsby in *The
Great Gatsby* was as bright and shining as the many suns mirrored in
the window of his automobile, as sad and lonely as his Long Island
mansion.

Like a moth by a candle, Scott Fitzgerald was dazzled by
wealth. The "era of extravagance" was still very much apparent in
New York and Newport in the teens and twenties, as the heirs of

the great nineteenth-century fortunes—the William Astors, the Vanderbilts, the Hydes, the Whitneys, the Ryans, the Guggenheims, the Schiffs, the Goulds, the Rockefellers, and the Morgans—lived like feudal lords. The newly rich could only imitate this type of royalty, predicating taste on money, manners on social position, and breeding on success in giving dinners and parties. Fitzgerald himself worshiped wealth, old or new, half wondering if those who had it didn't live off somewhere in a country as unreal as fairyland. Yet he privately disliked the rich, that leisure class which spent its time squandering money rather than earning it. Even though money did save them from selling their souls in the financial or commercial marketplace, the rich in Fitzgerald's fiction are damned anyway. They may have avoided the system, but they didn't dodge the devil.

Although he resented the rich, Scott Fitzgerald also understood their tragedy, as well as the tragedy of a capitalist society in which money, like nothing else, could produce such individual ruin and failure. But, portray failure though he did, Fitzgerald never offered an alternative to the money dream as London and Sinclair had. Those socialistic ideas preached by Amory Blaine in *This Side of Paradise,* for example, were not the novelist's. His own "political conscience had scarcely existed," nor had he ever done much "thinking save within the problems of his craft," as he frankly admitted in several self-dissecting articles toward the end of his life.

The portrait of the three generations of Patches in *The Beautiful and Damned* is a portrait of the newly rich class, the American plutocracy. In the genteel financial novels of Robert Grant and Edith Wharton, this new social species is identified strictly with Wall Street and capitalism. Where the old established aristocratic class is broken down and slowly replaced by the new in Grant and Wharton, the new moneyed class represented by the Patch family in Fitzgerald's fiction is doomed to extinction for lack of depth and roots. Each generation of Patches—grandfather, son, and grandson—is corrupted and weakened, not strengthened by money. Bequests, trusts, legacies, and Christmas gifts neither hold this family (or class) intact nor perpetuate it. Anthony Patch, in fact, is able to draw "as much consciousness of social security from being the grandson of Adam J. Patch as he would have had from tracing his line over the sea to the crusaders. This is inevitable; Virginians and Bostonians to the contrary notwithstanding, an aristocracy founded sheerly on money postulates wealth in the particular."[14]

Founder of the family fortune, Adam Patch is a personification of the vanishing nineteenth-century robber baron. At the conclusion of the Civil War he came home a major, "charged into Wall Street, and amid much fuss, fume, applause, and ill will he gathered to himself some seventy-five million dollars." Years later, basking in a moment of past glory, Old Adam boastfully recollects how he sent "three members of the firm of Wrenn and Hunt to the poorhouse." A vast store of Wall Street money, however, brings the Patch patriarch neither sweetness nor light, producing instead a deterioration of body, spirit, and mind. A stroke at age fifty-seven leaves Adam prematurely senescent. Suddenly, he turns remorseful about his past and grows obsessed with the hereafter. Aware of the selfishness of his misspent years and fearful that he must atone for their wickedness, the Wall Street millionaire, like a Mephistopheles converted to inscrutable good, consecrates "the remainder of his life to the moral regeneration of the world." Still another obsession takes hold in the shape of a strange idée fixe about reform, which prompts him to adopt a hypocritical moral righteousness completely without forbearance and a shallow philanthropy devoid of love and generosity. Patch is an Adam whose sins are never absolved. A fallen financier, he keeps reappearing unexpectedly in the novel like some dark avenging angel, an awful reminder of the damnation of money and a symbol of death. Actually the money lust has reduced him to a skeleton and toothless death's head, with all traces of life drawn out:

> It had sucked in the cheeks and the chest and the girth of arm and leg. It had tyrannously demanded his teeth, one by one, suspended his small eyes in dark-bluish sacks, tweeked out his hairs, changed him from gray to white in some places, from pink to yellow in others. . . .[15]

Patch resembles old Hargus in Frank Norris's *The Pit*, or old Henry Grimes in Upton Sinclair's *The Metropolis*, money and death figures who appear years beyond their actual age after a life of sin in high finance.

Adam Ulysses Patch, Anthony's father, did not live long enough to squander the Patch millions, although he managed to make a small dent in them and then compose a dull and smug set of memoirs entitled "New York Society as I have Seen It." [16] He passed his gaudy and dandyish habits on to his son, who, like Chauncey Chippendale, went to Harvard and made the Pudding. Expectations of a multi-million-dollar inheritance significantly weaken Anthony, as they did his own father, and strand him without character, purpose, or moral fiber. When the anticipated windfall fails to come, however, Patch, like young Chippendale and Lily Bart, resorts to the stock market in a symbolic revolt against the tyrannical money figure in the family. Chauncey, who had already turned to speculation before his uncle's will was invalidated, was in fact rebelling against his father's financial conservatism and authority. Lily made "investments" on Wall Street to free herself from her Aunt Peniston's financial control as well as to show defiance and independence when she was disinherited. Anthony Patch, when Old Cross Patch changes his will, is so dangerously becalmed in a sea of debt while still under full financial sail that he, too, turns to the stock market, but only to sell off bonds his grandfather had earlier set aside for him. Oddly enough, the Fall for these financial innocents occurs not when the family fortune is originally accumulated, but when they, the second or third generation, are deprived of their inheritance of it. Ironically, the "golden day" finally does arrive for Anthony Patch, when the court decision that took his $30 million away is reversed. The money comes too late, though. Headed at long last with Gloria for Italy aboard *The Berengaria,* but confined to a wheelchair as a result of his mental breakdown, Anthony's incapacitation is a haunting reminder of Old Adam's senility after he himself had become rich.

V

The nongenteel hero rises from obscurity into the genteel Garden in John P. Marquand's *Point of No Return* (1949). Charles Gray, son of poor New England Yankee stock, climaxes a long ascent into membership in the aristocracy by appointment to high position in an elite New York bank. As a counterpoint to Charles's success, John Gray, his father, had been caught years earlier in the 1929 Crash, fell into bankruptcy, and died. Charles Gray, therefore, when he accepts the role of underling in the old moneyed class, rises up like a Phoenix out of the embarrassing ashes of financial ruin.

Marquand slightly alters the familiar story of the financial hero who comes from the country to the city and finds Wall Street paved with gold. Gray does leave Clyde, Massachusetts for New York and rises in station, but the similarity to the typical Wall Street hero stops there. The stock market is not the source of his financial success; nor is there any Fall for this nonaristocratic Adam. He had already played the game of speculation in Clyde during the 1920s, and knew when to abandon it. If there is a Fall into original financial sin, Gray suffers it only vicariously through his father's unfortuitous ruin. Charles Gray's life, not without strife and competition for all its rewards, is actually a series of descents into pits and traps other than the stock market.

The bull market mania of the late 1920s swept the country like a wild river, "breaking all the dams of prudence and common sense." Small towns, including Clyde in Marquand's novel, were caught in its dangerous flow. The established aristocracy remained aloof from this fury swirling below them, which so muddied the financial waters that even the most worthy investment would not have been visible. The Lovell family of Clyde, shipping merchants of an earlier century, viewed inherited money as one thing, but stock market money as quite another. Like the Burton family of New York, who founded the well-known brokerage house of Burton & Fall, they withdrew from the hysteria into safe corporate and government bonds. Along with the masses who were suffering from boom fever, meanwhile, were John Gray and his son Charles. They plunged headlong into the frenzied current. Wary of impending disaster, though, Charles sold his stocks out in May 1929, after a tenfold increase over his original investment, and anchored the money in government bonds. His father, on the other hand, refused to sell, even when the market broke that October, and lost all his equity in the storm. His goal of a million dollars and dream of economic nirvana unattainable, John Gray died a shattered man.

The death of an earlier State Street financier in American fiction resembles if not foreshadows John Gray's demise, which occurred in the wake of the '29 Crash. Judge Jaffrey Pyncheon in Hawthorne's *The House of the Seven Gables,* like Gray, was discovered dead, utterly frozen and almost lifelike, keeping his business affairs and appointments in town waiting. Ironically, Charles remembers one summer afternoon as a boy when he had been reading Hawthorne's novel and "had reached the eloquent passage where old Judge Pyncheon was sitting motionless in his chair." Then Charles eerily "heard the front door slam and then the sound of his father whistling in the hall," as if fate were being foretold by chance association. Jaffrey Pyncheon had died within the gabled house under the stern gaze of Colonel Pyncheon's portrait. Mr. Gray passes quietly away beneath the portrait of his father, Judge Gray, which hung on the wall in his study. The evil capitalist died a victim of Maule's curse, and John Gray, the naive capitalist, dies bankrupt and broken, a victim of the curse of the stock market. The stock exchange in *Point of No Return,* like Maule's well, turns out to be the source that fouls this Yankee Eden.

Charles Gray fortunately renounces State Street, just as Silas Lapham had done in Howells's *The Rise of Silas Lapham,* and is spared tragedy. One commentator, however, who views Gray as a weak and flagging man of commerce, questions his triumph and success in relation to Lapham's:

> This is the issue of Charles Gray's crisis. See how precisely it contradicts the rise of Silas Lapham. Lapham's business failure perpetrates his control of himself; he presides over his own bankruptcy and salvages an honorable retirement. But Gray makes no decision. His success, already decided for him, measures his continued subservience to the business. Having lost the battle Lapham wins the campaign. But what of Gray? [17]

Gray's victory *is* Lapham's, in fact a more startling one if you consider that the stock market and temptation of easy money are the real enemies. Charles Gray left the market a richer man and overcame the desire to become even richer, things Silas did not do. Because Howells's hero falls and is restored to his native county seat, and Marquand's is established securely in the bosom of neo-genteel society, is really irrelevant. Both heroes make a decision to dispel the curse of the stock market, and by that act alone gain a type of salvation.

9.

The Devil and the Dollar

I

Theodore Dreiser cynically said that under "In God We Trust" on our dollar might as well be written "The Devil Take the Hindmost." The hindmost were the laborers in this country, the pawns and peons of big business; the devil, the American business kings and emperors who ruled over them. Dreiser often criticized America for its economic structure of subjects and sovereigns. Six years after he wrote *The Titan* (1914), a portrayal of the American capitalist at his most powerful and corrupt, the novelist was directly comparing the country to ancient commercial Rome, which was a material welter ruled by emperors.

In *Hey Rub-A-Dub-Dub* (1920), Dreiser viewed laissez faire capitalism as naturalism in the marketplace, an economic philosophy that allowed the strong to get stronger and the rich richer, all in the name of free and unrestricted trade. Under such a system, he worried that the making of money had become the national culture, intelligence, and purpose. He was bothered as well about the type of man the system had produced. Recounting world economic history, Dreiser drew a parallel between the financial rulers of America in the last fifty years and the powerful political rulers of mercantile Rome:

> And if you look back you will see that to-day, in another way, we have been repeating in Wall Street (or were until a few years ago), the type of man who occasionally sat as Emperor over all the Romans. If you are inclined to doubt this you might, if the opportunity offered, examine the collection of portrait busts of Roman Emperors of the highly executive and financial type (Hadrian, Trajanus, Titus, Caracalla and the rest) in the Vatican, the Musee del la Terme and the British Museum. Hadrian, for instance, was as much like the late Commodore Vanderbilt, side whiskers and all, as one man might be to another. . . . Any one of ten or fifteen portrait busts of ancient Roman Emperors might almost be mistaken for Armour, Morgan, Gould, Sage, Crocker, Stanford, Hearst. For example, compare Russell Sage to Julius Caesar; or William H. Vanderbilt to Augustus Caesar. Indeed, if you were to examine some of the major operations of the successful Roman Emperors you would find that their power to maintain their positions with the Praetorian Guard and the Patrician class (which was really the Roman world, so far as they were concerned) was largely financial and organizing in the same peculiar spirit in which we find those qualities operating to-day.[1]

Any assumption that Dreiser held the businessman or financier in undiminished admiration is false. On the contrary, even though he wrote without moral condemnation, the novelist pictured him as the coldest, most selfish, yet strangely the most useful of all living phenomena. In the trilogy of desire, the fictional financier-businessman Frank Algernon Cowperwood (as well as his real-life model, Charles T. Yerkes, the Philadelphia street railway king) belonged to that genus "robber baron" that Dreiser repudiated in *Tragic America* (1931). Captains of finance, in Theodore Dreiser's opinion, were little more than financial Captain Kidds, types who lived for themselves and chose a life of risk and danger that held the prospect of getting rich quickly. They were modern brigands, bolder, more ruthless, and less restrained by law or morality than seventeenth-century buccaneers who grew wealthy on the plunder of merchant vessels. In *Tragic America*, as it *Hey Rub-A-Dub-Dub* earlier, Dreiser vilified the financier as well as moneymaking and the methods of big business. He believed America had sadly fallen under the rule of the banks, the corporations, and Wall Street.

The history of Charles Tyson Yerkes is ordered for the illustration of selfishness, a symbol of nineteenth-century American rulership and piracy. Novelist Dreiser saw in Yerkes all the elements of success and power. He was a complex individual social organism supremely adept at numbers and mathematical calculations that enabled him to master his business environment. Partner in a syndicate that developed street railways and, to an extent, the public lighting companies in three great American cities—New York, Chicago, and Philadelphia—Yerkes became skilled in manipulating city politics as well as finance. Underhanded efforts in Philadelphia in 1873, however, when he assisted in embezzling municipal funds (an affair that also criminally involved the city treasurer, Joseph P. Mercer), earned the financier a seven-month jail term. It was this circumstance in Yerkes's career which forced him to remove to Chicago, where he started as a small broker. Amassing a sizable war chest of funds, Yerkes again branched out into the street railway business. His modus operandi was to purchase old street railway lines, arrange contracts for their reconstruction, issue large flotations of watered stock, and then pyramid heaps of securities and worthless paper upon previous heaps, all the while diverting the real assets into other businesses in a hundred devious and ingenious ways. Eventually, under the yoke of his rule, Chicago's power figures fell at his feet. City aldermen openly sold street rights of way for cash. Mayors and councilmen granted immunity from the law. Governors and legislators approved farreaching but often shady proposals. With the way made wide, financier Yerkes lined his pockets with pure gold. Before he permanently left Chicago for a life of pleasure in London and Europe, though, he sold the whole dilapidated, useless, rusting city railway system to New York financiers Thomas Fortune Ryan and William

C. Whitney for a king's profit, as if to finally reveal his own secret of success—"Buy old junk, fix it up a little and unload it upon other fellows."

Begin with an individual, and before you know it you find that you have created a type, wrote F. Scott Fitzgerald in his story "The Rich Boy." Dreiser began with Charles Yerkes, but created instead the type of the evil financier, a familiar figure in the American novel of high finance. The character of Frank A. Cowperwood in *The Financier* (1912), *The Titan* (1914), and *The Stoic* (1947), based on Yerkes, is a direct descendant in fiction of Hawthorne's evil capitalist, Judge Jaffrey Pyncheon, in *The House of the Seven Gables*. Cowperwood, in his devilish career in finance as an investment banker, represents the fallen and unredeemable moneyman who never seems to have had an origin in innocence. Moneymaking directs his steps before he ever places his first buy order on the Philadelphia Stock Exchange. "A financier by instinct," at the early age of ten he is attracted to money and learns all he can about high finance from his banker father. One incident dramatically confirms in young Cowperwood's mind how the practical and expedient govern the struggle for survival. When he has seen a lobster preying on a squid in a tank of water in a store window, he forever rejects the Bible as the source of truth in favor of this naturalistic lesson of life. By the time he is thirteen years old, Cowperwood already has engaged in sophisticated financial deals. In one business affair he bought seven cases of soap on borrowed money, then sold the whole load to a grocer for a nice profit. The grocer's thirty-day note, out of which he paid off the original loan, provided collateral against further borrowing, as the boy launched a career in trading on margin, or using profits from transactions not yet closed to leverage future buying and selling. Later, as an investment banker and broker on Third Street in Philadelphia, he perfects and masters the subtle art of hypothecating securities and pyramiding bank loans into portentous sums of capital.

Frank Cowperwood evolves into a Mycteroperca Bonaci, a healthy aquatic creature that grows to a weight of two hundred and fifty pounds and lives a comfortable existence because of its remarkable adaptability to its environment. The Mycteroperca's control over its appearance is so wonderful, Dreiser marvels in *Hey*

Rub-A-Dub-Dub, you cannot look at it long without feeling you are witnessing something spectral and unnatural, so brilliant is its power to deceive, change color, simulate, elude, lurk, or strike unseen. Devil iconography associated with the stockbroker or moneyman in the Wall Street novel is also assigned to Cowperwood. Cowperwood is Satan incarnate, a fiend of finance thoroughly engrossed in amassing money and power. Unlike Edith Wharton's stockbroker figures, whose evil is measured by blatant repulsiveness and frank carnality, Cowperwood's demonic qualities connote a more beguiling and indistinct form of evil. He is possessed of a mesmeric power, noticeable in the peculiar fire in his eyes and reinforced by a charming personality, which enables him to exert great influence over people. George Stener, the city treasurer in Philadelphia (and a reminder of poor Joseph Mercer, who was sentenced to the Eastern Penitentiary for his dealings with Yerkes), at first disarmed, then transfixed and paralyzed by Cowperwood, obediently places municipal funds at his disposal. An unseen darkness also broods over the financier, as if so much energy and passion were constantly gathering into a hundred thunderstorms that threaten whenever financial developments fail to go his way. Like Satan, Cowperwood rejects any form of subordinate role and aims to reign rather than serve in the capitalist system. He believes that "a man, a real man, must never be an agent, a tool, or a gambler—acting for himself or for others—he must employ such. A real man—financier—was never a tool. He used tools. He created. He led." [2]

Third Street, headquarters for the famed Jay Cooke & Company, and also the nation's investment banking center in the early 1870s, is the setting for *The Financier,* lead novel in the trilogy. Symbolically hell-like in the novel, Philadelphia's financial district recalls Norris's *The Pit,* in which Chicago's La Salle Street was all darkness and confusion. Third Street, however, is not suggestive of a fiery subterranean region as much as a shallow subsurface maze of social connections, financial partnerships, and political alliances, a thick labyrinthine web in which any innocent wayfarer would be ensnared and devoured. Cowperwood, to whom this subtle world is appealing, is "like a spider in a tangled net, every thread of which he knew, had laid, had tested," and in which "he had surrounded and entangled himself in a splendid, glittering network of connections, and he was watching all the details." [3] Not only survival in this diabolical realm, but loyalties in the friendships as well as plots of revenge are built on money. Financial recrimination is the punishment for any violation of the code. A powerful triumvirate of ruling lights eventually casts Cowperwood out of Third Street. Holding high council in hell after the Chicago fire of 1871, which raised pandemonium on the Philadelphia Stock Exchange and toppled Cowperwood's unsubstantial paper empire, the triumvirate judges him unfit even for this infernal region. The evil financier had been involved in an adulterous affair with a daughter of one of the city's rulers, a breach of trust far worse than any financial double dealing.

The saga of Frank A. Cowperwood as a financier is the account of a gradual descent into the reaches of hell from which there is no deliverance. Cowperwood first enters Third Street as a bookkeeper in a brokerage house, moves up to stockbroker, then note broker, finally becoming an underwriter with his own investment banking firm. Some of the biggest names in the city are his clients, including the municipal government. As an underwriter Cowperwood brings to the market a large debt issue for the city, a ten-year loan certificate yielding 6 percent. The public enthusiastically subscribes to the issue, giving the financier opportunity to secretly control its price in the aftermarket. Artfully manipulating the bid between ninety and par, he feasts on the fat short-term profits. Cowperwood also fraudulently uses certificates placed in his custody by customers as collateral for personal debts. More, this hellish financier manipulates Stener, the city treasurer, as if he were a puppet on wires, receiving a $500,000 loan from the public coffer at a low rate of interest. Cowperwood plows this money directly into risky streetcar stocks, hoping to reap a greater harvest. When he is fully invested and overextended in debt, the cataclysmic Chicago fire catches Cowperwood off guard, compelling him to embezzle $60,000 from the city just to maintain solvency. Exposure at the hands of the powerful triumvirate who are bent on revenge, as well as bankruptcy and a prison term, are Cowperwood's rewards for high financial crime. His journey into the nether world of Third Street ends only in material loss, though.

Stripped and naked in the prison baths before he's taken to his penitentiary cell, a symbolic state of humiliation for most men, Cowperwood "was not suffering from a consciousness of evil. As he saw it, he was merely unfortunate." [4] Without repentance and atonement, salvation and deliverance from the pit of destruction are not the hope for this evil financier.

Cowperwood is restored to the financial marketplace soon after serving his prison sentence, like Satan loosed again for a season after being bound in chains during the millennium. His dark dignity and evil character renewed, pride filling his heart to the full, the financier returns to Third Street and the pandemonium of the stock exchange just in time to benefit from the failure of Jay Cooke & Company. In the ensuing panic of 1873, Cowperwood sells short and swiftly recovers the money he had lost two years earlier. Then, "sick of the stock exchange as a means of livelihood, and now decided that he would leave it once and for all," [5] as Dreiser relates in *The Titan*, he quits Philadelphia and goes West—not to the backwoods as a fallen Adam figure would have done, but to La Salle Street, the marketplace of Chicago—to indulge in his financial demonism there.

Frank Algernon Cowperwood is the apotheosis of the evil American financier. Fictional capitalists such as J. G. Holland's Robert Belcher, Archibald Dexter, the Chicago gas king in Will Payne's *The Money Captain* (1898), or E. V. Harrington, the meatpacking magnate in Robert Herrick's *The Memoirs of An American Citizen* (1905), are adumbrations of Dreiser's satanic hero, Ur-Cowperwoods who fail to attain his epochal proportions. So colossal does Dreiser's financier become in the trilogy of desire that he seems to abuse, or at least temporarily forget, the privileges of immortality when he dies in *The Stoic*. He is a titan, not among the fabled race of mythological giants, but modeled after that storied breed of capitalists who ruled America from Wall Street in the decades following the Civil War.

II

Gullible, greedy, and belligerent, Jason Compson IV has all the necessary attributes of the financial fool in William Faulkner's *The*

Sound and the Fury (1929). Faulkner's perfect sucker is a Molièresque reproduction of Mark Twain's befuddled backwater financier, Nigger Jim, in *Huck Finn*. He also represents an ironic version of the evil financier in the American novel of high finance. Where Twain's ridiculous speculator is merely the comic victim of his own ignorance, or Dreiser's demonic capitalist is the destroyer, Faulkner's is both victim and destroyer, laughable yet despicable. The devil of finance in this novel, Jason Compson is duped and taken by his own craftiness, as his principal victims—Wall Street and Miss Quentin—turn around and make off with his money.

In the "April 6 1928" section (Jason's section) of *The Sound and the Fury,* Jason Compson is involved in a dizzying maze of financial ploys and maneuvers. On this day all his money dealings seem to sour at once. Jason first runs out of the dummy checks he has been substituting for Caddy's real checks, which Caddy regularly sends home for Quentin's welfare, and Mrs. Compson ceremoniously and sanctimoniously burns as "sin money." He is further vexed by the fact that Caddy this time has sent a money order because she correctly suspects Jason of finagling Quentin out of the money. Wall Street authors still more confusion for Compson when he discovers that the short sale of cotton he made that morning has turned against him.[6] Speculation in futures on the New York Cotton Exchange is one more thing that crosses and confounds him, as he battles to maintain the equilibrium of his fragile financial structure.

The Western Union Telegraph office in Jefferson is the comic target of Jason Compson's pent-up wrath as well as the scene of four visits he hurriedly makes there during this frantic day. The first visit occurs shortly after ten o'clock, the hour the Cotton Exchange opens in New York. Jason consults his telegram or market letter from a New York advisory service, for which he pays ten dollars a month and which, that morning has apparently predicted the market will decline. In the belief that the New York people who ran the service had all the necessary inside information, Compson sells a contract of cotton short. Although it is not certain when he actually places the order, neither is it important. He could have wired it at the close of the previous day's trading. Commodity prices, remember, always move inversely to estimates of the condition of a crop. Predictions of a successful crop drive prices down on the exchange, but expectations of a poor crop shoot prices up. In April, when Jason's narrative takes place, the cotton crop has barely been planted throughout the Mississippi Valley. Between the time of planting and harvest four to five months later, farmers can assume a speculative hedge with cotton futures against the possibility of an unsuccessful harvest. In other words, farmers are able to make up for losses in actual crop production with capital gains in cotton futures on the New York Cotton Exchange. Jason Compson, however, doesn't see it quite that way. "Cotton is a speculator's crop," he gloats in the hardware store that morning. Curiously, when his speculative margin account is closed out that afternoon during a strong market rally, Compson is on the side of the farmer, inveighing against Wall Street and the "damn Eastern crowd."

Remaining in the Western Union office long enough on his first stop to catch the market's opening, Jason reads the reports as they come in. Cotton rises two, then four points, and he says to himself, "But hell, they were right there and knew what was going on." He leaves before he remembers another purpose he has at the telegraph office, and so he returns. Jason instructs the telegraph operator to send this wire collect: "All well. Q writing today." The operator questions him and Compson sarcastically shoots back "Q. Can't you spell Q?" [7] This wire is intended for Caddy, because Jason is sending a message telling her that everything is all right. He wants to allay Caddy's suspicions that the checks she is sending are not reaching Quentin. The "Q" that the telegraph operator asks Jason about is puzzling to him only in the context of the message. Compson intends it to indicate to Caddy that Quentin will be writing today. There were specific telegraphic code letters for cotton futures, however, each month a different one. The letter U stood for September, V for October, X for November, Z for December, but Q was the code letter for August.[8] The operator may have recognized its significance in the form of an order to be wired in for a contract of cotton, but he is puzzled by the letter in this context. Doc Wright, though, who is sitting in the telegraph office at the time, overhears Jason's message. He perhaps catches the financial significance of the code letter, but consequently is mistaken when he takes the rest of the telegram to mean an order to a broker.

A short time after noon, Jason stops by the telegraph office again. His patience worn thin from rummaging around for an old blank check on a St. Louis bank and coercing Quentin into signing the back of the money order when she comes into the store moments earlier, he is in no mood for bad news. Cotton is three points below the opening price, but it had been down twelve points at noon. Angered because he could have covered his short sale for a twelve-point profit, he takes his ire out on the telegraph operator for not informing him. Then, Jason is quickly off once more, running out to the Compson homestead to give the phony substitute check to his mother for burning. Later, upon returning to town and going first to the bank to make some deposits, he stops at the telegraph office for the third time to check on the price of cotton. He finds it one point higher than the opening, or a gain of thirteen points from the day's low. Jason's thought when he is back at the store, that "I had already lost thirteen points," [9] refers to the gain he *could have* made had he covered at noon and closed out the contract.

Jason Compson's fourth and final visit to the telegraph office occurs at 5:10 P.M., two hours after the market ends trading. Cotton finished forty points down on the day, quoted at 12.21 (12.21 cents per pound). Commodity prices, incidentally, move one point at a time, from 12.23 to 12.22 to 12.21, for example. Because one point is the equivalent of $5 per contract, a forty-point drop, therefore, would be equal to a $200 gain on a single contract, if the trader were on the short side of the market. "Forty times five dollars," [10] thinks Jason as he mentally totals the paper profits he could have had. His margin account had been closed out that afternoon when the market rallied, however, causing him instead to suffer an unspecified loss from his short sale. The telegram Jason reads is a confirmation of the sell advice he had received in the morning from the advisory service. "Sell, it says. The market will be unstable, with a general downward tendency. Do not be alarmed following government report." [11] Such reports on the cotton crop were published monthly by the U.S. Department of Agriculture, projecting important data as well as estimating the size of the crop in the Cotton Belt. These figures, when released, had an immediate effect on trading in the cotton cash markets. In fact, so influential were these reports that the International Cotton Federation Committee meeting in Paris in early April 1928 (coincidentally almost the same day Jason's narrative takes place) passed a resolution that the government publication was detrimental to international trade and a cause of excessive speculation. The committee appealed to cotton manufacturing interests, farmers, and merchants to use their power to change legislation so that only one report would be issued during the growing season.[12] In the novel the report made public on April 6, which ignited a brief rally on the New York Cotton Exchange, presumably was pessimistic about crop prospects and, consequently, bullish for future prices. At any rate, Jason, furious his account was closed out on the upside of the market, hands the telegraph operator a message: "Buy, I wrote, Market just on point of blowing its head off. Occasional flurries for purpose of hooking a few more country suckers who haven't got into the telegraph office yet. Do not be alarmed." [13] He wires some of his own trading advice back to New York.

Like Nigger Jim in *Huck Finn,* who plunges his money into *live*-stock, Jason Compson's resistance to selling cotton short is as weak and based on as much careful research and analysis. He solicits trading advice from the New York service in the same manner Jim seeks guidance from "Balum's Ass," who had a reputation for being lucky. Jason, like Jim, is more upset at being cheated out of the trifle he paid for the service than for the larger loss of his principal. Just as he frets over the ten dollars he shells out for the market-letter subscription, Nigger Jim agonizes over his ten cents that Balum "invests" in the church plate for the poor. Jason's oath, "I just want my money back that these damn jews have gotten with all their guaranteed inside dope. Then I'm through," [14] sounds like Jim's promise that if he could just get his ten cents back he'd call it "squah."

Speculative excitement was high in the United States in the late 1920s. Stock trading in March 1928 set a new Wall Street record, with the heaviest monthly volume of transactions in the history of both the Curb (later the American Stock Exchange) and the New York Stock Exchange. Speculation on the commodity exchanges was also feverish. William Faulkner was sensitive to this atmosphere—particularly how it infected even remote rural pockets in Mississippi—and wove its effects into not only a burlesque of the irrational speculator in Jason Compson, but a satire of the invidious long-distance influence of Wall Street. The cotton speculation episode in *The Sound and the Fury* also offers a satire of the Western Union Telegraph Company, as well as of the populist distrust of Wall Street and Eastern finance that lingered on in the South until well after the Depression.

A specific target of Faulkner's ridicule in the novel is the crude facilities for trading in stocks and commodities readily available to every small-town farmer, field hand, and store clerk throughout the South. Market telegrams or advisory letters, for example, which contained information about the current trend of the market and probable future course of prices, were responsible in great part for stirring and fanning interest in speculation. The service Jason subscribes to is perfectly suited to his temperament, providing the sure "tip" that is based on little more than the enthusiasm of the sender. Western Union, the object of much of Compson's misdirected wrath, was highly instrumental in bringing the Wall Street mania into small towns such as Jefferson. Telegraph companies offered a service of reporting transactions and supplying quotations of market prices throughout the country, calling it "continuous quotation service." They also had a less expensive system that quoted prices every fifteen minutes. It is this slower, cheaper system that Jefferson, Mississippi is provided. Jason Compson's steady abuse of Western Union in the novel becomes comical. "Maybe your damn company's in a conspiracy with those damn eastern sharks" [15] he says on his second stop at the telegraph office. Or, on his third stop,

> "What time did that report come in? " I says.
>
> "About an hour ago," he says.
>
> "An hour ago? " I says. "What are we paying you for?" I says, "Weekly reports? How do you expect a man to do anything? The whole damn top could blow off and we'd not know it."
>
> "I don't expect you to do anything," he says. "They changed that law making folks play the cotton market."
>
> "They have," I says. "I hadn't heard. They must have sent the news out over the Western Union." [16]

After the market has closed and Jason makes his last stop, he looks at the message waiting for him, then at the clock.

> "Market closed an hour ago," he says.
>
> "Well," I says, "That's not my fault either. I didn't invent it; I just bought a little of it while under the impression that the telegraph company would keep me informed as to what it was doing."
>
> "A report is posted whenever it comes in," he says.
>
> "Yes," I says, "And in Memphis they have it on a blackboard every ten seconds," I says. "I was within sixty-seven miles of there once this afternoon." [17]

Jason's offer to spell out the letter "Q" or the word "b-u-y" later on elicits a further laugh at the operator's expense, insinuating his wits are as slow as his company's service. The operator inadvertently sets himself up as the butt of Compson's mordant remarks. Moreover, the telegraph office in Jefferson does just miss being a "bucket shop," as Jason contemptuously labels it. A bucket shop, by definition, is any brokerage office that merely bets with the customers on probable prices of stocks or commodities, rather than wiring in orders for execution on an exchange. A bucket shop is not formally connected with any exchange, much the same as a racetrack bookie operates independently from the parimutuel betting system at the site of a horse race. In this Jefferson Western Union Telegraph office, men sit around during trading hours of the cotton exchange in New York, buying and selling among themselves, not with the "house," at a nickel a point. Doc Wright is "cleaned out" on this day, getting caught twice, although I. O. Snopes exults because he had picked a "winner." Meanwhile, Jason, back at Earl's store, continues to berate the Telegraph Company:

> I'd just have to prove that they were using the telegraph office to defraud. That would constitute a bucket shop. And I wouldn't hesitate that long, either. Only be damned if it doesn't look like a company as big and rich as the Western Union could get a market report out on time. Half as quick as they'll get a wire to you saying

Your Account closed out. But what the hell do they care about the people. They're hand in glove with that New York crowd. Anybody could see that.[18]

Jason Compson's antagonism toward the New York and Eastern financial crowd, his anti-Semitism and xenophobia embody the lingering populist distrust of Wall Street common among many Southern farmers. Jason's feeling that the Telegraph Company is hand in glove with those sharks is a comic example of the conspiracy theory of Wall Street that was widely believed and actually lent credence to much of the populist literature written since the 1890s. The New York crowd, not he, Jason thinks, is to blame for his speculative losses. The populist hostility toward high finance, especially speculation, has been objectively described by one historian on cotton farming and Southern culture:

In the field of cotton economics the object of the farmer's particular wrath was the New York Cotton Exchange. It was believed that speculators established the prices ruinous to the cotton planters, and a particularly popular unwritten plank in the platform of the agrarian revolt was the extermination of the New York Cotton Exchange.[19]

The whole commodity market indeed was a vast bucket shop in the Southern mind.

Ultimately the cotton speculation episode in *The Sound and the Fury* affords insight into the evil nature of Jason Compson. With evil as its own reward, Jason's paltry and contemptible financial structure collapses—slowly, painfully, but certainly—bringing out by degrees his malicious character. The speculation in cotton futures is just one more thing that addles and prevents him from completing another day unhindered in his selfish and niggardly existence. Money for Jason, as for any evil financier, is his most valued possession; its loss his most vulnerable and secret weakness. Vexed primarily over the ten dollars he throws away on the advisory service, Jason's preoccupations are narrow and miserly as his spirit is mean and grasping. Not the Prince of Darkness figure such as Dreiser's Frank A. Cowperwood—whose fall is compared to a black eclipse of the sun—Jason Compson is gnomelike, groveling, more despicably malign.

William Faulkner occasionally casts figures of speech in the language of economics and finance. That terminology attracted him no doubt for its universal application to life rather than its suitability only to the world of buying and selling. Human love and sorrow are like a debenture bond in one such financial metaphor in *The Sound and the Fury*. Quentin Compson, a type of the sensitive young man in Faulkner's novels who bears in his soul the whole tortured conscience of the South, is on the verge of suicide. The virginity of his sister, Caddy, which had been purposelessly and senselessly yielded up, symbolizes in a way the purity of the virgin South heedlessly availing itself to traffickers in commerce and trade. Quentin, alone in his college dormitory room, recalls the end of a conversation about suicide he once had with his father. That dialogue rapidly flicks through his memory, punctuated by strokes of chimes in Harvard Square announcing the endless passage of time. He remembers that Mr. Compson told him his state of mind over Caddy would change, that it was only temporary and some day he would no longer feel the hurt as he did then. Pregnant at that time and forced to marry somebody, Caddy selected Sydney Herbert Head, a superficial, insensitive, and showy young man whom Quentin particularly detested. Mr. Compson philosophically told Quentin

> it is hard believing to think that a love or a sorrow is
> a bond purchased without design and which matures
> willynilly and is recalled without warning to be replaced
> by whatever issue the gods happen to be floating at the
> time no you will not do that until you come to believe
> that even she was not quite worth despair perhaps.[20]

According to Quentin's father, experiencing the deeper emotions of life is like blindly investing in a bond callable at any time and replaceable by any other bond the underwriter happens to be selling. No real investment objective is necessary; no duration or date of maturity is applicable. Mr. Compson had pointed out the impermanence and temporality of these emotions, arguing that overall they were a bad investment. By implication, he advised the short-term outlook on life rather than the long-term perspective required in bond investing. Struck by the nihilism of this point of view, Quentin at the time of the conversation seized on and repeated his father's word "temporary," as if that word alone violated the sanctity of his feelings toward his sister. Quentin's act of suicide actually is testimony of his belief in the long term, a strange and mute contradiction of his father's pessimistic philosophy.

In "The Bear," Faulkner creates an image based on a fundamental economic truth, which in turn sums up a larger truth about man. Old Carothers McCaslin in the story runs a supply store on his land and keeps meticulously recorded ledgers on

> the slow outward trickle of food and supplies and equipment which returned each fall as cotton made and ginned and sold (two threads frail as truth and impalpable as equators yet cable-strong to bind for life them who made the cotton to the land their sweat fell on).[21]

The basic metaphor stretches and expands until a universal truth about life is revealed. Food and supplies go out from Carother's commissary in return for cotton picked and baled. The outgo of food and supplies and the income of cotton grow into two threads that bind all those who work in the cotton fields to the land itself. The figure of these threads leads to the image of a huge bale of cotton, bound by cables. The word "equators" suggests the globe, further extending the scope of the metaphor. The picture that Faulkner creates, therefore, is of man in his age-old relationship with the land; the truth reached is that man, in his dependency upon the land, is established not just in McCaslin's cotton fields in Mississippi, but everywhere on this planet, as an economic being. Man's life, in part and in sum, is a bartering of what he produces for what he consumes.

Snopeses had been around in the South since the Civil War. But when the century turned, they began appearing out of nowhere,

multiplying and becoming successful. Yoknapatawpha County's
sewing machine agent as well as busybody at large, V. K. Ratliff,
reasons Snopeses were successful because they had all federated
unanimously to remove being a Snopes from just the zoological
category of wolf into a condition composed of success. Success and
money lift some members of the Snopes tribe in *The Hamlet* (1940),
The Town (1957), and *The Mansion* (1959) into local folklore and
legend. Flem Snopes, for example, rises to the position of economic
lord and ruler over Yoknapatawpha County. A central character
in the trilogy, his unscrupulous climb from field laborer to bank
president, filthy work overalls to dress shirt and snap-on black bow
tie, and small rented room to a large mansion in the county seat is
chronicled throughout these novels. A cousin, Wallstreet Panic
Snopes, one of the few clan members who represents simple honesty and hard work, builds a small business empire out of nothing
by un-Snopeslike fair dealing. Montgomery Ward Snopes, meanwhile, with neither Flem's intelligence nor Wallstreet's integrity,
thrives only for a season on sheer swagger. He also, however, possesses that instinctive snopes capacity for grasping the economic
rudiments of return on invested capital and bottom-line profits.

High as well as low finance characterizes these anthropoids, as
they inch their way into Yoknapatawpha County like mold over
cheese. As Faulkner had done with the Jason Compson cotton
speculation episode in *The Sound and the Fury,* again in the Snopes
trilogy he satirizes everything even remotely resembling finance.
Actually the financial satire reveals a deeper populist sentiment,
extant in the South since the 1890s, which regards the Northern
business establishment as a toothless money-sucking monster. The
Yankee money lord is seen as a heartless profiteer who takes away
from the Southerner without giving or returning anything. The
Snopeses, of such obscure origin that they are unconsciously associated with Yankee businessmen, are therefore condemned for economically exploiting the local townspeople as well as introducing
sophisticated financial practices into a rural barter economy.

Drawing the wily character of Flem Snopes, Faulkner probably
borrowed from a local banker-businessman named Joe W. Parks.
Parks, a relative latecomer to Oxford from the country, became
one of Lafayette County's shrewdest and most prosperous men. He

in fact eventually displaced Colonel J. W. T. Falkner (the novelist's grandfather) as president of the First National Bank of Oxford, and earlier he had taken over the Falkner family house called "The Big Place." Banker Parks, with his machine-made bow ties, may have been the original of Flem Snopes in *The Hamlet,* the first novel in the trilogy, which stood alone as a finished work of art for seventeen years. Flem grows to such monumental size in *The Town* and *The Mansion,* however, that any resemblance to Parks is lost or forgotten and replaced by the larger archetypal portrait of the genus "American Financier." Eternal symbol of the American financier is Wall Street banker J. Pierpont Morgan, Sr. Morgan portentously ruled over capitalism and the free enterprise system between 1870 and 1913. If he did not own something outright during his reign as America's most powerful banker, you could be sure Morgan had a controlling interest. After his death the Morgan name and aura lived on in his son, J. P. Morgan, Jr., as well as in his mighty institution, J. P. Morgan & Company, which squatted Sphinxlike at 23 Wall Street. As F. Scott Fitzgerald once wrote, begin with an individual and before you know it you have created a type. Joe Parks was no doubt the individual. Morgan became the type and shadow.

God made the world in 4004 B.C., but it was reorganized in 1901 by J. Pierpont Morgan, Sr. So jokes the caption of a popular turn-of-the-century cartoon about the famous banker. Similarly, William Faulkner created Yoknapatawpha County, the mythical postage stamp of soil in Mississippi, only to watch it taken over in time by Flem Snopes. Flem, who has no more friends than Blackbeard or Pistol, bears numerous resemblances to the imperious Morgan, enough in fact to suggest a convincing facsimile, even rebirth of the New York robber baron.

J. P. Morgan *père* almost alone revolutionized the American banking industry. Employing his Wall Street banking houses—Drexel, Morgan & Company and later J. P. Morgan & Company—as a power base, he discovered that direct control over corporations rather than outright ownership was a more effective means of influencing business and integrating industry and capital. Flem Snopes is the banker-conqueror who introduces "Morganization" to Jefferson, Mississippi and surrounding towns. Like Morgan, Snopes uses the Bank of Jefferson as a foothold for widening his sphere of influence and gaining economic control. Quietly removing enemies in his path while fiercely gripping the reins of money and credit, Flem's rule over his realm is every bit as totalitarian as the Wall Street financier's. Just as Morgan was one of the most ruthless capitalists in the world and an immense force in the dawn of American finance, Snopes becomes by "ruthless antlike industry" the virtual master of this small Southern community and the mightiest power in its business life.

From youth, J. P. Morgan, Sr.'s imagination was tantalized and nurtured by the unlimited possibilities of wealth and power. Son of international banker Junius S. Morgan, he was educated in mathematics at the University of Göttingen in Germany. Apprenticed in London at J. S. Morgan & Co. and its successor, Morgan Grenfell & Co., Ltd., he received training from the Rothschilds and later from powerful investment bankers in Wall Street. Flem Snopes's banking education by contrast is absurdly coarse and rudimentary, his financial vision constricted by a mean and currish nature. He learns about the banking business over a teller's shoulder in Colonel Sartoris's bank, watching greenbacks handed through the window. Then he somehow employs his crude knowledge of banking to exploit and strangle the entire community. Despite startling differences in backgrounds, however, the ethics of these bankers are remarkably alike. Each saw the bank as a means to circumvent basic right and wrong. Flem, for instance, demands "no more and no less than his legal interest according to what the banking and civil law states in black and white is hisn." Moral law is never mentioned. Also, Flem's

> association with banks had been too brief even to have
> occurred to him that there was a morality to banking, an
> inevictable ethics in it, else not only the individual bank
> but banking as an institution, a form of social behavior,
> could not endure.[22]

Whatever acknowledgment of a banking morality he does make (actually a grudging respect for certain legal and social limitations) might also have been Morgan's. Like Morgan, Snopes mocks virtue and morality because he is a paradox. He, like the Wall Street banker, often operates on the very edge of scandal and illegality. What is the difference between Flem Snopes's conceiving his "tenant-farmer panic" to frighten depositors into switching over from Sartoris's bank to the Bank of Jefferson so that he could have more control, and J. Pierpont Morgan's engineering the panic of 1907 (as Upton Sinclair claimed on good authority) to eliminate competition from the small independent trust companies? Or how does Snopes's attempt to destroy Wallstreet Panic's business by running it into insolvency differ from Morgan's infamous "reorganization" of the once-rich New York, New Haven & Hartford Railroad, which left that line a bankrupt shell for years afterward? Beyond morality, Flem Snopes's half-cocked idea of a bank might well have summed up Morgan's own beliefs, as history shows.

> His idea and concept of a bank was that of the Elizabethan tavern or a frontier inn in the time of the opening of the American wilderness; you stopped there before dark for shelter from the wilderness; you were offered food and lodging for yourself and horse, and a bed (of sorts) to sleep in; if you waked the next morning with your purse rifled or your horse stolen or even your throat cut, you had none to blame but yourself since nobody had compelled you to pass that way nor insisted on your stopping.[23]

Snopes himself bears a likeness to his Wall Street prototype, particularly in personality traits and habits. Both financiers are domineering, proud, and secretive. Carrying silence to the point of rudeness, they conduct their affairs with manners that are execrable. Neither Morgan nor Snopes had many friends, but both could boast countless enemies. Neither brooked any opposition, and each never forgave. Lincoln Steffens, who covered the New York financial district as a newspaper reporter, told in his *Autobiography* (1931) how Morgan reigned over his empire from his office at 23 Wall Street, how he "sat alone in a back room with glass sides in his banking house with his door open, and it looked as if anyone could walk in upon him and ask any question." [24] If anyone dared dis-

turb the banker, however, Steffens describes how such an inter-
loper would summarily learn that Mr. Morgan was none too
accommodating. Flem Snopes's habit also is to sit alone in a back
room, not reading and not doing anything except silently brooding
over his fief of land, loans, and mortgages. The images of these
bankers in their lairs are so close, in fact, that they could almost be
interchanged. Morgan could pass for Snopes, Snopes Morgan.
Consider John Dos Passos's "Biography" of J. P. Morgan, Sr., in
Nineteen Nineteen:

> J. Pierpont Morgan was a bullnecked irascible man with
> small black magpie's eyes and a growth on his nose; he let
> his partners work themselves to death over the detailed
> routine of banking, and sat in his back office smoking
> black cigars; when there was something to be decided he
> said Yes or No or just turned his back and went back to
> his solitaire.[25]

Then compare Faulkner's portrait of Flem Snopes as

> a thick squat man of no establishable age between twenty
> and thirty, with a broad still face containing a tight seam
> of mouth stained slightly at the corners with tobacco, and
> eyes the color of stagnant water, and projecting from
> among the other features in startling and sudden pa-
> radox, a tiny predatory nose like the beak of a small
> hawk.[26]

Snopes is a rougher copy of the Wall Street investment magnate.
Instead of smoking expensive black cigars, he chews; rather than
looking indomitable and remote, he appears greedy and downright
vicious. Each is ill-humored and monosyllabic. Like Morgan,
Snopes's only words are "no" and "foreclose." Snopes, as Morgan
does, plays solitaire, only Flem's version is with mortgage deeds,
not playing cards, and his opponent is the whole town of Jefferson.
  The parallel between the elder Morgan and Flem Snopes does
not end with their roles as businessmen or financiers. Church ac-
tivities, strangely, occupy a part of both men's lives. Each estab-

lishes a public, almost pious personality, while remaining privately inscrutable and inaccessible. Morgan was a "tireless vestryman and church warden, a giver of parish houses and cathedral chapels, an energetic attender of triennial Episcopal Conventions." [27] The financier, however, who once stated flatly "I owe the public nothing," actually served Mammon with at least equal zeal and worshiped the golden calf. Likewise, Snopes becomes a deacon of Jefferson's Baptist Church, yet his only auspices are financial, not fraternal, civic, or religious. Even the bankers' dwellings suggest similarities. Snopes's antebellum mansion in Jefferson, symbol of wealth and power, crowns his ignoble rise to the pinnacle of the bourgeoisie, even though it mocks the respectability for which it once stood. The mansion, in fact, "might have been the solid aristocratic ancestral symbol of Alexander Hamilton and Aaron Burr *and Morgan* [italics mine] and Harriman and Hill and ever [*sic*] other golden advocate of hard quick-thinking vested interest." [28] Morgan's aristocratic ancestral symbol, a richly furnished Renaissance castle on a full Madison Avenue block in New York, is the marble monument of his triumphant empire.

Faulkner's central character in the Snopes trilogy, therefore, is a Southern exponent of the Yankee cult of the great speculator, a variant of the nineteenth-century robber baron. The financier is a luring theme in the novel, and the satanic histories of many capitalists are traced in American fiction. In the quiet backwaters of Jefferson, Mississippi, an unlikely spot far from the frenzied finance of corporate mergers and stock market corners, the story of Flem Snopes is the chronicle of still another evil captain of American industry.

One clan member actually bears the name of that legendary and far-off place where mountains of money are made—Wallstreet Panic Snopes. Wallstreet Panic was not given a name when he was born. He had always been referred to as "Eck's boy," "that boy of Eck's," or called by his grandfather's name. When his father gave him the name Wallstreet, V. K. Ratliff asks if Eck had changed his boy's name lately. Eck tells him that last year, after he had gotten settled down, "I thought maybe he better have a name. I. O. [Snopes] read about that one in the paper. He figured if we named him Wallstreet Panic it might make him rich like the folks that run that Wallstreet Panic." [29] "That one" Eck refers to is the panic on Wall Street that Ratliff mentions occurred a year or two ago, probably the panic of 1907. I. O. Snopes and Eck are unsophisticated about high finance, but they do know that panics *are* run by somebody, especially "that one" in 1907 supposedly engineered by J. P. Morgan, Sr. They know, too, that whoever does run them gets rich. Faulkner, in naming this Snopes, makes an elaborate joke at Wall Street's expense, a reflection of the Southern populist bias against Eastern finance and men like Morgan who are in control there. Wallstreet's second grade teacher, Miss Vaiden Wyott, tells him later what Wallstreet Panic means—almost as if dishonest money is not just wrong but something filthy—and that he doesn't have to be named that. She tells him to change it to Wall because that was a good family name in Mississippi, and he doesn't need the Street.

Wallstreet Panic Snopes represents the new economic man in the South who rises by hard work and honest industry, qualities rare enough in any breed but particularly unusual because he is a Snopes. A self-made success, he builds up a chain of self-service grocery stores scattered about a three-state area. Wallstreet's start actually comes from a profit on his father's bizarre death. Investing indemnity money paid by the oil company for a fatal accident, he opens a little back-alley store and expands it into a local monopoly. Wallstreet is so successful that cousin Flem quickly picks up the scent of money and makes a devious attempt to take control of the business. First, Flem gets him to overbuy his stock from a wholesale house in St. Louis, which pushes Wall to the brink of insolvency. The scheme fails when Wallstreet discovers his purchasing error in time, but not before he is forced to go to Flem for a private loan. Flem agrees to make the loan, then as a director of the bank officially acts to block it. Wall is able to save his business from Flem's Morganlike raid and thereafter stay out of his clutches. The contrast between these Snopeses is startling. Wall's moral integrity is high; so high, in fact, that Ratliff humorously speculates about the chastity of his grandmother as the only possible source of his break from the Snopes tradition. He achieves a respectability and even a fortune that is greater than Flem's without recourse to financial manipulation or extortion.

Another Snopes associated with Wall Street and big American

business is Montgomery Ward Snopes. Like Flem and Wall, he has the Snopes nose for profits. He also has the Snopes knack for setting up in business with little capital outlay or risk. Montgomery Ward entered the canteen business in Châlons, France after he quit the army. His canteen became the most popular in town because in the establishment's backroom a young French girl was provided for the soldiers' entertainment. Montgomery Ward soon found profits from this mode of business were ridiculously large. He also learned the marketing principle that ice cream and candy, once consumed, cost money to produce and replace, "where in just strict entertainment there ain't no destructive consumption at all that's got to be replenished at a definite labor cost: only a normal natural general overall depreciation which would have took place anyhow." [30]

A successful track record as an entrepreneur encourages Montgomery Ward Snopes to plunge into business when he returns home to Mississippi. The photography shop he opens on the main street in Jefferson is speedily converted into a pornography studio, as Montgomery Ward sets about applying the same economic formulas and marketing techniques that served him so well in France. In fact, his studio is more like an X-rated backroom movie house, except that the pictures are slides made out of French postcards magnified onto a sheet with a magic lantern. High profits, low overhead, and minimal depreciation characterize his operation, until the town sheriff finally shuts him down.

The economic basis on which Montgomery Ward Snopes operates his business suggests his namesake company, Montgomery Ward. Montgomery Ward & Company was the first firm in the nation to conduct its business through catalog orders. It was founded in 1872 by Aaron Montgomery Ward (he never used his first name), who applied the mail-order concept of selling specifically to the rural trade. Ward always wanted to be a drummer and traveled about the Mississippi Valley for a St. Louis firm selling goods to country stores. He set himself up in the mail-order house business in Chicago a year after the great fire. Proud of the fact that he did not pay enormous rent, Ward also boasted he had no agents or middlemen and bought and sold strictly for cash. Faulkner's Montgomery Ward Snopes, with his backroom pornography business in Jefferson, copies A. M. Ward's mail-order formula for success. Sales costs are kept low because he too doesn't use salesmen, production expenses are negligible, turnover of goods is brisk, the product is standardized, and transactions are for "cash only." Montgomery Ward & Company and Montgomery Ward Snopes have similar marketing campaigns, creating value and awakening consumer interest with pictorial illustration rather than by displaying goods. Instead of eye-catching advertising copy and pictures glamorizing the product, as in the A. M. Ward catalog, Snopes's gimmick is to attract attention simply with eye-filling photos of nude men and women "experimenting with one another." In fact, the photographs themselves are the final product. Snopes is under no obligation to deliver further goods or services.

William Faulkner certainly was aware of the presence of big companies like Montgomery Ward, because "the geographical center of mail-order house selling was in the Mississippi Valley." [31] Rural and semirural communities throughout Mississippi, "where it was not easy for townspeople to secure the variety, quantity, or type of merchandise desired from local retail stores," [32] grew dependent on Montgomery Ward & Company, whose existence to some must have been as intrusive as the ubiquitous Coca-Cola sign, billboard ads for shaving cream, or any other blatant form of product commercialism. The satirical inference is that the quality and value of goods purveyed as well as the retailing methods employed by Montgomery Ward & Company, that Northern Yankee mail-order house, are essentially the same as those of Montgomery Ward Snopes. Once again, on the subject of economic exploitation of the South, Faulkner's tongue may not have been entirely in his cheek. Beneath the comedy and satire of the Snopes saga lay a conspicuous anti-Wall Street and anti-Big Business feeling, quite common in rural Southern areas, which resisted any infringement upon the unspoiled Garden peace.

10.

Familiar as an Old Mistake

I

When the New York Stock Exchange fell under New Deal investigation in the 1930s, the U.S. Senate committee in charge saw signs of a pool in alcohol stocks operating right under their noses. Alcohol stocks, of course, were market favorites, because every small-time speculator was gambling on liquor making a comeback after the repeal of Prohibition. Richard Whitney, stock exchange president, was asked to look into this situation. He duly reported that no evidence of any pool could be found, yet his own figures clearly demonstrated as classic an example of one as you could find anywhere in the history of American finance. The floor specialist, of all people, was the pool manager. Later, a fellow governor of the exchange said he had seen Whitney working pools himself on the floor while he was president. Such longstanding "insider" shenanigans, especially after the 1929 Crash, earned Wall Street a reputation as the Slum District of American Business. The old guard, headed by caste-proud men like Whitney who regarded the stock exchange as a private club, staunchly opposed any Washington interference in exchange affairs. The battle began, however, when the Securities and Exchange Acts of 1933 and 1934 established the SEC and brought the securities industry under its control—and ended when Richard Whitney was cast out of Wall Street and sentenced to prison for embezzlement.

Since the sweeping liberal reform of Wall Street during the Depression, excesses and exuberances that made headlines in an earlier day are largely prevented from occurring. Epic scandals like Equity Funding, or swindles on the grand late nineteenth-century scale such as Investors Diversified Services, Inc. and Homestake Oil still upset the public's trust in high finance. The stock exchange, though, is no longer a private club but an open public institution. The stock market itself, no more the source of good times and bad times, is a scientific economic index or barometer of the future trend of the nation's business. Also the frontier character of Wall Street has long since vanished and the New York Stock Exchange has settled down to become more sedate and mundane. Even the character of money is changed. Fortune, the speculator's goddess, has humbled herself into the modern balance sheet or consolidated financial statement, and cash, rather than floating down like manna, means AT&T debentures accumulated in safe deposit boxes or Treasury Bills and certificates of deposit rolled over every six months. And the lone stock market operator, awesome for his financial derring-do and fearsome in a double-breasted suit with gold watch chain dangling from a vest pocket, has disappeared as well, leaving behind an unseen, anonymous corporate type in dark pinstripes whose humdrum heroism amounts to outperforming the Dow Jones industrial average or Standard & Poor's 500-stock index. For all these changes, just as the bedraggled Bewick Finzer in E. A. Robinson's poem is as familiar as an old mistake when he shows up at the bank for yet another loan, so also is each new American novel about high finance an old familiar form of fiction. There is no new thing under the sun in Wall Street literature. No new temptation, no new trial, no new defeat await each new Wall Street hero. The old drama that continues to play on the shadowy stage of the stock exchange is the Fall of Man.

The economic theme in Saul Bellow's novels, if without roots directly in the Puritan-Calvinistic culture, is not without its origin in the American experience. Bellow, a Jewish-American novelist who grew up in the Humboldt Park section of Chicago's West Side in the early 1930s (he describes Chicago then as a "colossal industrial and business center, knocked flat by unemployment)" [1] knew what hard times and struggling for existence were really like. That anxiety over money and fear of economic failure are themes throughout his fiction is no surprise, therefore. A motif found in nearly every Bellow novel—perhaps a lingering Depression hang-up—involves juxtaposition of a worldly success figure, often an older member of the hero's own family, with the protagonist, usually an economic failure figure. The father, brother, cousin success figure, counterpoint to the underdog hero, is self-sufficient, aggressive, moneymaking, and safe from those corrosive craters of the American spirit which develop out of material nonaccomplishment. The presence of this family symbol of success, off in the background yet omnipresent, accentuates not only the hero's financial plight, but also his psychological feelings of inadequacy and worthlessness.

Despite economic miasmas into which nearly every Bellow protagonist sinks, the success figure, most often the elder brother, rushes to the financial rescue. Amos in *Dangling Man,* Simon March in *The Adventures of Augie March,* Shura Herzog in *Herzog,* and Julius Citrine in *Humboldt's Gift,* in one way or another, offer their younger brothers a helping hand. Only when the father holds the family purse strings is the underdog hero protectorless, left alone to make his own way. Dr. Adler, the success figure in *Seize the Day* (1956), turns a deaf ear toward his son, Tommy Wilhelm, who, more than any other Bellow character, is in desperate need of financial assistance. Tommy must fend for himself in the shark-infested waters off Upper Broadway, stranded by a father who believes love, like money, is limited and must be closely guarded.

The economic failure figure in *Seize the Day* is Tommy Wilhelm. He is out of work, having quit his job as a toy salesman after ten years of steady employment. In contrast, Dr. Adler, considered one of New York's best diagnosticians, is retired and extremely wealthy. A second success figure in the novel who underscores Wilhelm's failure is Tommy's cousin, Artie, an honor student at Columbia (Wilhelm had dropped out of college in his sophomore year) and now a college professor. Tommy Wilhelm's world is the crowded, bustling, commercial world of New York City, essentially the same money society in which Melville's Bartleby or Wharton's Lily Bart were trapped and struggled to survive. "Uch! How they love money," thinks Wilhelm. "They adore money! Holy money! Beautiful money! It was getting so that people were feeble-minded about everything except money." [2] New York is a world in which to be written up in *Fortune,* as Dr. Tamkin claimed he once was, is enough to establish one's image and worth; a world in which *The Wall Street Journal* is looked to as the sacred text of daily happiness; a world in which money and death are closely associated. The money society, with its allurements, promises, and glories, ultimately deceives and disappoints individuals like Tommy Wilhelm.

Seize the Day is a fable of failure in a prosperous world. A modern financial Adam, Bellow's hero culminates his painful fall from innocence by plunging into the sin of high finance. Commodities, speculation, margin accounts, and brokerage houses draw him deeper into the pit. Wilhelm's fall, however, can be likened to an inconsequential drop off the bottom step of the cellar stairs, so low is he already when the final descent occurs. Separated from his wife and children and confronted by a flood of unpaid bills, lawyers' fees, and insurance premiums, Tommy's emotional as well as financial reserves are nearly depleted. He can ostensibly fall no lower. Yet, from the very outset of the story, when the elevator that carries him down from the twenty-third floor of New York's Hotel Gloriana "sank and sank," he continues to slide further.

A series of tempters in the story are strewn across Wilhelm's path, effortlessly luring him into confusion. Not only do they attract and entice, these ministers of the devil also attach themselves to their victim like deadly parasites. Maurice Venice, the charlatan talent scout who stirs visions in Tommy's mind of a glittering career in films, is the first of these destructive leeches. He seduces Wilhelm into abandoning college to go out to Hollywood, where Tommy soon discovers a recommendation from him is the kiss of death. Venice is later exposed as a fraud when he is indicted for connection with a ring of call girls. Another Devil parasite is Tommy's wife, Margaret. She lures him into marriage, bleeds him financially, and, once grasping him in her deadly claws, refuses to let go by consenting to a divorce. Dr. Tamkin, quack, swindler, combination healer and prophet, inventor, sage, scientist, and "confuser of the imagination" also gains a hold over Wilhelm. He conjures up out of his bag more disguises and tricks than even Melville's confidence man. Tamkin's eyes glitter hypnotically, with sight so powerful not only can he read the microscopic figures of commodity prices from the back of a crowded brokerage office, he is able to see directly into Tommy Wilhelm's soul. As aware of his victim's hunger for freedom as he is of his need for money, Tamkin is the devil as arch-psychologist from whom no secrets can be hidden. His "seize-the-day" philosophy quite literally is a destructive system of seizing, an ideology of hate, of grab. Tamkin tempts Wilhelm into a binding agreement, then sucks and feeds on his money.

Tommy Wilhelm, dupe of Tamkin's wiles, is a type of the financial innocent who yields to the temptation of easy money. He is a perfect target and pawn for the tempter. Earlier, when Wilhelm quit college to go to Hollywood, he was oblivious to the hard times of the Depression. "I didn't seem even to realize that there was a depression. How could I have been such a jerk as not to prepare for anything and just go on luck and inspiration?" [3] he recalls. That same economic unawareness plagues him later on when he jumps into speculation in the commodity market. He ingenuously reasons "why not?" because it is 'way beyond 1929, year of the Crash, and the market is still on the rise. Dr. Tamkin shrewdly perceives this naïveté while inducing Tommy into the belief that they will be "equal partners" in trading commodity futures.

The commodity futures market, most volatile and hazardous of all trading markets, is certainly its own form of hell. If one last vestige of American nineteenth-century finance remains, this is it! A man can become rich and poor in commodity trading, almost in the same day. "Have you stopped to think how much dough people are making in the market?" Tamkin provocatively asks Wilhelm. "And can you rest—can you sit still while this is going on?" [4] Tommy has to concede there is money everywhere, that everyone in the market is shoveling it in. Agreeing to a joint margin account with Tamkin, he places his last seven hundred dollars in the tempter's hands. Wilhelm also signs a power of attorney, an "even more frightening document," which gives Tamkin authority to speculate with his money. That document symbolizes Tommy Wilhelm's pact with the devil and consummates his fall. The bottom of his decline as well as a glimpse of the pit of hell are now not far off. As if suddenly aware of the magnitude of his folly, this Adam-Faust financier hurries back to the manager of the brokerage office to ask if in signing his name he has granted Tamkin control over any of his other assets. Relieved by the manager's answer, Wilhelm is innocent of the truth that it is his soul over which he has given Tamkin power of attorney and influence.

Saul Bellow's beleagured hero, confused by the wild gyrations of commodity futures, parallels another muddled speculator, Jason Compson, in Faulkner's *The Sound and the Fury*. Like Compson, Wilhelm spends a nerve-racking day watching pork belly prices as well as attending to a variety of troublesome matters. Both Jason and Tommy are on the dead run, trying to keep their respective financial schemes from scattering into disarray. Whereas Jason is finally driven to frustration and fury by the cotton market, Tommy Wilhelm however panics at the dread prospect of being wiped out. Wiped out he is, though. Wilhelm's fear-stricken search for the elusive Dr. Tamkin, who mysteriously disappears into the muddy shoals along upper Broadway, proves as futile as Jason Compson's rage at Wall Street and Eastern finance. Wilhelm's collapse does bring about a catharsis, a poignant moment of grief, as well as an anagnorisis. Although fallen, Tommy is liberated from that pretender soul which sheltered him from responsibility, and may now be headed for rebirth and redemption.

II

The president of the Investment Bankers' Association, mirroring the optimism of the speculative decade (1919-1929), said in 1924, "We are a nation of investors, and class distinctions are rapidly disappearing." New York's old guard, set apart by class distinctions, is threatened with extinction in Louis Auchincloss's fiction, as it slowly sells its aristocratic birthright to the newly rich, moneyed class. Old established values disappear, and former social distinctions ebb as the holy seed is mingled with strangers and outsiders. The victim in Auchincloss's novels is the *ancienne noblesse,* the genteel families who have descended from the city's founders and settlers. They gradually relinquish their ancestral estates by failing to heed changing economic trends, or lose their place in society by being engulfed in wild periods of financial speculation. Speculation and economic change, history shows, inevitably lift new ruling classes into existence.

Wall Street is the source of both new manners and old allegory in Louis Auchincloss's novel of high finance, *The Embezzler* (1966). The manners are of men who play the money game on the New York Stock Exchange. The allegory is of the Fall of Man. Money values and ideals that New York's aristocracy adopts are suggested by the manners. The allegory of the Fall, on the other hand, emphasizes not the conspicuous truth that sin, evil, and corruption are conditions of modern urban life as much as it shows how the old ideal of innocence has gone sour and how an old culture is breaking down. The established nobility of New York, represented in the novel by the family of the Primes, is subjected to forces that have been steadily transforming society into a less distinctive and more common form of affluence. The Primes, with roots back to the merchant and patroon class in the eighteenth century, are remnants of old Knickerbocker New York. The Prime clan is the primal or ancestral family of America, the first inhabitants of the Garden who cultivated it and laid out its boundaries. The last glorious member of the family, Guy Prime, retains the newness and freshness of innocence, the brightness and spontaneity of youth. But he is an anachronistic Adam in a vanishing Eden. In the years of the New Deal, the modern corporate or industrial man had all but replaced the individual economic man of an earlier period, in the same way as the corporation had overshadowed the partnership as the standard organizational form of American business. Guy Prime, who individually struggles to succeed in this modern world ruled by corporate giants, represents the final Fall for the financier in American fiction into a classless obscurity from which there is no hope of regaining paradise.

Guy Prime's fall from place and eminence is neither tragic nor pathetic, for it is long anticipated and prepared for. What were the accomplishments of Edwardian elegance and sophistication of this family, anyway, in the dawn of Standard Oil or in the age of the great fortunes of the Morgans, the Fisks, and the Goulds? Guy's father, Percy Prime, while preserving his pride of family and nobility, worshiped money like all the rest and genuflected to the golden calf. His son, shallow, gaudy, a moth with a penchant for "the deadly heat of the candle" and the product of growing family decadence, bears merely the name and outward semblance of upper-class respectability. Angelica Prime, whom Guy married, from a less effulgent social background than the Primes but with more instinctive sensitivity and perception, exposes the myth of the ancestral clan. The figure of Eve in the novel, whose earthy passions and lusts are subdued by her Catholicism, she is an iconoclast who also sees through Guy's innocence and romantic nature with characteristic pique and hauteur. Like the Chippendale family in *The Chippendales* by Robert Grant, a novel that may have influenced *The Embezzler,* the Primes have been steadily falling behind in a commercial world, abandoning their principles on the way and emulating the more practical morals and values of the rising new class of ambitious bankers and businessmen.

Guy's section, that first of several first-person narratives by central characters in the novel, is a lengthy memoir that resembles an atonement for sin as much as it does a confession or *mea culpa.* Guy is moved by a sense of guilt and conscience when he openly admits that "I know what I did and why I did it, and I believe that I have paid the penalty and should be quits with society." [5] Not a religious man, Prime, however, does have a curious regard for his soul. In church one morning where he, like Soames Forsyte in John Galsworthy's *The Man of Property* (a novelist Guy much admired), was in the habit of going to contemplate his business affairs, he notices in the altar window that the most colorful figure is the image of Christ. He wonders if the resplendence of the Son, in relation to the four evangelists who flank Him, could mean that salvation was possible for a colorful Prime like himself. Believing in himself as he does, he associates his own glory with some redemptive force that will quite naturally save him from falling into evil. Guy might never have fallen into the sin of the financial marketplace had he heeded his mother's prayer for forgiveness when he came home drunk one evening during Christmas vacation. She fervently asked God to lead him from the gutters of Mammon and the cesspools of society. But Guy's father, who had ambitions for his son to become a broker and go into the stock market, intervened and overruled both Guy's mother and God. A romantic, a dreamer, and an inveterate actor who saw himself in different roles, Guy Prime was Adamically innocent about money. "My view of Wall Street may have been naive compared to his," he reveals, thinking of himself in relation to Rex Geer. "I admit that I took a childish pleasure in the crisp heavy paper on which securities were engraved and in the promises of fairy tale wealth that they seemed to contain." [6] He derives more satisfaction and fulfillment in comparing himself to Count Landi (a mysterious international financier who fails in some great unknown scheme and commits suicide), or earlier to Tamburlaine (a poetic symbol of the lust for conquest and love of splendor), than from devoting his time to the practical details of managing money. Rather than keep an accurate accounting of his assets and liabilities, or an estimate of how much he can borrow before overextending himself, Guy prefers to record the stories he tells at the Club so that he can be sure of never repeating one. As head of the brokerage firm of Prime King Dawson & King (the novelist may have borrowed this name from Prime, Ward & King, the first great banking house in New York City in the early nineteenth century), Guy Prime is the figure of Adam as broker, a financial innocent misplaced in the nether world of Wall Street. Although Auchincloss reverses the role of the stockbroker as devil in *The Embezzler,* a departure from the usual pattern in the novel of high finance, the theme of the Fall remains.

Guy Prime is a symbol of light as well as innocence in the novel. His glory is uncertain and intermittent, however, like an April sun eclipsed by darkening clouds. Angelica, seeing Guy for the first time in Europe, falls in love with his luster, his crown of blond hair, his sky-blue eyes, and his Apollonian beauty—the same "negotiable securities" possessed by Herbert Melson, with whom Lily Bart was enamored in *The House of Mirth.* When Guy makes love to her, she, like Eve, is subdued by passion and delivered into his power. Prime always dresses brightly (if not slightly dandified), behaves ostentatiously, and has a habit of putting "gilded frames on everything." An incorrigible hero-worshiper, he idolizes old cynics and hypocrites like Judge Stedman, or dark, foreboding, and humorless individuals such as Rex Geer. Guy thinks of Rex, a Harvard classmate from humble and spare beginnings in Vermont, as handsome, "not with the bursting blondness of my brief moment in the sun, but with a taut, tight cleanness that has lasted through the years." [7] At the time of his embezzlement trial, observers searching for an explanation for his sudden fall conclude that Guy Prime "suffered from megalomania," that he must have thought of himself as "a kind of sun king of stockbrokers" who strutted about the imperial regions of heaven "between Trinity Church and the East River declaiming: 'Wall Street, *c'est moi.*' " [8] Guy's light is not the burnished radiance of Dreiser's epic devil figure in *The Financier,* Frank A. Cowperwood, but a natural brilliance that suggests qualities of innocence and naiveté.

Whatever the motive, the American novelist usually models a financier upon an actual person. Frank Norris had Joseph Leiter, the "boy plunger" who tried to corner the Chicago wheat market in the winter of 1896-1897, as a type for Curtis Jadwin in *The Pit.* Jack London used speculator and pool operator James R. Keene, the "Silver Fox of Wall Street," for his hero Burning Daylight in *Burning Daylight.* Theodore Dreiser researched financier Charles T. Yerkes in Philadelphia newspaper files for his character Frank Algernon Cowperwood, in the trilogy *The Financier, The Titan,* and *The Stoic.* Louis Auchincloss draws upon New York broker Richard Whitney for his character Guy Prime in *The Embezzler.*

Who was Richard Whitney? He was once regarded as nothing less than the voice of Wall Street and moral turpitude. Cast as public hero in halting the stock market Crash of 1929, he went on to become the youngest man ever chosen president of the New York Stock Exchange, an office he held five consecutive terms between 1930 and 1935. Whitney also ran his own bond firm on Wall Street, Richard Whitney & Co. No demigod, however, he was convicted of embezzlement in 1938 and sentenced to a five-to-ten year term at Sing Sing Prison.

Guy Prime in *The Embezzler* is the very ghost of Richard Whitney. He handles the brokerage for an important New York banking house in the novel, de Grasse Brothers, as Richard Whitney did for J. P. Morgan & Co. Old Marcellus de Grasse, "son of the founder of the firm whose name he bore," is modeled after J. Pierpont Morgan, Jr. An Adamic financier, Prime, like Whitney, invests in a variety of outside ventures, all of which suddenly collapse from under him. When a series of simultaneous disasters and reversals shake his paper empire, he borrows heavily from a number of sources to protect loans already outstanding, the principal security of which, Georgia Phosphates, has suffered a ruinous drop of the exchange. Richard Whitney's *raison de fiasco* was Distilled Liquors Corp., the prop of his unsteady empire, for which he borrowed and embezzled money to peg its price on the New York Curb Exchange at $15, then $9. Whitney, along with thousands of small-time speculators, had dreamed of netting a fortune when liquor was about to come back in 1933, and envisioned Distilled Liquors as another Hiram Walker or Somerset Importers. Anyway, Prime King Dawson & King in the novel, like Richard Whitney & Co., is finally suspended from operations when irregularities are discovered. Guy Prime, like Whitney, is plunged into personal bankruptcy. The prison sentence he receives, following a highly publicized trial (parallel to Whitney's sensational 1938 trial) is symbolic punishment for his Fall into the sin and evil of speculation. Guy Prime's bankruptcy in fact brings the history of the ancestral Primes to an end "in a hell as bright as any in the Bishop's [Guy's grandfather, Reverend Chauncey Prime] sermons." When his three years in the penitentiary elapse (the same number Whitney served before being paroled), the disgraced and humiliated financier exiles himself to Panama to live out his days in seclusion. Guy retains even there a luminescence, local color as it were, created mostly by reflected light.

Auchincloss shaped the character of Rex Geer, the banker-antagonist in *The Embezzler,* on not one but two real-life financiers close to Richard Whitney—Whitney's brother and partner at J. P. Morgan & Co., George Whitney, and Thomas W. Lamont, another Morgan partner. George Whitney and Lamont, Tweedledum and Tweedledee under J. Pierpont Morgan, Jr., for many years, knew about Richard Whitney's borrowings and illegal use of funds to support his wild speculations, but said nothing to exchange officials. Instead, Thomas Lamont, who in 1946 published reminiscences under the title "My Boyhood in a Parsonage" (Rex Geer's memoirs in the novel were similarly called "My Boyhood in a New England Rectory"), covertly approved a $1,082,000 private loan to Richard Whitney in November 1937 to replace monies taken from the stock exchange's Gratuity Trust Fund. George Whitney, who was thunderstruck by news of his brother's Trust Fund embezzlement, but O.K.'d the loan just the same, insisted upon immediate liquidation of the bond firm of Richard Whitney & Co., as Rex Geer does in the novel with Guy Prime. Richard Whitney, as does Prime, however, ignored his promise to get out of the brokerage business and leave Wall Street. He stayed on until his whole hypothecated house of cards fell in, less than a year later. Like Prime, Whitney was convicted of felony charges that netted him a prison term.

If Guy Prime is associated with light and life, Geer represents darkness and death in *The Embezzler.* Contrasted to the mercurial Prime, Rex is colorless, saturine, and somber. An aura of evil surrounds him. He has no dreams or illusions, only cold ambition; no romantic imagination, only an uncanny memory for facts and numbers. Guy is the naive idealist and dreamer, and Rex is relentlessly logical, a philosopher of finance. In the 1920s, when every innocent investor was making money, Rex felt that too many Guy Primes existed. During the darkness of the Depression that followed, Rex Geer, who "brilliantly . . . had avoided the general ruin," shone and flourished. If the devil figure in the novel, Rex is a strangely moral one. He retains the strict Puritan-Calvinist morals of his clergyman father in Vermont, even when he is carrying on a love affair with Guy's wife, Angelica. In his love as in his business dealings, however, there is neither light nor warmth.

Guy Prime may have been more than simply bitter and angry, but absolutely accurate when, just before his fall, he summed up Rex's role as his antagonist:

> You envied me my popularity, my family, my whole bright little place in the sun. You hated those things because they weren't yours. You had to have them, not to enjoy them, but to destroy them. You grabbed the fortune that *I* should have made, and what have you ever

done with it but build a big house that's as dreary as yourself and prate about morals while you practiced adultery? You made a world that's more sordid than the old Prime world that you sneered at, only yours isn't even gay. It's drab as a crow! [9]

In his own narrative, although a logical and careful rebuttal of the Adamic hero's accusations against him, Rex Geer devilishly but unconvincingly shifts the blame for the fall on Guy. He is clearly motivated by pride, envy, and a desire for revenge against the ancestral family of the Primes. Ever since that day when the gateway into the Prime family was forever shut to him, effectively casting him out of the Prime heaven, Rex has plotted his revenge. His courtship with Alix Prime, Guy's lovely cousin, had ended for him in abject humiliation and rejection. He was called a swineherd in the disguise of Prince Charming by old Chauncey Prime, Alix's father, who cruised up the coast to Bar Harbor to take her away from Rex. Aboard the spotlessly white yacht *The Wandering Albatross,* from which he never deigned to set foot on shore unless it was at Newport, Chauncey Prime resembled God, who Himself had never set eyes on Chauncey before ten in the morning. His wrath and fierce administration of judgment dashes any hopes Geer had of marrying Alix. "So long as she chooses to make her home with me—and she still does, sir, and of her own free will—there will be no further visitations or harassments from you," [10] he sternly informs Rex, who had rowed out to the yacht after Alix. Saved from the evil and ambitious Rex Geer, Alix, who herself "knew her opera plots, down to the last villain's disguise," later marries the good and innocent Freddy Fowler, another Adamic financier in the novel. Fowler loses his own and his parents' money in the stock market before shooting himself in a Manhattan hotel.

The object of Rex Geer's misdirected hatred of the Primes is Guy, who, he felt ever since the Bar Harbor episode, had a part in his humiliation and defeat. In the Garden of Eden, Guy's country home at Meadowview, Geer carries out his revenge. There he seduces the "dark pale beautiful" Angelica, Prime's wife. Also at Meadowview, Rex, in return for Guy's promise to terminate his business affairs and leave Wall Street, loans him $350,000 to keep him from being crushed under the weight of his borrowings. Always self-seeking, Rex actually saves himself, not Guy Prime, with this loan. He wishes to protect the Prime name because his own son, George, is to marry Guy's daughter. At the same time, Rex thinks he has found a way to put this colorful Wall Street personality and long-time secret adversary out of business. The "Meadowview Pact" that Guy refers to, "when I bargained away my birthright to engage in business (my very manhood, by the standards of downtown) in return for a loan that was the merest pittance to him," [11] further suggests Faust's bargain with Mephistopheles. Guy Prime, both Adam and Faust in this allegory of high finance, is the arch-victim of the devil's wiles. That Meadowview is the Garden in which the serpentine Geer maneuvers is hinted at by Mrs. Hyde, Angelica's mother, in a conversation she has with Guy:

> Doesn't she have everything a sane woman could want?
> A beautiful house, an assured position, plenty of money
> and a husband who does not begrudge her the company
> of Mr. Geer. In my day that would have been regarded as
> a kind of Paradise.[12]

After Guy's fall and banishment, Meadowview, or Paradise, is symbolically condemned by the state to make way for a new highway. The Garden is abandoned and paved over.

Guy Prime's devotion to and admiration for Rex Geer is testimony to the devil's irresistible allurement and attractiveness. He's not the only member of the ancestral family to find him appealing. Alix is drawn to Geer before her father is forced to intervene. Even Bertha, Guy's spinster sister, has a crush on him at Bar Harbor, while Rex is off pursuing Alix. Angelica Prime, when she makes the discovery of the profligate and degenerate side of her husband's romantic nature, flatly acknowledges that "I would have preferred the devil." Her passionate acquiescence to and subsequent marriage with Rex Geer suggest that, although Guy was bearable, her instinctive choice was, like Eve's, for the dark and foreboding figure of Satan. Guy's unseen grandsons, the scions of Adam, not only inherit original sin but are the children of an intermarriage between the Primes and their evil antagonist, for Guy's daughter, Evadne, marries Geer's son. Also, Angelica marries Rex, which makes her her own daughter's mother-in-law, further complicating the interrelationship and suggesting man's deep commitment to evil after the Fall.

Rex Geer's narrative, the devil's point of view, is meant to be a self-justification, a defense, but instead becomes a stronger self-indictment. In working for Marcellus de Grasse, a man who boasts "I betray my essential self in taking sides between the cops of government and the robbers of business," Geer associates himself with the evil titans and barons of high finance. He seems to sense that when he comes to work for de Grasse Brothers after Harvard, "I had betrayed the principles of my Puritan forebears and sold my birthright for a meretricious success." On the subject of Guy Prime, Rex is singularly devious and unconvincing. Angelica says of his memoir that, in fact, despite its "straight, honest, Rex-like approach . . . it is still misleading. Rex never understood anyone's sincerity but his own." Geer jealously calls his Adamic enemy a Wall Street Robin Hood, or more inaccurately, an actor who chose the role of Othello for his own memoir (the first narrative section, which Rex has already read) but bore a closer resemblance to Iago. Prime is sufficiently cavalier and impulsive in his affairs that Rex Geer can, with some authority, speak evil of his good. But Guy represents neither the darkness of the Moor, nor does he, like Othello, or even Alix's husband, Freddy Fowler, kill himself when his universe collapses. The Iago in the drama is not Guy, but Geer himself. Rex's purpose in his narrative is only to sully and discolor Guy's image as thoroughly as he can, hoping to make his own shade of evil look brighter by comparison. He pictures Guy as an incurable embezzler who must be stopped and a Machiavel who wanted either to be the richest man on Wall Street or to bring Wall Street down in ruins with him if he failed. The real Rex Geer, however, shows through the lies in spite of their persuasive appeal. Recalling the Bar Harbor affair, origin of his envy and hate and an episode he never forgets, Rex says

> Had he not cheapened his cousin Alix by making me see
> her only as an heiress and myself as a fortune hunter?

> Had he not cheapened the whole trade of banking until I
> had had to drive him out of de Grasse? Oh, yes, I had
> driven him out—I saw that now! Had he not debased
> Angelica by winking at our love? And had he not now
> cheapened her again, hideously, unbearably? I could
> think of no nook or cranny of my life that had not been
> degraded by Guy Prime.[13]

Accomplishment and worldly position do not mask Rex Geer's evil
nature. He is as dissimulating as his Rembrandt portrait of a moneylender, found to be fake. Geer gains in eminence in the financial
underworld by ascending into the ruling echelons of the de Grasse
bank. But Guy Prime, prompted by weakness of character, lack of
will, and an innocence that proves fatal, falls into ruin and disgrace. Bankruptcy, prison, long years of self-imposed exile, these
and untold other sufferings are symbolic punishment for the sin of
speculation in the financial marketplace. Prime, like many heroes
in Wall Street fiction, is damned with no hope of regeneration of
his former brilliance.

An expansion of an earlier story, "The Money Juggler" *(Tales of
Manhattan,* 1967), the novel *A World of Profit* (1968) again reflects
Louis Auchincloss's interest in the disintegration of aristocratic
New York. The novelist's distaste for the principles and manners of
the *arriviste* in society uptown as well as downtown in Wall Street is
reminiscent of Edith Wharton, whose aversion to the barbarians
and invaders who began infiltrating New York in the 1880s is well
documented in *The Custom of the Country.* As newcomers like the
Spraggs settled on Fifth Avenue, speculated on the stock exchange
with their newly made fortunes, and hunted for titles on the Washington Square reservation, so do outsiders in Auchincloss's fiction
rise in society by their exploits on Wall Street and poach on the
preserves of the upper class. Both novelists portray the slow assim-
ilation of the parvenu class into the "Four Hundred," a form of
death and a cause of natural extinction of the aristocratic species.

Auchincloss repeats the allegorical pattern of *The Embezzler* in *A
World of Profit.* Shallcross Manor, a baronial estate on Flushing
Bay, New York, with a large pillared house and lawn majestically
descending to the water, is a Garden of Eden from a former age. It

represents the ancestral home of the Shallcross family, who, like the Primes, are descendants of the merchant and landed class of old New York. Eben Shallcross (who has a paradisiacal ring to his name like Guy Prime) is the patriarch of the family, the last remnant of the golden epoch of eighteenth-century New York. His son, Martin, shallow and without substance, is another Guy Prime, a weak financial innocent who jeopardizes his own aristocratic breed and places it on the endangered list. He urges the sale and subdivision of Shallcross Manor, not because he lacks loyalty to the family or fidelity to his past, but because a real estate scheme proposed by a developer seems the more attractive and profitable alternative. Martin Shallcross, caught up in this fatal business partnership, eventually is plunged into bankruptcy and commits suicide.

Another financial innocent who falls in the novel is Martin's brother-in-law, Thaddeus Kay. Kay, who inherits his family's brokerage firm, is tinged with the same weakness of financial cupidity characteristic of the Shallcrosses. He is buried beneath the debris when he suffers an avoidable reversal and his firm goes bust. Tenderly guided into the financial arena by his father but unable to mature in that environment, Kay seems too childish and effete for Wall Street: "In his boyhood in the darkling moneyed world of the nineteen thirties, on a disillusioned and frightened Long Island, the young Thaddeus Kay, who had won all the cups and all the medals, had been deemed an angel child with a divine mission to redeem the wanderers in the financial wilderness." [14] Auchincloss's heroes are not cast in the same rough mold as the real-life Jay Cookes, the Fisks, and the Goulds, titans who stole fire from the gods of the stock exchange and escaped retribution. Instead they are educated, sophisticated society types who regard Wall Street as a gentleman's club, an extension of their fraternity life on an Ivy League campus. Unprepared for this rough and uncivil world, their careers in high finance are brief and doomed to failure.

Jay Livingston, son of a Jewish banker, is the social alien or outsider in *A World of Profit*. An obvious parallel to Rex Geer in *The Embezzler* and a literary descendant of Simon Rosedale in *The House of Mirth*, Livingston is dark, ominous. His goals are not only to displace the Shallcross family, but to own the Garden lock, stock, and barrel and develop it into a huge moneymaking corporate complex after his own blueprint. In his deceptively quiet and determined way, he attracts and allures members of the doomed Shallcross clan, as Geer had done with the Primes. Sophie, the youngest daughter, is the first to be drawn to him, then her married sister, Elly Kay, who succumbs later on. Martin Shallcross naively enters into Livingston's employ as his first lieutenant and tool. The legend of the novel taken from *Doctor Faustus* presages the fatal Shallcrossian partnership with the devil for profit: "O, what a world of profit and delight, / Of power, of honour, and omnipotence, / Is promised to the studious artizan!" By devious and wily means, Livingston convinces even Mrs. Shallcross, who originally snubbed him as a déclassé intruder, that he is more worthy as a man for Elly than her husband, Thad Kay. The only Shallcross who is never impressed by him is old Eben, the father. At the farewell party for Shallcross Manor, before it is sold for development, Eben hears there is talk about his daughter, Sophie, marrying Livingston. The old man's reply is an appropriate anecdote about the exiled queen of Naples in Napoleonic times. When the queen was told of the proposed marriage of her granddaughter to the Corsican usurper, Judge Eben relates how she cried—"The final humiliation has been reserved for me! To become the devil's grandam."

The raid on Atlantic Corp., a favorite blue chip of the upper class, is Jay Livingston's financial *coup de maître*. A lucrative conglomerate with interests in parking lot franchises, movie theaters, a chain of cigar stores, shopping complexes, and a bus line, Atlantic Corp is the plum, the crown that will establish Livingston in high place among the business elite. This devilish financier harbors a secret vision "to be nothing less than master of the boundary between the city and Nassau County, with magnificent bargaining power, between the political entities, as to what improvements were placed on which side of the line." [15] Control of Atlantic is not Livingston's only objective, though, because he also makes a conquest of Elly Kay. Discovery of their affair leads her husband to enlist with the dissident stockholders of Atlantic. No longer able to count on Thaddeus Kay's block of stock, which would have ensured control, Livingston insidiously buys shares with money from Atlantic's own treasury in a maneuver that recalls Frank Cowper-

wood's embezzlement of $60,000 from the municipal treasury in
The Financier. When Judge Eben Shallcross, guardian of the old
morality, learns of these crooked wheelings and dealings, he visits
the former district attorney and the whole scheme is exposed. Atlantic Corp. plunges from a speculative high of 190 down to practically nothing on the exchange, and the Adamic financiers Martin
Shallcross and Thad Kay are swept away in the panic.

The world of Wall Street is the fallen world of Babylon in Louis
Auchincloss's *I Come as a Thief* (1972). Like the great city in Revelation, Wall Street continues to be in the American financial novel a
habitation of devils, hold of every unclean spirit and place where
merchants grow rich as well as drunk. Religion and money, God
and Mammon once again are conjoined in the Wall Street novel.

I Come as a Thief offers a rare view of the Wall Street sinner. No
American novelist since William Dean Howells portrays the moral
struggle of the financier or businessman as Auchincloss does in this
novel. Money, speculation in the stock market, and, worst of all, a
bribe accepted as a public official from the Mafia underworld, give
Tony Lowder a sense of personal damnation and awareness of the
evil within himself. Fallen into sin, his only escape is to confess and
ease his troubled conscience.

A partnership—bête noire for the financier or businessman in
Wall Street fiction—begins Tony Lowder's decline. Urged by his
law partner, Max Leonard (whom he calls Max Satanicus),
Lowder ventures into politics, then stocks as a means of paying off
political expenses. Together, they speculate in a joint margin account, like Wilhelm and Dr. Tamkin in *Seize the Day*, and get
hooked on a risky new computer stock called Herron Products.
When prices tumble dramatically in the 1970 bear market, Max
borrows more money from a shady Mafia character named Jerry
Lassatta to forestall margin calls. Lassatta, one of a multitude of
demons inhabiting the region of Wall Street, is merely the contact
man for the brokerage house of Menzies, Lippard & Co., a firm
tied to organized crime and facing suspension by the SEC. The
boss man, Menzies, combines the underworld of the Mafia with
the dark world of high finance and represents a more awful Mephi-
stophelean figure in the novel. He proposes to Tony Lowder,
mixed up in Max's stock market borrowings, a "little silent part-

nership. Our little silent exclusive and very profitable partnership." The Mafia is aware of Lowder's position as special assistant with the SEC and hopes to buy him off. Lowder accepts and soon finds himself damned, cast into a strange limbo where he avoids everybody. Eventually he goes to the U.S. Attorney to admit his crime, the guilt is so great. Lowder's confession and craving for atonement, if not with God, then at least with his own conscience, take him significantly beyond Guy Prime's feckless attempt at exoneration in *The Embezzler*.

Escaping the devil who laid snares for his soul through the enchantment of high finance, Tony Lowder's salvation is still imperfect. His legal admission is merely a form of repentance, his deliverance from sin and evil at most a temporary freedom. Auchincloss's view of redemption, like that of many American novelists who write about Wall Street, is similarly imperfect and incomplete, as if any washing could take place in Christian doctrine without the blood and the water. However, by turning away from the stock market and speculation—a source of evil—as many financial heroes do, a redemptive step is taken.

Notes

Chapter 2

1. Granville Hicks, *The Great Tradition. An Interpretation of American Literature since the Civil War* (New York: Macmillan, 1933), pp. 174-75.
2. See Edwin Cady, *The Road to Realism: The Early Years (1837-1885) of William Dean Howells* (Syracuse, N.Y.: Syracuse University Press, 1956), p. 231. Cady reiterates the point in his introduction to *The Rise of Silas Lapham* (Boston: Houghton Mifflin, 1957), p. vi.
3. Cotton Mather, *The Magnalia Christi Americana* (Hartford, Conn.: Silus Andrus, 1820), Book V, p. 57.
4. *The Journal and Miscellaneous Notebooks of Ralph Waldo Emerson*, ed. William H. Gilman and J. E. Parsons (Cambridge, Mass.: Belknap Press of Harvard University, 1960), VIII, 290.
5. Nathaniel Hawthorne, *The House of the Seven Gables: A Romance* (1850; reprinted Boston and New York: Houghton Mifflin, 1903), p. 392.
6. Ibid., p. 393.
7. Ibid.
8. Ibid., p. 236.
9. Ibid., p. 237.
10. Herman Melville, *Moby-Dick*. The Standard Edition of the Works of Herman Melville (New York: Russell & Russell, 1963), VII, 91.
11. Herman Melville, *The Confidence Man: His Masquerade*. The Standard

197

Edition of the Works of Herman Melville (New York: Russell & Russell, 1963), XII, 63.
12. Ibid., p. 53.

Chapter 3

1. Herman Melville, *Moby-Dick.* The Standard Edition of the Works of Herman Melville (New York: Russell & Russell, 1963), VII, 135-36.
2. Ibid., p. 203.
3. Ibid., p. 267
4. Theodore Dreiser, *Hey Rub-A-Dub-Dub: A Book of the Mystery and Wonder and Terror of Life* (New York: Boni and Liveright, 1920), pp. 58-59.

Chapter 4

1. John W. De Forest, *Honest John Vane,* intro. by Joseph Jay Rubin (1875; reprinted State College: Bald Eagle Press, 1960), p. 224.
2. Ibid., p. 92.
3. Ibid., p. 84.
4. Ibid., p. 78.
5. Ibid., p. 172.
6. Ibid., p. 132.
7. Ibid., p. 168.
8. Josiah G. Holland, *Sevenoaks: A Story of To-Day* (1875; reprinted New York: Charles Scribner's Sons, 1901), p. 275.
9. Ibid., pp. 186-87.
10. De Forest, *Honest John Vane,* p. 182.
11. Holland, *Sevenoaks,* p. 148.

Chapter 5

1. Mark Twain, "Pudd'nhead Wilson's Calendar," *Pudd'nhead Wilson.* Authorized Edition of *The Complete Works of Mark Twain* (New York: Harper and Brothers, 1922), III, 108. Oddly, a similar bit of investment advice was offered by Edwin LeFèvre in 1932, when the country was sinking deeper into the Great Depression: "When is it safe to invest? There are two answers. Both date from the beginning of the investment business: (1) Never! (2) Always! 'Never' for the coward or the visionary. 'Always' for the reasonable man; for it all depends upon what you call 'safe,' in a world peopled by fallible human beings."

2. Mark Twain, *The Gilded Age*. Authorized Edition of *The Complete Works of Mark Twain* (New York: Harper and Brothers, 1922), I, 199-200.

3. Mark Twain, *The Adventures of Huckleberry Finn*. Authorized Edition of *The Complete Works of Mark Twain* (New York: Harper and Brothers, 1922), IX, 63.

4. Selling out at the bottom is an example of the same financial acumen Colonel Beriah Sellers displays in *The Gilded Age*. The Colonel plunges into a sugar speculation on the heels of a great success with his mule crop, but he gets wiped out. Twain describes it: "If he had kept out of sugar and gone back home content to stick to mules it would have been a happy wisdom. As it was, he managed to kill two birds with one stone—that is to say, he killed the sugar speculation by holding for high rates till he had to sell at the bottom figure, and that calamity killed the mule that laid the golden egg . . ." (p. 67).

5. Twain, *Huckleberry Finn*, pp. 64-65.

6. Mark Twain, "Sold to Satan," *Europe and Elsewhere*. Authorized Edition of *The Complete Works of Mark Twain* (New York: Harper and Brothers, 1922), XX, 326.

7. Mark Twain, *The Innocents Abroad*. Authorized Edition of *The Complete Works of Mark Twain* (New York: Harper and Brothers, 1922), II, 78.

8. Ibid.

9. Henry James, *The Art of the Novel: Critical Prefaces*, intro. by R. P. Blackmur (New York: C. Scribner's Sons, 1934), p. 193.

10. Henry James, "Daisy Miller: A Study," *The Complete Tales of Henry James*, ed. with intro. by Leon Edel (Philadelphia and New York: Lippincott, 1962), IV, 148.

11. Henry James, *The American* (1877; reprinted Boston: Houghton Mifflin, 1889), pp. 32-33.

12. Henry James, *The Reverberator* (1888; reprinted London: Rupert Hart-Davis, 1949), p. 20.

13. Henry James, "The Jolly Corner," *The Novels and Tales of Henry James* (New York: Charles Scribner's Sons, 1922), XVII, 449.

14. Henry James, *The Ivory Tower* (New York: Charles Scribner's Sons, 1916), p. 114.

15. Ibid., p. 212.

16. Henry James, *The Ambassadors*. New York Edition (1902; reprinted New York: Charles Scribner's Sons, 1909), I, 44.

17. William Dean Howells, *Their Wedding Journey* (1872; reprinted Boston and New York: Houghton Mifflin, 1895), p. 273.

18. William Dean Howells, *The Rise of Silas Lapham* (1885; reprinted Cambridge, Mass.: Houghton Mifflin, 1957), p. v.

19. Granville Hicks, *The Great Tradition: An Interpretation of American Literature since the Civil War* (New York: Macmillan, 1933), pp. 76-77.

20. William Dean Howells, *The Rise of Silas Lapham*, ed. with intro. by

George Arms (1885; reprinted New York and Toronto: Rinehart, 1955), p. 218.
21. Ibid., p. 46.
22. Richard Coanda, "Howells' *The Rise of Silas Lapham*," *The Explicator*, 22, No. 3 (November 1963). Coanda's note touches briefly on a number of similar points about the demonism of Milton K. Rogers.
23. Howells, *Silas Lapham*, p. 48.
24. Cady, *The Road to Realism*, pp. 236-37.
25. Ibid., p. 237.
26. Howells, *Silas Lapham*, p. 141.
27. Ibid., p. 138.
28. Ibid., pp. 306-7.
29. Ibid., p. 319.
30. Ibid., p. 320.
31. Ibid., p. 101.
32. Ibid., p. 45.
33. Ibid., p. 20.
34. Ibid., p. 56.
35. Dixon Wecter, *The Hero in America: A Chronicle of Hero-Worship* (Ann Arbor, Mich.: University of Michigan Press, 1941), p. 314.

Alexander Turney Stewart was the originator of "selling off-at-cost" or the discount style of merchandising. Just a block away from Cooper Union in New York City, he constructed his mammoth Business Palace, which became Wanamaker's after Stewart died a decade later. Like many New York merchants, he made a practice of hiring as store clerks businessmen whose financial luck had gone sour, forcing them into bankruptcy. Most were honest, devoted tradesmen who had either become overinvolved in the stock market or just failed to succeed commercially. In fact, Stewart's department store, by 1862 the world's largest, employing more than 2,000 persons, came to be widely known as the "hospital for decayed traders." Unlucky businessmen from such distant points as Philadelphia, Buffalo, Chicago, and Boston came to accept a job already waiting for them if they failed without dishonor. Stewart was certainly evidence of de Tocqueville's observation in 1835 about "the strange indulgence that is shown to bankrupts in the United States; their honor does not suffer by such an accident."

It is ironic that Silas Lapham, who obviously emulated the princely merchant, most definitely could have found employment clerking in Stewart's New York store when his own luck turned. Instead, Lapham takes his cure in Vermont and begins over again in business.

36. Howells, *Silas Lapham*, p. 329.
37. Ibid., pp. 329-30.
38. Ibid., p. 379.

39. Ibid., p. 392.
40. Ibid., p. 393.
41. William Dean Howells, *The Quality of Mercy* (New York: Harper and Brothers, 1892), p. 13.
42. Ibid., p. 422.
43. Edwin H. Cady, *The Realist at War: The Mature Years (1885-1920) of William Dean Howells* (Syracuse, N. Y.: Syracuse University Press, 1958), p. 103.
44. William Dean Howells, *A Hazard of New Fortunes* (New York: Harper and Brothers, 1890), p. 89.

Chapter 6

1. The Ghost Dance religion, in which believers sang, danced, and fell into trances, was not a war dance but a medicine dance, explains Hamlin Garland in *Companions on the Trail*. Sioux Indians supposed the Great Spirit would bring back the old days of the buffalo if they put away all weapons and renounced everything they had gained from the white man.
2. *The Life and Letters of Lafcadio Hearn,* ed. Elizabeth Bisland (Boston and New York: Houghton Mifflin, 1906), II, 182.
3. Frank Norris, "The True Reward of the Novelist," *The Responsibilities of the Novelist* (1903; reprinted New York: Hill and Wang, 1967), p. 201.
4. Frank Norris, *The Pit: A Story of Chicago* (1902; reprinted New York: Doubleday, Page & Co., 1903), p. 86.
5. Ibid.
6. Ibid., pp. 86-87.
7. Ibid., p. 332.
8. Ibid., p. 345.
9. Ibid., p. 346.
10. Ibid., p. 411.
11. Ibid., p. 216.
12. Ibid.
13. See Howells, *The Rise of Silas Lapham,* Rinehart edition, p. 101.
14. Norris, *The Pit,* p. 255.
15. See Warren G. French, *Frank Norris* (New York: Twayne, 1962), p. 125.
16. John K. Swensson, " 'The Great Corner in Hannibal & St Jo.': A Previously Unpublished Short Story by Frank Norris," *American Literary Realism, 1870-1910,* 4, No. 3 (Summer 1971), 205-26.
17. Franklin D. Walker, *Frank Norris: A Biography* (Garden City, N. Y.: Doubleday, Doran, 1932), p. 275.
18. John K. Swensson's supplementary analysis of "The Great Corner"

should be noted. Its exhaustiveness is far out of proportion to the length of Norris's story, barely five printed periodical pages, or the story's significance. More important, Swensson has several weak conclusions that need emendation, or oversights that should be corrected. For further comment, see Wayne W. Westbrook, " 'The Great Corner in Hannibal & St Jo.'—Another Look," *American Literary Realism, 1870-1910*, 10, No. 2 (Spring 1977), 213-14.

19. Swensson, "The Great Corner," p. 210.
20. Ibid.
21. Edwin LeFèvre, *Sampson Rock of Wall Street* (New York and London: Harper and Brothers, 1906), 107.
22. Matthew Josephson, *The Robber Barons: The Great American Capitalists, 1861-1901* (New York: Harcourt, Brace & World, 1934), p. 46.
23. LeFèvre, *Sampson Rock of Wall Street*, p. 226.

Chapter 7

1. David Graham Phillips, *The Master-Rogue: The Confessions of a Croesus* (1903; reprinted Ridgewood, N. J.: Gregg Press, 1968), p. 9.
2. Ibid., p. 98.
3. Gustavus Myers, *History of the Great American Fortunes* (Chicago: C. H. Kerr, 1910), III, 89.
4. David Graham Phillips, *The Cost* (1904; reprinted New York and London: Johnson Reprint Corp., 1969), p. 241.
5. Ibid., p. 176.
6. Ibid., p. 324.
7. Ibid., p. 399.
8. Thomas Lawson also wrote an anti-Standard Oil novel ominously entitled *Friday, the Thirteenth* (New York: Doubleday, Page, 1907). The villain is the broker for the "System," portrayed as a cutthroat brigand of the New York Stock Exchange, a devil of finance. The hero of this revenge fantasy—for Lawson is still obsessed with "Frenzied Finance"—crucifies "Standard Oil" and the "System" that spiked him to the cross earlier in a bear raid. He smashes the call loan market by offering $100 million at 4 percent, a full 146 percent below Standard Oil's rate, putting the "System" to rout. With its messianic hero and Day of Judgment atmosphere in which the stock exchange is miraculously cleansed, *Friday, the Thirteenth* brings the Wall Street novel closest to Armageddon.
9. David Graham Phillips, *The Deluge* (1905; reprinted New York and London: Johnson Reprint Corp., 1969), p. 244.
10. Ibid., pp. 12-13.
11. Ibid., pp. 172-73.
12. Ibid., pp. 124-25.

13. Myers, *History of the Great American Fortunes*, III, 254.
14. Upton Sinclair, *The Autobiography of Upton Sinclair* (New York: Harcourt, Brace & World, 1962), p. 91.
15. Upton Sinclair, *The Metropolis* (New York: Moffat, Yard, 1908), p. 233.
16. Sinclair overstates Montague's profit. If he averaged almost 19 points on 6,000 shares, his net gain would have been $114,000, not the "profit of a trifle under a quarter of a million dollars" *(The Metropolis,* p. 247).
17. Sinclair, *The Metropolis*, p. 296.
18. *Mark Twain in Eruption: Hitherto Unpublished Pages about Men and Events,* ed. with intro. by Bernard De Voto (New York and London: Harper and Brothers, 1940), p. 5. Twain lost money when the Knickerbocker Trust Company failed: "—it was just my luck. I had fifty one thousand dollars there. I feel hurt. I feel abused" (p. 6).
19. Upton Sinclair, *The Moneychangers* (New York: B. W. Dodge, 1908), p. 208.
20. Ibid., p. 265.
21. Jack London, *Burning Daylight* (1910; reprinted New York: Macmillan, 1959), p. 264.
22. Ibid., p. 131.
23. Ibid., p. 132.
24. Ibid., pp. 131-32.
25. Ibid., p. 133.
26. Ibid., p. 136.
27. Ibid., p. 361.

Chapter 8

1. Robert Grant, *The Chippendales* (New York: C. Scribner's Sons, 1909), p. 81.
2. Ibid., p. 141.
3. Ibid., p. 133.
4. Ibid., p. 479.
5. Ibid., p. 496.
6. Ibid., p. 600.
7. Edith Wharton, *The House of Mirth* (New York: Charles Scribner's Sons, 1905), p. 418.
8. Ibid., p. 194.
9. R. W. B. Lewis, in his *Edith Wharton: A Biography* (New York: Harper & Row, 1975), reports that *The House of Mirth* was both a huge and immediate commercial success. The first edition of 40,000, published October 14, 1905, was followed two weeks later by a second printing of 20,000, and again on November 11 by another printing of 20,000.

William Crary Brownell, a literary consultant for Scribner, told Mrs. Wharton it was "the most rapid sale of any book ever published by Scribner." Lewis states further that "over the first two months of 1906, Edith could several times record that *The House of Mirth* was still the best-selling novel across the country, as it continued to rival or surpass such other current successes as *The Garden of Allah*, *The Clansman*, and Upton Sinclair's *The Jungle*" (p. 151).

10. Curtis Dahl, "Edith Wharton's *The House of Mirth:* Sermon on a Text," *Modern Fiction Studies*, 21, No. 4 (Winter 1975-1976), 572-76.

11. Report of the [New York] Legislative Insurance Committee, 1906, x: 16. For full historical accounts of the New York insurance scandal of 1905, see Gustavus Myers, *History of the Great American Fortunes*, III, Chapter XXIII, entitled "Morgan at his Zenith," and Louis Filler, *Crusaders for American Liberalism* (New York: Harcourt, Brace, 1939), Chapter XV, entitled "Insurance on Trial."

12. *Mark Twain in Eruption*, ed. with an intro. by Bernard De Voto (New York and London: Harper and Brothers, 1940), pp. 77-79.

13. Edith Wharton, *The Custom of the Country* (New York: C. Scribner's Sons, 1913), p. 78.

14. F. Scott Fitzgerald, *The Beautiful and Damned* (1922; reprinted New York: Charles Scribner's Sons, 1950), p. 4.

15. Ibid., p. 14.

16. Fitzgerald modeled Adam Ulysses Patch after real-life New York socialite Ward McAllister. McAllister was court chamberlain for Mrs. William Backhouse Astor, grande dame of Manhattan society in the 1870s and 1880s. A fop and dilettante, he wrote his memoirs, entitled *Society as I Have Found It* (1890). McAllister is most remembered for inventing the term "the Four Hundred," often used in reference to the elite of New York Society. A fuller discussion of this source can be found in the *Fitzgerald/Hemingway Annual* (1979), "Portrait of a Dandy in *The Beautiful and Damned*," by Wayne W. Westbrook.

17. Albert D. Van Nostrand, "Fiction's Flagging Man of Commerce," *The English Journal*, 48 (January 1959), 8.

Chapter 9

1. Theodore Dreiser, *Hey Rub-A-Dub-Dub: A Book of the Mystery and Wonder and Terror of Life* (New York: Boni and Liveright, 1920), pp. 75-76.

2. Theodore Dreiser, *The Financier* (1912; reprinted Cleveland and New York: 1946), p. 44.

3. Ibid., p. 157.

4. Ibid., p. 433.

5. Theodore Dreiser, *The Titan* (New York: John Lane, 1914), p. 1.

6. William W. Cobau, "Jason Compson and the Costs of Speculation," *The Mississippi Quarterly*, 22, No. 3 (Summer 1969), 257-61, observes that Jason Compson in *The Sound and the Fury* sold a cotton contract short on the New York Cotton Exchange on April 6, 1928. This essential fact escaped such critics as Dorothy Tuck, *Crowell's Handbook of Faulkner* (New York, 1964) and Edmond L. Volpe, *A Reader's Guide to William Faulkner* (New York, 1964), who, as Cobau says, erroneously argued that Jason bought a contract long. Compson's dealings in cotton futures, like the rest of his financial affairs, are not all that obvious—either to the Compson family or the reader. His money transactions are so cloaked in secrecy that in fact they appear entirely different from their real nature.

7. William Faulkner, *The Sound and the Fury* (1929; reprinted New York: Modern Library, 1946), p. 210.

8. W. Hustace Hubbard, *Cotton and the Cotton Market* (New York: D. Appleton, 1928), p. 236.

9. Faulkner, *The Sound and the Fury*, p. 243.

10. Ibid., p. 260.

11. Ibid., p. 261.

12. *The Wall Street Journal*, April 4, 1928, p. 4.

13. Faulkner, *The Sound and the Fury*, p. 261.

14. Ibid., p. 252.

15. Ibid., p. 235.

16. Ibid., pp. 243-44.

17. Ibid., pp. 261-62.

18. Ibid., p. 244.

19. Rupert B. Vance, *Human Factors in Cotton Culture: A Study in the Social Geography of the American South* (Chapel Hill, N. C.: University of North Carolina Press, 1929), p. 141.

20. Faulkner, *The Sound and the Fury*, p. 196.

21. William Faulkner, "The Bear," *Go Down, Moses and Other Stories* (New York: Random House, 1942), pp. 255-56.

22. William Faulkner, *The Town* (New York: Random House, 1957), p. 262.

23. Ibid.

24. Lincoln Steffens, *The Autobiography of Lincoln Steffens* (New York: Harcourt, Brace, 1931), p. 188.

25. John Dos Passos, *Nineteen Nineteen* (1932; reprinted New York: Modern Library, 1937), p. 338.

26. William Faulkner, *The Hamlet* (1931; reprinted New York: Vintage Books, 1940), p. 52.

27. Frederick Lewis Allen, *The Great Pierpont Morgan* (New York: Harper, 1949), p. 13.

28. William Faulkner, *The Mansion* (New York: Random House, 1959), p. 154.

29. Ibid., p. 272.
30. Faulkner, *The Town,* p. 115.
31. Verneur Edmund Pratt, *Selling by Mail: Principles and Practice* (New York: McGraw-Hill, 1924), p. 373.
32. Ibid., p. 371.

Chapter 10

1. Saul Bellow, "Starting Out in Chicago," *The American Scholar,* 44, No. 1 (Winter 1974/75), 71.
2. Saul Bellow, *Seize the Day with Three Short Stories and a One-Act Play* (New York: Viking Press, 1956), p. 36.
3. Ibid., p. 15.
4. Ibid., p. 9.
5. Louis Auchincloss, *The Embezzler* (Boston: Houghton Mifflin, 1966), p. 11.
6. Ibid., p. 58. Guy Prime's childlike fascination with elaborately engraved stock certificates echoes the excitement that Marcel Proust's narrator experiences in *Within a Budding Grove:* "The sight of them enchanted me. They were ornamented with cathedral spires and allegorical figures, like the old, romantic editions that I had pored over as a child" (New York: Modern Library, 1951, I, 35).
7. Auchincloss, *The Embezzler,* p. 41.
8. Ibid., p. 124.
9. Ibid., pp. 133-34.
10. Ibid., pp. 177-78.
11. Ibid., p. 125.
12. Ibid., p. 114.
13. Ibid., p. 220.
14. Louis Auchincloss, *A World of Profit* (Boston: Houghton Mifflin, 1968), pp. 189-90.
15. Ibid., p. 132.

Index